Hallo und herzlich willkommen bei Red Line!

Hi! I'm Tom.

Englischlernen macht Spaß! Damit es dir möglichst leicht fällt, möchte ich hier kurz erklären, wie dein neues Englischbuch aufgebaut ist.

Es beginnt mit **Welcome to Red Line**. Hier löst du ein Quiz, mit dem du das Buch kennen lernst.

In den folgenden sieben Units (Kapiteln) lernst du die vier Hauptpersonen und ihre Familien kennen. In jeder Unit findest du:

Check-in: Hier geht es los! Auf zwei Seiten lernst du als Einführung in die Unit neue Wörter und Landeskunde.
Language: Hier geht es um Redemittel und Grammatik. Auf der letzten Language-Seite gibt es besonders viele Hör- und Wiederholungsübungen.

Story: Hier findest du eine Geschichte mit den Hauptpersonen.
Wordwise: Alles rund um Wörter! Hier machst du Wortarbeit und Wortspiele.
Check-out: Alles klar? Am Ende der Unit überprüfst du selbst, was du gelernt hast.

Auf den Link-up (Verbindungs)-Seiten und in Unit 1 kannst du dein Wissen aus der Grundschule anwenden. Im Anschluss an die sieben Units folgt Passing on information (Sprachmittlung). Unter Extras findest du im hinteren Teil des Buches ein Gedichtprojekt, eine spannende Fortsetzungsgeschichte, ein Theaterstück und Texte über Festtage in Großbritannien. Im Anschluss folgt Grammar (der Grammatikanhang) mit Regeln, vielen Beispielen und Tipps. Am Ende des Buches findest du auch den Vocabulary -Teil (die Vokabelliste). Hier stehen alle neuen Wörter einer Unit mit ihren deutschen Übersetzungen. Das Dictionary (Wörterbuch) listet die Vokabeln des ganzen Buches alphabetisch auf. Es ist auch zum Nachschlagen gedacht, wenn du einmal ein Wort vergessen hast.

Alles klar? Dann mach dich bereit für die Reise nach Greenwich.
Aber bevor es losgeht, *let's sing a song!*

Hi, hi, hi, hello!
Good morning! How are you?
Hi, hi, hi, hello!
I'm fine, and how are you?

Text: K.-H. Böttcher

Erläuterungen:

	Real talk	Wir sprechen echtes Alltagsenglisch.
	Listening	Wir hören zu.
	Your turn	Hier kannst du über dich, deine Familie und Freunde sprechen oder schreiben.
	Revision	Wiederholung
◉		Diese Teile sind auf den Begleit-CDs enthalten.
👥		Partnerarbeit
👨‍👩‍👧		Gruppenarbeit
📄		Hier entsteht ein Produkt für deine Sammelmappe.
✎		Wir schreiben.
*		Diese Übungen sind besonders knifflig.
( )		Diese Übungen sind fakultativ.
→ G1		Grammatik-Verweis

Contents

Section	Pages	Topic/Content	
Rally	10–11	Welcome to Red Line	
Unit 1		**Thomas Tallis School**	
Check-in	12–13	*sich begrüßen*	Hello! My name is … .
		sich vorstellen	What's your name?
		sagen, woher du kommst	I'm from … .
		fragen, wie alt jemand ist	How old are you?
Language 1	14–15	Old friends and new friends	This is Emma.
Language 2	16–17	Sam	Here's Mrs Carter.
Language 3	18–19	The school bag	Here is a ruler.
		Zahlen bis 100	What's 7 and 17?
Language 4	20–21	The classroom	There's a pen on the table.
Story	22–23	No problem!	
Wordwise	24	School and classroom	
Check-out	25	*Selbstkontrolle: Die Lernziele der Unit 1 überprüfen.*	
Link-up A		**Home sweet home**	
	26–27	*Familie, Farben, Zimmer*	That's his brother.
Unit 2		**Families in Greenwich**	
Check-in	28–29	*über Familien in GB lesen*	Four families
Language 1	30–31	Sam's family tree	Tim is Sam's uncle.
Language 2	32–33	Emma, you're in big trouble!	Where's my new T-shirt?
Language 3–4	34–35	At home with Lisa	Make your bed.
Story	36–37	A fun project!	
Wordwise	38	Family and furniture	
Check-out	39	*Selbstkontrolle: Die Lernziele der Unit 2 überprüfen.*	
Link-up B		**The hobby gardens**	
	40–41	*Hobbys und Wochentage*	I can play football.
Unit 3		**Clubs and hobbies**	
Check-in	42–43	*Über Schulclubs lesen*	Clubs at Thomas Tallis
		Uhrzeiten	What time is it?
Language 1	44–45	A phone call in the morning	I go to dance lessons.
Language 2	46–47	Terry likes Alison	Alison lives on our street.
Language 3–4	48–49	That's my game	Computer games
Story	50–51	Barker's story	
Wordwise	52	Pairs and sounds	
Check-out	53	*Selbstkontrolle: Die Lernziele der Unit 3 überprüfen.*	

Contents

Structures	Skills	Activities in unit
	Kennenlernen des Buches	A song: Let's get started!
G1 – G11		
		A poster
To be *in Aussagen*; *Personalpronomen; Fragen; Verneinung; Unbestimmter Artikel; Plural; Präpositionen*		A song: Alphabet rap A game: Words and numbers A game: Where is it?
		Act the story
	Vocabulary skills: Mind maps	
		A song: Room rap
G12 – G19		
Possessivbegleiter; have got; *Aufforderungen; Verbote;* can/can't		A game: Who is where?
		Act the story
	Vocabulary skills: Picture words	
		A game: What can you collect? A song: Seven days in a week
G20 – G24		
Simple present *in Aussagen;* Adverbs of frequency; this and that		A game: I often go …
	Reading skills: Useful questions	
	Vocabulary skills: Prepositions	

five **5**

Contents

Section	Pages	Topic/Content	
⟨ ⟩ Revision 1			
	54–55	*Selbstkontrolle: Die Lernziele der Units 1–3 überprüfen.*	
Link-up C		**In town**	
	56–57	Places in Mousetown	
Unit 4		**Greenwich project week**	
Check-in	58–59	*über Greenwich lesen*	Places in Greenwich
Language 1	60–61	A Greenwich project	It's project week!
Language 2	62–63	At the Cutty Sark	How long is the ship?
Language 3	64–65	The ghost driver	The DLR is cool.
Language 4–5	66–67	The Greenwich quiz	You can win a prize.
Story	68–69	Terry's dream	
Wordwise	70	Transport and sounds	
Check-out	71	*Selbstkontrolle: Die Lernziele der Unit 4 überprüfen.*	
Unit 5		**Shopping for a birthday**	
Check-in	72–73	Different shops	How much are they?
Language 1	74–75	Sam's party	My birthday is on 21st May.
Language 2	76–77	A present for Sam	It's too expensive!
Language 3–4	78–79	Shopping for Sam's party	20 packets of crisps
Story	80–81	Happy Birthday, Sam	
Wordwise	82	Birthdays	
Check-out	83	*Selbstkontrolle: Die Lernziele der Unit 5 überprüfen.*	
⟨ ⟩ Revision 2			
	84–85	*Selbstkontrolle: Die Lernziele der Units 4–5 überprüfen.*	
Unit 6		**At the farm park**	
Check-in	86–87	A school trip	It's a great place to visit.
Language 1	88–89	Not that pullover!	It's not cool.
Language 2	90–91	At the Cotswold Hostel	We're in the orange room.
Language 3–4	92–93	Breakfast at the hostel	It's Sunday morning.
Story	94–95	Pet pig Polly	
Wordwise	96	Shopping	
Check-out	97	*Selbstkontrolle: Die Lernziele der Unit 6 überprüfen.*	

| Structures | Skills | Activities in unit |

Grammar skills: Grammar pages

A game: Where am I?

G 25 – G 29

Project: Your town

Object pronouns; simple present *in Fragen und Verneinung*; question words

Project: Your town

Listening skills: Questions

A quiz about the friends

Vocabulary skills: Example sentences   A game: Word game

G 30 – G 37

Would like and want to; present progressive; expressions of quantity with of; much and many

A game: What are you doing?

Reading skills: Headings   A song: It's your day

Vocabulary skills: Use a dictionary

Grammar skills: Grammar pages

G 38 – G 41

Irregular plurals; simple present vs. present progressive; must and needn't

Communication skills: Poems

Vocabulary skills: Words and things

seven **7**

Contents

Section	Pages	Topic/Content	
Unit 7		**The school year**	
Check-in	98–99	Events at Thomas Tallis	There's a disco in March.
Language 1	100–101	Sports day at Thomas Tallis	Emma runs a race and wins!
Language 2	102–103	A summer fair at Thomas Tallis	The games are fun.
Language 3–4	104–105	Behind the scenes	They're painting the scenery.
Story	106–107	Two great actors!	
Wordwise	108	Phrases and sounds	
Check-out	109	*Selbstkontrolle: Die Lernziele der Unit 7 überprüfen.*	

Passing on information			
	110–113	*Sprachmittlung*	

Extras			
A project	114–115	Poems and chants	Poetry in motion
Reading Skills	116–117	*lernen, wie man gut liest*	Learning to read
A story	118–123	Paul and Jason on a ship to China.	A great story
A play	124–127	Turn again, Whittington!	A short play
A calendar	128–129	Around the year	Special days

Grammar			
	130–159	*Grammatikanhang*	G1–G43

Vocabulary			
	160–194	*chronologische Vokabelliste*	

Dictionary			
	195–205	*Wörterbuch*	English–German
	205–206	*Eigennamen*	
	207–215	*Wörterbuch*	German–English

Numbers	216	*Zahlen und Mengen*
Classroom Phrases	217	*Wendungen für den Unterricht*
Lösungen	218–222	*Lösungen zu den* Check-out *und* Revision-*Seiten*
Bild- und Textquellen	223	

8 eight

| Structures | Skills | Activities in unit |

G 42 – G 43

Conjunctions; word order

A game: Do you know?
A game: A school quiz
A song: Turn again, Whittington

Vocabulary skills: Words with two meanings

Communication skills

Group skills; Presentation skills

Reading skills (vor, während und nach dem Lesen)

A song: We wish you a Merry Christmas

Vocabulary skills — Word games

Selbstkontrolle

nine **9**

Welcome

Welcome to Red Line

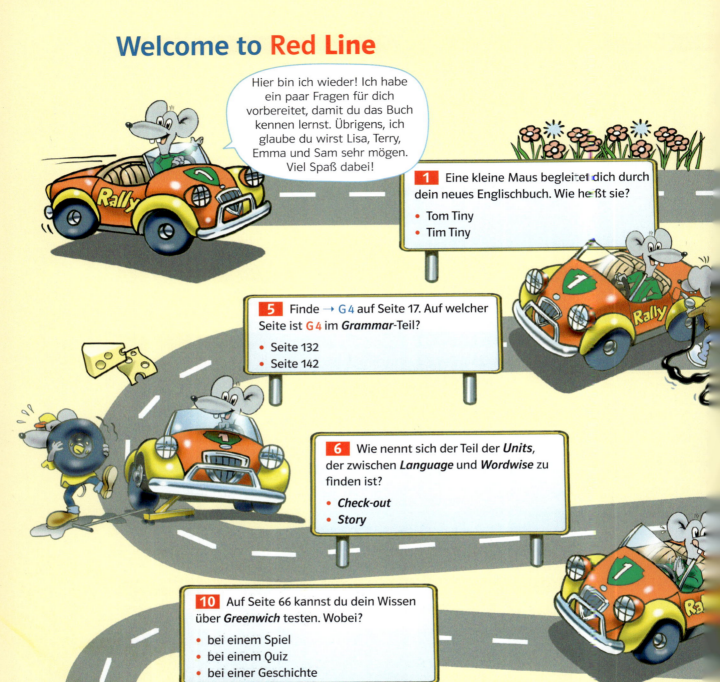

Hier bin ich wieder! Ich habe ein paar Fragen für dich vorbereitet, damit du das Buch kennen lernst. Übrigens, ich glaube du wirst Lisa, Terry, Emma und Sam sehr mögen. Viel Spaß dabei!

1 Eine kleine Maus begleitet dich durch dein neues Englischbuch. Wie heißt sie?
- Tom Tiny
- Tim Tiny

5 Finde → G 4 auf Seite 17. Auf welcher Seite ist G 4 im *Grammar*-Teil?
- Seite 132
- Seite 142

6 Wie nennt sich der Teil der *Units*, der zwischen *Language* und *Wordwise* zu finden ist?
- *Check-out*
- *Story*

10 Auf Seite 66 kannst du dein Wissen über *Greenwich* testen. Wobei?
- bei einem Spiel
- bei einem Quiz
- bei einer Geschichte

11 Hier siehst du einen Ausschnitt aus der *Story* in Unit 6. Worum geht es in der Geschichte?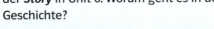
- ein Schwein in der Stadt
- ein Schwein im Farmtierpark

12 Wofür steht p. (z. B. auf S. 163, p. 16) im *Vocabulary* am Ende des Buches?
- *page*
- *please*

Welcome

2 In den *Units* des Buches lernst du die vier Hauptpersonen Emma, Lisa, Terry und Sam richtig gut kennen. Ein Haustier, Barker, spielt ebenfalls eine große Rolle.
Wer ist Barker?

- ein Meerschweinchen
- ein Hund
- eine Katze

3 Wie viele *Units* hat dein neues Englischbuch?

- sieben *Units*
- acht *Units*

4 Was bedeutet GRAMMAR?

- hier findest du einen Trick
- hier findest du Grammatik-Hinweise

7 Wozu dienen die *Revision*-Seiten?

- zur Wiederholung der *Units*
- hier findest du Regeln und Beispiele

8 In einem *Check-in* Teil des Buches werden dir die Familien der Hauptpersonen vorgestellt. In welcher Unit geschieht dies?

- in *Unit* 2
- in *Unit* 3
- in *Unit* 4
- in *Unit* 5

9 Wie heißt die Schule von Lisa, Sam, Emma und Terry?

- **Thomas Tiny School**
- **Thomas Tallis School**

10, 9, 8, 7, 6, 5, 4, 3, 2, 1 –
Let's go!
Let's get started!
We're on our way.
We're learning English!
Let's go! Hooray!

Let's go to England!
It's time, you know.
We're learning English.
Come on, let's go!
Text: Sheila McBride

eleven **11**

Unit 1 Thomas Tallis School

 **1** Real talk: Hello

"Hello. I'm a mouse. My name is Tom Tiny. I'm from Thomas Tallis, in Greenwich. I'm one. And you?"

USEFUL PHRASES
Hello. / Hi!
My name is … .
I'm ten. / … .
I'm a … at … .
I'm from … .
I'm in Year 5.

→ WB 4,1

12 twelve

Check-in 1

2 What's your name?

A: Hello. I'm Peter. What's your name?
B: Hello. My name is … .
A: Where are you from?
B: I'm from … .
A: How old are you?
B: I'm … .

→ WB 4, 2

3 Listening: Phone numbers

a) *Listen and write.*

Lisa: ???
Terry (home): ???
(mobile): ???

b) *What's your phone number or your mobile number?*

My … is … .

 zero (phone number: 'oh')

 one   two   three

 four   five   six

 seven   eight   nine

Mobile is *Handy* in German. My mobile number is 076540 915462.

→ WB 4, 3

4 Your turn: A poster

My name is … .
I'm … .
I'm from … .
I'm in Year 5.
My phone number is … .

My name is Julia.
I'm eleven.
I'm from Berlin.
I'm in Year 5.
My phone number is 030 …

My name is Marion.
I'm ten.
I'm from Stuttgart.
I'm in Year 5.
My phone number is 0711 …

My name is Sven.
I'm ten.
I'm from Leipzig.
I'm in Year 5.
My phone number is 0341 …

thirteen 13

1 | Check-in | Language 1 | Story | Wordwise | Check-out

Old friends and new friends

→ WB 5,1

New friends Language 1 1

1 Thomas Tallis School

Example: Thomas Tallis is a big school.

| Thomas Tallis
Terry
Emma
Mrs Carter
Mr Newman | is | a tutor.
a big school.
new in Greenwich.
the caretaker.
in Year 7. |

2 This is Mrs Carter

She's … .

- a tutor
- at Thomas Tallis
- cool
- a German teacher
- from London

Mrs Carter

3 This is Nina

1. A: This is Nina. **She's** eleven.
   She's from Stuttgart.
   B: Hello, Nina. My name is … .

2. B: This is Mehmet. **He's** … .
   He's … .
   A: Hello, … . *Go on, please.*

→ WB 5, 2

Nina, 11, Stuttgart   Mehmet, 12, Istanbul   Alexandra, 11, Athens   Marco, 12, Rome   Kadar, 11, Paris

4 Your turn: This is my friend

This is … .
She's/he's … .
…

… eleven.

… from Stuttgart.

… cool.

…

… my friend.

→ WB 5, 3

fifteen 15

1 | Check-in | **Language 2** | Story | Wordwise | Check-out

🔊 Sam

Lisa: Are we in the right classroom, Terry?
Terry: Yes, we are. But Mrs Carter isn't here.
Lisa: Is Sam here?
Terry: Oh, no, he isn't.
5 Emma: Who's Sam? Is he a friend from your old school?
Lisa: Yes, he is. He's nice but he's always late!
Terry: Here's Mrs Carter.
10 Mrs Carter: Good morning, girls and boys.
Lisa: And here's Sam.
Sam: Sorry I'm late, Mrs Carter.
Mrs Carter: That's OK. What's your name?
Sam: I'm Sam Spencer.
15 Mrs Carter: Where's your bag?
Sam: It's in Cardiff.
Mrs Carter: Oh! Your home is in Cardiff?
Sam: No, it's in Greenwich. But my mum – she's in Cardiff with my bag.
20 Mrs Carter: OK. But you're here.
Sam: Yes, Mrs Carter. I'm here.

1 Right or wrong?

Example: Sam is late. – That's right.

1. They are in the wrong classroom.
2. Mrs Carter is the teacher.
3. Sam is a friend.
4. Sam is from Greenwich.
5. Terry is late.
6. Emma is from Cardiff.

GRAMMAR	
Verb: to be	
short form	long form
I'm	I am
you're	you are
he's	he is
she's	she is
it's	it is
we're	we are
you're	you are
they're	they are

→ G1–3

2 Short forms

What are the short forms?

Example: He's nice but he's always late.

1. He ☐ nice.
2. Here ☐ Sam.
3. Sorry I ☐ late.
4. That ☐ OK.
5. It ☐ in Greenwich.
6. She ☐ in Cardiff.

→ WB 6, 1–2

3 Short and long forms

Write the sentences.

Example: I'm late. → I am late.

1. She's eleven.
2. We're new here.
3. You're at Thomas Tallis School, too.
4. He's from Greenwich.
5. I'm in your tutor group.
6. They're friends.
7. It's a big school.
8. You're late.

16 sixteen

Verb: to be Language 2 1

4 Emma and her diary

Put in: am, is *or* are.

I ☐1 new at Thomas Tallis. I ☐2 in Year 7.
Sam ☐3 so nice! He ☐4 in my tutor group at school.
Terry and Lisa ☐5 my new friends, too.
They ☐6 very nice. My new school ☐7 big, but the
teachers ☐8 OK! And the pupils at Thomas Tallis
☐9 OK, too.

5 That isn't right

Finish the sentences.

Example: The bag **isn't** here. It**'s** in Cardiff.
The pupils **aren't** in Year 9. They**'re** in Year 7.

1. Tom ☐ five. He ☐ one.
2. Emma ☐ from Greenwich. She ☐ from Bristol.
3. Terry and Sam ☐ girls. They ☐ boys.
4. Mr Newman ☐ a teacher. He ☐ the caretaker.
5. Lisa ☐ in Year 8. She ☐ in Year 7.
6. Tom ☐ a pupil. He ☐ a mouse.
7. Thomas Tallis ☐ in Berlin. It ☐ in Greenwich.
8. Mrs Carter and Mr Newman ☐ eleven.
   Lisa and Sam ☐ eleven.
9. I ☐ a teacher. I ☐ a pupil.

GRAMMAR	
Verb: not to be	
short form	long form
I'm not	I am not
you aren't	you are not
he isn't	he is not
she isn't	she is not
it isn't	it is not
we aren't	we are not
you aren't	you are not
they aren't	they are not

→ WB 6, 3   → G 4

6 Make questions and answers

Example: | Is | Sam | ten? | No, he isn't. |

Is	Tom	Terry	from Greenwich?	Yes, she is.	No, she isn't.
Are	Sam	Emma	eleven?	Yes, they are.	No, he isn't.
	Lisa	and	a mouse? ten?	No, they aren't.	Yes, he is.

→ WB 7, 4–5   → G 5

7 Your turn: At your school

a) Write five sentences about your school.

   Example: My school is new.

b) Ask your partner three questions about
   your school.

   Example: Are the classrooms big?

→ WB 7, 6 – 8, 7

seventeen **17**

1 | Check-in | Language 3 | Story | Wordwise | Check-out

The school bag

1 Listening: In the bag

a) *Copy the grid in your exercise book. Listen and fill in your grid.*

b) *What is in the bag in the picture?*
A pencil, a ruler, …

In the bag	Lisa	Terry	Emma
a pencil case	✓		
a pen	✓		
a pencil			
a rubber	✓		
a ruler			
a book			
an exercise book			
a sandwich			
an apple			
a mobile			

2 A or an?

1. Here's ☐ exercise book.
2. And here's ☐ pencil case.
3. This is ☐ English book.
4. Here's ☐ shoe.
5. And that's ☐ old ruler.
6. Mmm, ☐ apple.

→ WB 9,1

GRAMMAR
an + a, e, i, o, u
an apple a pen

→ G 6

3 Sounds: [ðə] and [ði]

Listen and write the words in two lists.

[ðə]	[ði]
the pencil	the apple
…	…

→ G 7

4 Listening: Numbers

a) *Listen and say the numbers.*

b) *Listen and write the numbers.*

c) A: What's 5 and 19?
   B: 24. – What's … and …?
   A: That's … .
   B: … . Go on, please.

d) *Play 'Buzz!' Say numbers in the right order, but say 'Buzz!' for numbers with seven.*
   one • two • three • four • five • six • Buzz! …

10 ten	16 sixteen	22 twenty-two	50 fifty
11 eleven	17 seventeen	23 twenty-three	60 sixty
12 twelve	18 eighteen	24 twenty-four	70 seventy
13 thirteen	19 nineteen	25 twenty-five	80 eighty
14 fourteen	20 twenty	30 thirty	90 ninety
15 fifteen	21 twenty-one	40 forty	100 a/one hundred

→ WB 9,2

18 eighteen

In a school bag

5 One ruler – two rulers

Here is one ruler.   Here are two rulers.   Go on, please.

→ G 8

6 Sounds: [z], [s] and [ɪz]

Listen and say.   zzzzzzzzz   sssssssss   izzzzzzzzz

[z]	[s]	[ɪz]
bag – bags: The bags aren't new.	book – books: My books are in my bag.	pencil case – pencil cases: The pencil cases are new.
friend – friends: My friends are OK.	tutor group – tutor groups: The tutor groups are big.	sandwich – sandwiches: Mmm – two big sandwiches!

7 A song: Alphabet rap

A, (clap) B, (clap) C, D, E,
Here's a rap for Thomas T.

F, (clap) G, (clap) H, I, J,
English lessons are OK.

K, (clap) L, (clap) M, N, O,
Are you new here? Hi, hello.

P, (clap) Q, (clap) R, S, T,
Say the numbers one, two, three.

U, V, W, shout and clap
X, Y, Z, (clap) do the rap.

8 A game: Words and numbers

a) What's your favourite number?

b) Read and spell the numbers.

   fifteen • forty • twenty-one

c) Make number puzzles for your partner.

   A: Here are the letters:
      What's the number?
   B: It's 'fifteen'.

9 Your turn: What is in your bag?

Example: Two exercise books, a rubber, …
            Go on, please.

→ WB 9, 3

TIP
one pen   one sandwich
two pens   two sandwiches

1 The classroom

1 Listening: What's in the classroom?

a) *Listen and point.*
b) *What's the word for A? – The word is **door**.*
   What's the word for B? – ... .

2 What is where?

Example: There is an apple **on the table**.
             There are posters **on the wall**.

1. on a chair
2. under the table
3. behind a chair
4. on the table
5. in the cupboard
6. on the cupboard
7. on the door
8. in the classroom

GRAMMAR
there is	es gibt, da ist
there are	es gibt, da sind

→ G 9

→ G 10
→ WB 10, 1

3 Your turn: Your classroom

There is ... • ... in the cupboard. • There are ... •
The classroom is (not) ... • ... on the wall. •
... under a desk.

My classroom

The classroom is nice.
There are 20 tables and a desk.
There are ... on ...
There is ...

20 twenty

In the classroom
Language 4

4 A game: Where is it?

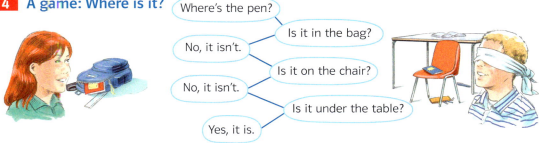

Where's the pen?
Is it in the bag?
No, it isn't.
Is it on the chair?
No, it isn't.
Is it under the table?
Yes, it is.

5 Who or what?

1. … 's TTS? – It's Thomas Tallis School.
2. … 's Mr Newman? – He's the caretaker.
3. … 's Emma? – She's a girl from Bristol.
4. … 's mobile in German? – It's *Handy*.
5. … 's from Greenwich? – Lisa and Sam.
6. … 's in the school bag? – A pencil case.
7. … 's Tom? – The school mouse.
8. … 's under the table? – A bag.

6 Questions and the answers

1. Who's Tom?
2. What's your favourite sport, Lisa?
3. Where's Greenwich?
4. Who's always late?
5. Who's twelve?
6. Who's Mr Newman?
7. What's 7 and 7?
8. Where's Thomas Tallis School?

GRAMMAR		
what?	=	was?
where?	=	wo?
who?	=	wer?

→ WB 10, 2   → G 11

He's the caretaker. • Terry. • He's a mouse. • Sam is always late. • It's 14. • It's in London. • It's football. • It's in Greenwich.

7 Real talk: Classroom talk

Sam, Lisa, Emma and Terry are in the German classroom with Mrs Carter.

a) *Listen. Match the numbers to the letters.*

USEFUL PHRASES

You:
1. Good morning.
2. Are we on page nine?
3. What's the homework?
4. Thank you.
5. What's *hinter* in English?

Your teacher:
a) It's *behind*.
b) No, turn to page ten.
c) You're welcome.
d) Good morning, boys and girls.
e) No homework.

b) *Practise the phrases with a partner.*

No problem!

A Emma is in the cafeteria with Lisa.

Emma: It's Terry. He's cool.
Lisa: Cool? He's –
Emma: Sssh!
5 Terry: Listen, you two. Here's a new joke. What's a word with twenty-six letters?
Emma: That's easy! The word is 'alphabet'. Right?
Terry: Uh, yes.
10 Lisa: That isn't a new joke, Terry. It's a boring old joke. Your jokes are always boring.
Terry: Lisa, that isn't very nice. Goodbye.
15 Lisa: Goodbye, Terry.

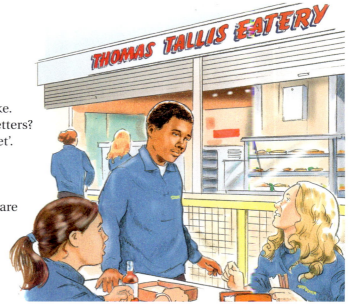

B Lisa and Emma are in the playground now.

Lisa: Let's play. Here you are!
Emma: Oh, no! I'm not good at –
Lisa: Oops! The ball is in the tree. 20
Emma: Oh, Lisa. I'm sorry!

C Now Sam and Terry are in the playground, too.

Sam: Hi. What's the problem?
25 Emma: It's the ball. It's in the tree.
Sam: That's no problem.
Terry: Is it your ball, Emma?
Emma: No, it isn't.
Lisa: It's my ball.
30 Terry: Hm. Your ball – your problem.
Sam: Terry! You and Lisa are friends.
Terry: Friends? No, we aren't. –
My jokes are boring.
Lisa: I'm sorry, Terry. Your jokes are OK.
35 Emma: Please, Terry.
Terry: OK, OK.

D Terry is in the tree.

Terry: Oh, no. Sorry, Mrs Carter!
Lisa: Terry! You're an idiot!

1 No problem!

Talk about the story with your partner.

Example: The story is …

2 What's the right order?

Put the sentences in the right order.

Example: 1. The girls are in the cafeteria.
            2. … .

- Lisa and Emma are in the playground with a ball.
- Here is Terry with a new joke.
- Lisa is sorry now.
- Emma is not good at football.
- The girls are in the cafeteria.
- The ball is in the tree.
- The ball is in the classroom.
- Terry is in the tree.

▸ WB 11, 1

3 Sort the phrases

☺	☹
Oh, I'm sorry.	That's wrong.
…	…

You're not cool. • Here you are. • Your jokes are boring. • You're cool. • No! • Thank you. • Very nice. • That's no problem. • You're an idiot! • Oh, I'm sorry! • That's wrong.

b) *Make a poster for your classroom.*

✱ 4 A picture

*Look at the picture in the story with Mrs Carter.
Write what Mrs Carter says.
Then write what Terry says.*

✱ 5 Act the story

Make groups and act the story.

▸ WB 11, 2

twenty-three 23

1 | Check-in | Language | Story | Wordwise | Check-out

1 Mind maps

VOCABULARY SKILLS

Neue Wörter behältst du am besten, wenn du sie im Zusammenhang lernst. Dabei kann dir ein *mind map* helfen. Übertrage diese *mind maps* auf ein Blatt Papier und lege es in deinen *English folder*. Lass Platz für weitere Wörter, damit du die *mind maps* im Laufe des Schuljahres ergänzen kannst.

a) school: teacher, caretaker, playground, cafeteria, classroom
b) classroom
c) school bag

2 Pairs

Find six pairs: old – new

yes	thank you
on	new
girl	goodbye
old	boy
hello	no
please	under

3 The wrong word

Example: ruler • rubber • mouse • pencil
The wrong word is **mouse**.

1. girl • boy • chair • teacher
2. cafeteria • playground • classroom • caretaker
3. who • what • hi • where
4. pen • on • under • in
5. sandwich • apple • chocolate • homework
6. wall • window • joke • door

4 Word list

Who?	Where?
girl	classroom
...	...

girlpartnerclassroomboyplaygroundteachercafeteriacupboardfriendhomebagcaretakerschoolEngland

5 Find the right adjectives

Example: Tom is a **nice** mouse.

1. My ... sport is football.
2. TTS is a ... school.
3. Lisa is not ... .
4. Sam is always ... .
5. Emma is a ... girl.
6. How ... are you?
7. Here's Terry. He's ... .
8. Your jokes are ... , Terry.
9. The caretaker is ... !
10. My English book is ... .

favourite, OK, boring, late, nice, big, old, new, cool

6 Listening: Words

Write the letters. What are the words?

→ WB 12, 1–3

Check-out 1

1 A new school

*Here is a letter from Emma to her friends in Bristol. Fill in: **am**, **is**, **are**.*

Hello there,

Here [1] three pictures of my new friends and school in Greenwich. Picture number one [2] in the playground – it [3] big. I [4] with Lisa and Sam. They [5] nice. In picture number two we [6] in the cafeteria. The boy at the door [7] Terry. He [8] in Year 7, too. In picture three he and Lisa [9] in the classroom. Sam [10] not there. He [11] always late. My new school [12] OK but you [13] in Bristol and I [14] in Greenwich. That [15] not OK.

Love, Emma

2 Questions and answers

Example:

A: **Is** Mrs Carter the German teacher?
B: Yes, she **is**.

1. Is Thomas Tallis a big school? • Yes, …
2. … Mr Newman a teacher? • No, …
3. Hi, Terry and Lisa! … you from Greenwich? • Yes, …
4. Oh, I'm sorry. … I late? • Yes, …
5. … the girls in the classroom? • No, …
6. … your school bag new? • No, …
7. … Mrs Carter a teacher? • Yes, …
8. Hello, Mrs Carter. … we in the right classroom? • No, …

3 What is different?

Example:

In A there are two posters
  in the classroom.
In B there is one poster
  in the classroom.
In A there …
Go on, please.

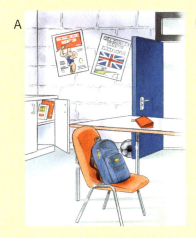

→ G 9

4 Who, what or where?

1. … is from Greenwich?
2. … is Mr Newman?
3. … is in the tree?
4. … is Emma from?
5. … is your mobile number?
6. … is Greenwich?

→ WB 13, 1–3

NOW YOU CAN

✓ Talk about your school. → Stelle deine Schule in 5 Sätzen vor.
✓ Say your name. → Stelle dich und einen Partner/eine Partnerin vor.
✓ Talk about your desk. → Beschreibe deinen Schreibtisch.
✓ Say the numbers. → Zähle bis 100.
✓ Spell → Buchstabiere *teacher, pencil, exercise book*.

twenty-five 25

Link-up A Home sweet home

1 Listening: Rooms

a) Listen and write the words on cards.

b) Look at the picture and listen. Where is Tom?

bedroom   dining room   bathroom
kitchen   living room

2 Colours

a) Look at the picture for one minute.
Then pupil B close your book.
Pupil A: Ask questions.
Pupil B: Answer the questions.

b) Now pupil B asks the questions.

Example:
A: What colour is the kitchen?
B: It's … .
A: What colour is the … ?   Go on, please.

Link-up A

3 A song: Room rap

I'm Tom and here's my home sweet home
with table, chairs and bed.
Green and yellow, blue and purple
and my favourite colour, red.
Tiny pictures, tiny sofa,
in my funny, tiny house.
Tiny TV and computer –
this is my home for Tom the mouse.

4 Funny furniture

Write and say the words.

1. so • a
2. com • • t • r
3. • ha • r
4. ta • • e
5. • e •
6. pi • tu • e

→ WB 14, 1

5 My dream house

a) Draw your dream house. Use your favourite colours.

b) Write the words for the furniture and the rooms in your picture.

c) Put your picture and the new words in your English folder.

d) Talk to a partner.

1. What are the rooms in your dream house?
2. What furniture is in the rooms?
3. What colours are in the rooms?

Example: 1. There are … .

6 Listening: Tom Tiny and his family

Look at the pictures. Then listen and answer the questions.

Example:

1. Who is in picture 1?
   That's his brother, Tim.

2. Who is in picture 2?
   Go on, please.

BROTHER Tim
FATHER (DAD) Tony
GRANDFATHER (GRANDAD) Thomas
SISTER Tess
MOTHER (MUM) Tamara
GRANDMOTHER (GRANDMA) Tilly

7 Happy family!

a) Write the family words.

1. adragnd
2. itress
3. rchemt
4. tadogenrrmh
5. aertfh

b) Write more family words.

→ WB 14, 2

8 Link-up quiz

1. What rooms are in the mouse house?
2. What furniture is in the rooms?
3. What colour are the rooms in the mouse house?
4. Who is in the Tiny family?

twenty-seven 27

| 2 | Check-in | Language | Story | Wordwise | Check-out |

Unit 2 Families in Greenwich

B The Taylor family

A The Brook family

This is my family – my parents, Rob and Farah Brook, and my half-sister, Nasreen. Nasreen is fifteen, and my dad is her stepfather. Our flat is in Holburne Road and it's over a computer shop.
5 The shop is cool. My dad is its new manager. But the flat is very small, so Nasreen and I are in one room. And that's a big problem!

This is my family: my mum and dad, Sue and Richard, and my brother and sister, Ben and Jade. Oh! And our dog, Barker. And our car is blue and very big!

1 The families

Look at the pictures and texts.
Match the sentences with the names.

Example: I'm an only child.
                – That's Terry Jackson.

1. Nasreen is my half-sister.
2. Our house is in Wendover Road.
3. There are drums in my room.
4. Our car is very big.
5. Grace and Ted are my parents.
6. My sister and I are in one bedroom.

→ WB 15, 1 – 2

2 The Taylor family

Look at the text about the Taylors.
Write a family text about Lisa.

This is her family. Her parents are … .
Her sister is … and Ben is her … .
Barker is her … . Her house is … .
The family car is … .

in Pond Road   dog   Jade

brother   Sue and Richard   big

→ WB 15, 3

28 twenty-eight

Check-in **2**

D The Spencer family

This is my dad and my grandma. Our house is in Wendover Road.

C The Jackson family

My parents are Grace and Ted Jackson. They're OK, but it can be boring at home. I'm an only child. There's our cat, Tiger, but he's only interested in mice. Our house with a big garden
5 is in Hither Farm Road. There are drums in my room and there's a shed in the garden.

3 Listening: In Wendover Road

a) *Draw this house.*

b) *Listen. Draw the windows on the house. Then write the number on the door. Now colour the house.*

upstairs

downstairs

4 Your turn: My home

A: Where's your home?
B: It's in … Street.
A: Is it a house or flat?
B: It's a .. .

A: What's the number?
B: It's number … .
A: What colour is the door?
B: It's … .

twenty-nine **29**

Sam's family tree

1 Make sentences about Sam's family

Example: Tim is Sam's uncle.

→ WB 16,1

GRAMMAR
Sam's family
Mum's cousin

→ G 12

2 A game: Who is where?

There is a big family dinner in Sam's dining room.
Read the sentences. Then find the names for the letters at the table.

1. The girls next to Sam are his cousins.
2. Tracy's book is on the table.
3. Sam's dad is next to Tracy.
4. Sam's aunt is next to his dad.
5. His aunt, Rachel, is next to her son Phil.
6. His aunt's son Phil is next to Grandma Spencer.
7. Grandma Spencer is next to Sam's uncle.

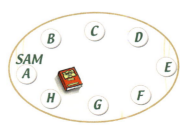

Families Language 1 2

3 A European family

Sam's family tree is on the computer.

Sam: My grandparents' name is Spencer. The Spencer family is from Britain. But I'm British and Italian because my mum is from Italy. And here are my cousins. My cousins' name is Spencer, too. Their house is in London.

Write sentences.

Example: 1. The Spencers' house is in Wendover Road.

1. The (Spencers) house is in Wendover Road.
2. His (grandparents) name is Spencer.
3. His (cousins) name is Spencer, too.
4. A family tree is on the (Spencers) computer.
5. The (Spencers) car is blue.

→ WB 16, 2

Look! This is my family tree.

GRAMMAR

the **Spencers'** house
his **cousins'** home

→ G 12

4 Find the right words

Example: **Our** house is OK.

Sam: ☐1 house is OK. That's Dad's bedroom. ☐2 room is next to the bathroom. And this is Grandma's room.
Emma: Oh, is the house ☐3 home, too?
Sam: Yes, it is. Grandad Spencer is dead. And ☐4 parents are divorced. Mum is in Cardiff now.
Emma: Where's ☐5 bedroom, Sam?
Sam: Here. It isn't very big, and the cupboard is old. Look – there's ☐6 computer.
Emma: ☐7 house is great. You're lucky.
Sam: The Jacksons are lucky. ☐8 house is big!

→ WB 16, 3

GRAMMAR

my	mein, meine
your	dein, deine, Ihr, Ihre
his	sein, seine
her	ihr, ihre (Einzahl)
its	sein, seine
our	unser, unsere
your	euer, eure, Ihr, Ihre
their	ihr, ihre (Mehrzahl)

→ G 13

5 Real talk: Your family tree

a) *Draw your family tree. Put it in your folder.*

b) *Talk about your family.*

USEFUL PHRASES

This is my family.
My parents are … and … .
I'm an only child.
My brother / sister is … .

6 Your turn: Countries and languages

Example: Flag number one is from Germany. The language is German.

1 2 3 4 5 6

Greece/Greek • Russia/Russian • Germany/German • Turkey/Turkish • France/French • Italy/Italian

thirty-one 31

2 | Check-in | Language 2 | Story | Wordwise | Check-out

◉ Emma, you're in big trouble!

Emma has got a big sister, Nasreen. Their flat is small, so Emma has not got her own room. Nasreen has not got a lot of time. Her friends are outside, so she is in a hurry. But her new T-shirt is not in the wardrobe. Where is it?

5 Nasreen: Emma? Where's my new pink T-shirt? I'm late. Have you got the T-shirt?
   Emma: No, I haven't.
   Nasreen: Has Mum … ?
   Emma: No, she hasn't. Hmm. Look in the wardrobe
10   where I've got my magazines.
   Nasreen: It isn't here. Where is it? You've got two seconds!
   Emma: OK, OK! Maybe it's on my chair with …
   Nasreen: On your chair? Aargh! Here it is, with your dirty old T-shirts! What a mess!
15   Emma, you're in big trouble!
   Later in the living room:
   Emma: Mum, Dad! Where's Nasreen? Has she got my discman?
   Mr Brook: Yes, she has.
   Emma: Oh, no! Just because her silly T-shirt –
   Mr Brook: Well, that's your problem, Emma. Sort it out with your sister.

GRAMMAR

Verb: have got

short form	short form + not
I've got	I haven't got
you've got	you haven't got
he's got	he hasn't got
she's got	she hasn't got
it's got	it hasn't got
we've got	we haven't got
they've got	they haven't got

→ G 14 – 15

1 Emma

She**'s got** a big sister.
She **hasn't got** her own room.
She … . *Go on, please.*

- a new pink T-shirt
- a stepfather
- her own room
- a discman
- a big sister
- magazines in the wardrobe

2 The girls' room

Make sentences about the girls' room.

Examples:

They**'ve got** beds.

They **haven't got** a sofa.

1   2  3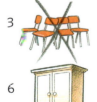

4 5 6

▸ WB 17, 1 – 2

📖 3 Your turn: In your room

Example: **I've got** a wardrobe in my room, but I **haven't got** a computer.
Go on, please.

32 thirty-two

Verb: have got — Language 2

4 Write the sentences with long forms

Example: **H**e's got a nice grandma.
He has got a nice grandma.

1. They've got a small flat.
2. He hasn't got a big room.
3. You've got a nice T-shirt.
4. I've got new shoes.
5. She's got a problem.
6. We haven't got a computer.
7. He hasn't got a sister.
8. I haven't got your magazines.

→ WB 17, 3 – 18, 4

GRAMMAR	
short form	**long form**
I've got	I have got
I haven't got	I have not got
he's got	he has got
he hasn't got	he has not got

→ G 14 – 15

5 Questions about Nasreen's father

Lisa is with Emma and Nasreen in their room.

Nasreen: My dad isn't in London. He's in Leicester.
Lisa: Has he got a new family?
Nasreen: Yes, he has.
Lisa: Has he got a flat?
Emma: No, he hasn't.   *Go on, please.*

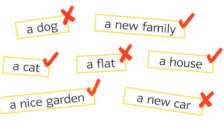

→ G 16

6 Family quiz

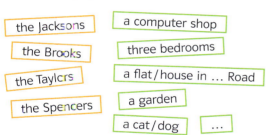

A: My questions are about the [Brooks].
   Have they got a [computer shop]?
B: **Yes, they have.**
A: Have they got a [cat]?
B: **No, they haven't.**   *Go on, please.*

→ G 16

7 Have you got a pen?

A: Have you got a pen?
B: No, I haven't.
A: Have you got a book?
B: Yes, I have.

→ WB 18, 5

8 Your turn: Your home

a) *Put in the right forms for the questions. What are your answers?*

Example: Has your family got a car? – Yes, it has. / No, it hasn't.

1. … your house … a garden? – …
2. … you … a computer? – …
3. … you … brothers or sisters? – …
4. … your friends … mobiles? – …
5. … you … your own room? – …
6. … your family … a cat or a dog? – …

b) *Write two questions. Ask a partner.*

→ WB 18, 6 – 19, 7

At home with Lisa

GRAMMAR
Clean your room, Lisa.
Don't take my football, Mum.

→ G 17

1 Family rules

a) *Say Mum's rules for Lisa.*

Take		your bed.
Clean		Barker for a walk.
Help	+	your homework.
Make		Jade with her homework.
Do		your room.

b) *Say Lisa's rules for her mum.*

Don't	+	use come into make read	+	my football. calls on my mobile. my new computer. my diary. my room.

→ WB 20, 1–2

c) *Make rules for your brother, sister or parents.*

Example: Don't come into my room, Mum. Go on, please.

2 Be polite, please

Say the same thing with polite words.

Example: Listen. → **Can** you listen, **please**?

1. Take the dog for a walk.
2. Help your brother with his homework.
3. Make your bed.
4. Clean your room.
5. Take your sister to school.
6. Phone your dad.
7. Help your mum in the kitchen.
8. Play with your sister.
9. Clean the living room.

→ G 19

3 Your turn: At home

a) *What can and can't you do at home?*

Example: I can phone my friends.
I can't play football in the house.

b) *Ask your partner.*

Example: A: Can you play computer games in your room?
B: Yes, I can. / No, I can't.

have a party • phone your friends •
play music • play with your friends

→ WB 20, 3   → G 13–19

34 thirty-four

Family rules

Language 4

2

1 Listening: Emma at Lisa's house

a) *Look at the picture. Talk about the picture.*

b) *Listen to the text. Which words are in the text?*

good | homework | football
Tiger | dog | door | kitchen

c) *Listen and answer the questions.*

Example: Is Lisa in the park?
No, she isn't. She's at home.

1. Has Lisa got a lot of homework?
2. Can Emma help Lisa with her homework?
3. Where is Barker?
4. What is Emma's problem?
5. Can Barker open a door?
6. Is Barker a good dog?

2 A song: We're a funny family

Now here's my uncle Fred,
His home is in a shed,
And look at his TV –
it's up there in a tree.

We're a funny family,
my relatives and me.
I think you can agree,
we're a funny family.

Words: Ernst Klett Verlag

3 Revision: Barker's bedroom → G 9

*Barker's place is in the Taylors' kitchen.
What's in Barker's bed in the kitchen?*

Example: There is … .
There are … .

4 Revision: What is missing? → G 1

Find the right words for Nasreen's e-mail to a friend in Bristol.

Hi, Nicola.
Are [1] and your family OK? (Please say hello to your big brother – [2] 's so cool!) [3] 'm with my father and his new family in Leicester. [4] 've got a house here. [5] 's a nice house because the rooms are nice and big! My two brothers are very funny. [6] 're four and six years old. [7] 's not easy in Greenwich because my sister and [8] are in one room. The flat is small, so [9] haven't got our own rooms. And there are always problems with Emma.
Bye, Nasreen.

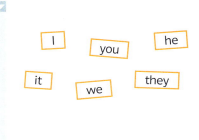

I | you | he
it | we | they

thirty-five **35**

2 | Check-in | Language | Story | Wordwise | Check-out

◎ A fun project!

A It is Saturday afternoon. Emma and Lisa are at Terry's house. Barker is alone in the garden. The friends are in Terry's room but they are too loud. Mrs Jackson is not happy. What can the friends do?

Terry: Let's listen to music.
Mrs Jackson: No, Terry. No music. You can play in the garden.
Terry: Aw, Mum. What can we do in the garden?
Mrs Jackson: Terry … .
Terry: OK. Let's go.

B The friends are in the garden but what can they do? It is boring! Then Emma has got an idea.

Emma: Hey! Come over here. Look at this!
Lisa: What, Emma? What is it?
Terry: Oh, it's the garden shed, Emma. That's boring, too.
Emma: It can be our clubhouse!
Terry: That's a really good idea, Emma.
Emma: Thanks, Terry!

C The friends are in the shed now. "Meow!" Tiger is in the shed but he is not happy.

Terry: Don't be a pain, Tiger. It's our shed now.
Lisa: Look at all the things in the shed. It's a mess.
Emma: Yes, it's really dirty, but we can clean it together.
Terry: I can send Sam a text message. He can come over and help.

Story 2

D Sam is there now and all the friends are in the shed. They are very busy because the shed is very dirty.

Sam: There are a lot of funny things in this shed. Look at this funny old picture!
Lisa: And look at this old table. We can use it in our clubhouse.
Terry: And I can bring my drums in here, too.

Now the shed is clean, and there are four old chairs and a big table in it. The friends are very happy because they have got a great clubhouse! Only Tiger is not happy. Why? Because he hasn't got a bedroom now.

1 The new clubhouse

Answer the questions.

1. It is Saturday afternoon. Where are the friends?
2. Why is Mrs Jackson not happy?
3. Has Emma got a good idea?
4. What is Emma's idea?
5. What can Terry send Sam?
6. What is in the dirty shed?
7. Who is happy? Why?

▸ WB 21, 1

2 Act the story

Act part B of the story in groups.

▸ WB 21, 2

thirty-seven **37**

2 | Check-in | Language | Story | Wordwise | Check-out

1 New words

VOCABULARY SKILLS

Besorge dir bunten Karton und schneide Kärtchen aus. Schreibe darauf die Wörter, die du lernen willst. Vielleicht kannst du noch eine Zeichnung hinzufügen.

Befestige die Kärtchen an verschiedenen Plätzen in deinem Zimmer. Immer wenn du an den Wörtern vorbeikommst, wirst du sie sehen, lesen und auf diese Weise besser behalten.

Example:

2 What can you do?

Make lists.
1. You can play: a game, …
2. You can write: an e-mail, …
3. You can open: a bag, …
4. You can use: a pen, …
5. You can …

3 Funny words

a) *Can you make the words right?*

   Example: bedroom

b) *Make your own funny words.*

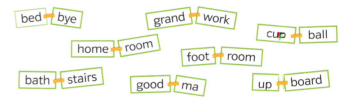

4 A word puzzle

What is the missing word?

1. grandad – grandma
   uncle – ☐
2. wardrobe – bedroom
   sofa – ☐
3. school – teacher
   computer shop – ☐
4. he – his
   they – ☐
5. Greece – Greek
   Russia – ☐
6. CD – play
   homework – ☐

5 Sounds: [uː] and [əʊ]

[uː]	[əʊ]	[uː] - [əʊ]
Who are you?	Oh, no!	Please do your homework.
Hey, cool shoes!	That's an old joke.	Who's got a mobile?
It's a school rule.	My poster is over my bed.	We've got two folders!

→ WB 22, 1–4

38 thirty-eight

Check-out **2**

1 Find the right words → G13

my | your | her | his | its | our | their

Lisa: Let's look at ⓵ pictures from Bristol, Emma. Who's the girl here?
Emma: She's a friend from ⓶ old school. ⓷ name is Fiona Green. The Greens have got a funny house. ⓸ house has got a living room upstairs – and ⓹ walls are pink and yellow!
And Fiona's dad is funny, too. He's always got funny pictures on ⓺ T-shirts!
Lisa: Ha, ha! Is that a dog with Fiona – or a mouse? We've got a dog, but ⓻ dog is big.
Emma: Yes, ⓼ dog is very big – but Fiona's dog is nice, too.

2 Six pictures → G12, G14–15

a) *Example:* 1. That's Terry's shed.
   2. That's … .

b) What have the people got? *Write sentences.*

   Example: Terry has got a shed.   *Go on, please.*

3 Funny questions → G16

Example: I / tree / in my bedroom – Have I got a tree in my bedroom? – No, you haven't.
My / dad / drums / in his car – Has my dad got … ? – No, he hasn't.

1. my cousins / shed / in the playground
2. we / sofa / in our bathroom
3. my grandma / computer / in her garden
4. our school / garden / in the cafeteria
5. I / cupboard / in my school bag
6. Barker / window / in his bed

→ WB 23, 1–3

NOW YOU CAN

✓ Talk about your family. ➔ Stelle deine Familie in 5 Sätzen vor.
✓ Talk about where your friend is from. ➔ Stelle eine Person vor und sage, woher sie kommt.
✓ Talk about your room. ➔ Beschreibe dein Zimmer.

thirty-nine **39**

Link-up B The hobby gardens

1 Hobbies in the gardens

a) Look at the hobby gardens.
Listen to the CD.
Then answer the questions.

Example:

1. Where can you ride a bike?
   You can ride a bike in garden A1.

b) Ask your partner.

Example:

A: What can you do in garden D?
B: You can draw a picture.

→ WB 24, 1

2 Listening: What can Tom do?

What can Tom do? What can't he do?

Example:

Tom can play basketball. But he can't … .

→ WB 24, 2

40 forty

Link-up B

3 Your turn: Your hobbies

a) *Collect hobbies with your partner. Make a poster.*

b) *Now say your hobby.*

Example: I can play football and I ... .

4 Role play: Fun or boring?

*Make dialogues about hobbies.
What is fun and what is boring?*

A: Let's play computer games.
B: That's boring!
A: OK. Then let's watch videos.
B: No, that's boring, too.
  But I've got an idea. Let's ride our bikes.
A: Yes, that's fun! Let's go!

Go on, please.

play computer games	watch videos	go swimming
play the guitar	draw pictures	play football
ride our bikes	read books	...

5 A game: What can you collect?

What can you collect? Start like this in your group:

"I can collect CDs." "I can collect CDs and books."
"I can collect CDs and books and ... ."

Go on, please.

6 A song: Seven days in a week

Text: K.-H. Böttcher, Sheila McBride

7 Funny week

Write the days of the week. Example:  = Saturday

1. nduays   2. auetsyd   3. adonym   4. dnedawesy   5. yadrif   6. yhrdusta

→ WB 24, 3

8 Link-up quiz

1. What can you play in the hobby gardens?
2. What are your favourite hobbies in the hobby gardens?
3. Spell the days of the week. Start like this: M-O-N- ... .

forty-one 41

Unit 3 Clubs and hobbies

Greenwich Band

How about music?
Play in the band!

When: Fridays at 3:00
Where: the music room

Come to the Thomas Tallis
Sports Club
in the sports hall on Mondays at 3:30.

There is a different sport every week! You can learn to play basketball, badminton and volleyball.

The T.T.S. Football Club

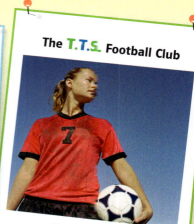

Every Tuesday at
4 o'clock in the field.

Computer Club

Computer games and more ...

Tuesdays at 4:30
in the computer room.

Drama Club

Can you **sing**? Good!
Can you **dance**? Great!
Can you **sing and dance**? WOW!

We have got the right thing for you!
In the hall on Wednesdays at 3:30

How about you?

TIP

Mondays = every Monday
2:00 = two o'clock
2:30 = half past two

1 Clubs at Thomas Tallis

What clubs are there at Thomas Tallis?
Where are they?

Example: You can go to the Football Club.
It's in the field.

→ WB 25,1

2 Listening: Let's find a club

1. What can't Emma do?
2. What has Emma got on Tuesdays?
3. Who can't find a good club?
4. Who is in the band and the Sports Club?
5. What's Emma's idea?

42 forty-two

Check-in **3**

3 Can you tell the time?

a) *What time is it, please?*

1. 3:00: It's **three o'clock**.
   a. 4:00   b. 8:00   c. 11:00
2. 3:15: It's **quarter past** three.
   a. 2:15   b. 4:15   c. 7:15
3. 3:30: It's **half past** three.
   a. 5:30   b. 9:30   c. 1:30
4. 3:45: It's **quarter to** four.
   a. 4:45   b. 8:45   c. 11:45
5. 3:05: It's **five past** three.
   3:40: It's **twenty to** four.
   a. 4:05   b. 8:25   c. 11:50

b) *Or you can use only numbers.*

1. 5:30: It's **five thirty**.
   a. 3:45   b. 9:15   c. 7:43   d. 11:30
   e. 2:45   f. 6:25
2. 1:09 It's one – '**oh**' – nine.
   a. 2:07   b. 3:02   c. 12:01   d. 5:05
   e. 12:08   f. 8:05

→ WB 25, 2 – 3

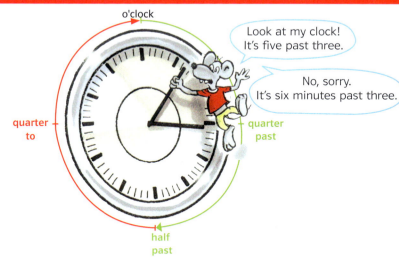

GRAMMAR
4:00 = four o'clock
4:15 = quarter past four
4:20 = four twenty / twenty past four
4:30 = half past four
4:45 = quarter to five

→ G 20

4 Real talk: Let's meet

What can you do at the weekend? Make sentences and talk to a partner.

Examples: A: Can we play basketball on Saturday?
B: Oh no! Let's go to the park.
A: Cool idea! Let's meet at four o'clock.

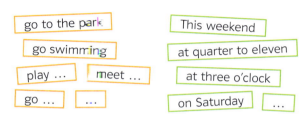

USEFUL PHRASES	
	🙂
Can we … ?	OK!
Let's …	Cool idea!
	Great!
	☹
	Oh no!
	That's boring!

5 Your turn: Hobbies and clubs

What are your hobbies? What clubs are you in?
Make a poster of your hobby, club or dream club.

forty-three **43**

3 | Check-in | Language 1 | Story | Wordwise | Check-out

⦿ A phone call in the morning

Emma and Nasreen get up at seven o'clock every morning. Then they make their beds. After that they eat breakfast. It is now 7:30 on a Wednesday morning in the Brooks' flat.

Emma:	Greenwich 84007433.
Mr Brook:	Hello, Emma. It's Dad.
Emma:	Oh, hi, Dad. Where are you?
Mr Brook:	I'm in the shop. Can I speak to Mum, please?
Emma:	OK. Mu-um! Mum! It's Dad. Bye, Dad. See you at eight o'clock tonight.
Mr Brook:	Why eight o'clock, Emma?
Emma:	Dad, today is Wednesday. You and Mum work on Wednesdays, and I usually go to Lisa's house after school for two hours. You know that.
Mr Brook:	But your dance lesson is today.
Emma:	No, Dad! I always go to dance lessons on Thursdays.
Mr Brook:	Oh, yes! What about your homework?
Emma:	We sometimes play games or take Lisa's dog, Barker, for a walk in the park. But we never forget our homework.
Mr Brook:	Sorry, Emma. I always forget.
Emma:	Here's Mum. Bye.
Mr Brook:	Bye, Emma.

1 Emma on the phone

Write the sentences and finish them.

1. Emma's dad is in the ☐.
2. Emma is home at ☐ o'clock on Wednesdays.
3. Emma has got dance lessons on ☐.
4. Emma and Lisa sometimes take Barker for a ☐.
5. Lisa and Emma never forget their ☐ on Wednesdays.

GRAMMAR		
I	play	basketball.
You	play	basketball.
We	play	basketball.
They	play	basketball.

→ G 21

2 Write Emma's sentences

Example: We sometimes play games.

I We You	+	always usually sometimes never	+	go to Lisa's house on Wednesdays. go to dance lessons on Thursdays. play games. take Lisa's dog for a walk. forget our homework. do our homework. work late in the shop. forget about my dance lessons.

I always do my homework.

→ WB 26, 1   → G 22

44 forty-four

Free time   Language 1   3

3 Their free time

Say what they do in their free time.

Example: 1. On Mondays Sam and his father sometimes play cards.
2. On Tuesdays …

1. Monday   2. Tuesday   3. Wednesday   4. Thursday   5. Friday

Sam – his father sometimes   Emma – Sam often   Lisa – Emma usually   Terry – his friends sometimes   Emma – Nasreen always

→ WB 26, 2

4 Word order

Example: always • I • on Mondays • go swimming
I always go swimming on Mondays.

1. sometimes • We • at the weekend • play basketball here
2. on Fridays • go to dance lessons in Greenwich • usually • You
3. sometimes • on Fridays • call my German grandfather • I
4. do their homework • on Fridays or Saturdays • never • They
5. in the park • I • take our family dog for a walk • always
6. on Sundays • We • go to Thomas Tallis School • never

> **TIP**
> I always go swimming on Mondays.
>
> ~~I go always~~ swimming on Mondays.

5 Listening: On the phone

Right or wrong?

Example: Ben is Lisa's father.
That's wrong! Ben is Lisa's brother.

1. There is a new film at the cinema.
2. The film is *From Here to Chelsea*.
3. The film is on Sunday.
4. It is at the Bristol Cinema.
5. The film is at six o'clock.

6 Real talk: A phone call

USEFUL PHRASES

A: Hello.
B: Hello, it's (Ben) here.
A: Oh. Hi, (Ben). How are you?
B: Fine thanks. And you?
A: OK.
B: Can you ☐ on ☐?
A: I always ☐ on ☐.
B: How about ☐?
A: Cool. See you on ☐. Bye.
B: See you. Bye.

play football
watch TV
play basketball
go swimming …

Sunday/Sundays
Monday/Mondays

→ WB 26, 3

7 Your turn: After school

Example: I always play football with my friends. We sometimes play basketball, too.

→ WB 27, 4

forty-five **45**

Terry likes Alison

Terry plays the drums in the Thomas Tallis School Band. On Saturdays he always plays basketball. Then he practises his drums. Today Lisa, Sam and Emma are there.

Emma: Wow! You're great, Terry.
Terry: No, I'm not, but Alison is great.
Emma: Who's Alison?
Sam: I know Alison. She's in Year 8.
Terry: No, Alison is in Year 9. She plays in the band, too.
Lisa: I know Alison. She lives in our street. She goes on the bus with Ben after school.
Terry: She's cool. She plays the drums and the guitar, and she knows a lot of songs.
Emma: I play the guitar, too.
Terry: *And* she tells funny jokes, too.
Lisa: Oh, Terry likes Alison.
Sam: Is that right, Terry?

1 Find the right sentences

Terry plays	the guitar.
Terry practises	a lot of songs.
Terry likes	Lisa's street.
Alison lives in	his drums.
Alison knows	about Ben.
Emma plays	Alison.
Lisa talks	in the band.

GRAMMAR

He, she, it –
das s muss mit!

she likes
he plays
she sees

→ G 23

2 Say who it is

Example:

A: He **plays** the drums in the school band. –
B: It's Terry. He plays the drums in the school band.

1. She plays the guitar in the school band. It's …
2. She knows Alison.
3. She lives in Lisa's street.
4. He plays the drums in the school band.
5. He asks Terry a question.
6. He likes Alison.

3 Emma's diary

Emma comes home from Terry's house. She writes in her diary.

Put in the correct verbs.

Dear Diary,
Terry [1] (like) Alison. He [2] (talk) about Alison a lot. He [3] (see) Alison every day. She [4] (play) in the band, too, and she is great.
Terry [5] (practise) with Alison in the band. She always [6] (talk) to Terry after practice, and she [7] (tell) funny jokes.

→ WB 28, 1

46 forty-six

Play, lives, goes ... Language 2 **3**

4 In Blackheath Park

Put in the correct forms.

Lisa often ⟨1⟩ (go) to Blackheath Park with Barker. She ⟨2⟩ (love) Barker and he ⟨3⟩ (love) Lisa. Sometimes Lisa ⟨4⟩ (meet) Terry or Emma in the park. Barker usually ⟨5⟩ (chase) a cat and Lisa ⟨6⟩ (shout) at Barker. Lisa often ⟨7⟩ (watch) TV with Barker. He is a happy dog.

→ WB 28, 2

GRAMMAR
she goes
he chases
she watches

→ G 23

5 Finish the sentences

Example: Emma and Lisa read a lot of magazines in their free time.
Nasreen reads a lot of magazines in her free time, too.

1. Lisa and Emma go to school by bus.
   Alison ... .
2. Terry and Sam play computer games.
   Lisa ... .
3. Alison and Ben tell funny jokes.
   Terry ... .
4. Ben and Lisa like Alison.
   Terry ... .
5. Terry and Alison know a lot of songs.
   Emma ... .
6. Nasreen and Emma sometimes make dinner.
   Sam sometimes ... .

6 A game: I often go ...

1. I often go to the cinema.
2. She often goes to the cinema. I always play basketball on Thursdays.
3. She often ... . He always ... .
4. She ... . He ... . She ... . I ... .

7 Sentences

Example: He never does his homework on Fridays. (do)

1. I always ... .   (play)
2. He never ... .   (talk)
3. You usually ... .   (ask)
4. She sometimes ... .   (ride)
5. They ... .   (go)
6. You ... .   (call)
7. It ... .   (write)
8. They ... .   (watch)
9. We ... .   (help)

→ WB 29, 3

8 Your turn: About my weekends

Write about your weekends.

→ WB 29, 4

At weekends I always go to ... .
I sometimes/never/often ... .

forty-seven **47**

That's my game

Sam and Terry sometimes play on the computer at Sam's house.

Sam: Let's play a computer game.
Terry: OK. What have you got?
Sam: Well, these are my new games here.
I've got football and basketball.
But this game here is my favourite.
It's *Power Ball*.
Terry: Are those your old games on the bed?
Sam: Yes, but those games over there are boring. These are cool.
Terry: And what's that on the cupboard?
Sam: Oh, that's my cousin's game. He plays baby games. Let's play *Power Ball*.
Terry: OK. But can I take your old games to my house?
Sam: OK.

1 Right or wrong?

1. Sam is at Terry's house.
2. Sam's favourite game is *Power Ball*.
3. *Power Ball* is a computer game.
4. Sam's old games are on the bed.
5. The old games are cool.
6. Sam's cousin's game is great.
7. There is a game on the cupboard.
8. Terry can't take Sam's old games.

Those apples over there are for my friends.

GRAMMAR
this / these *(here)*
that / those *(over there)*
→ G 24

2 This isn't your bag!

a) Example: "**This** isn't his bag! **That's** his bag."

1
2
3
4
5
6

b) *Practise in your classroom.*

→ WB 30,1

48 forty-eight

This and that — Language 4 — 3

1 Listening: In the park

a) *Look at the picture.*
Then answer the questions.

   Who is in the picture?
   Where are they?

b) *Listen to the text.*
Put the sentences in the right order.

   a. Lisa and Terry meet Alison in the park.
   b. Lisa and Terry can't see Barker.
   c. Barker finds Alison and her dog.
   d. Alison is late.
   e. Lisa and Terry play football in the park.

c) *Answer the questions.*

   1. What day is it?
   2. Who has got a new football?
   3. Who is Lucy?
   4. What does Alison's uncle play?

→ WB 30, 2

2 Revision: Has got or have got?   → G 14, 16

a) *Ask questions with* **Has ... got ...?** *or* **Have ... got ...?**

   1. Have the Jacksons got a house in Greenwich or Bristol?
   2. Has Tiger ☐ a mouse or a sandwich?
   3. ☐ Lisa ☐ a dog or a cat?
   4. ☐ Emma ☐ a brother or a sister?
   5. ☐ Sam ☐ a grandma or a grandpa?
   6. ☐ Emma and Nasreen ☐ a computer or a TV in their room?
   7. ☐ Terry ☐ drums or a guitar?
   8. ☐ Lisa and Terry ☐ the same teachers?

b) *Now make answers for the questions in a).*

   Example: 1. They've got a house in Greenwich.

3 Revision: In Greenwich   → G 12

Write the sentences with the correct s-genitive.

Example: Lisa ☐ football is new. → Lisa**'s** football is new.

1. The Jackson ☐ house at Greenwich is at 39 Hither Farm Road.
2. Terry ☐ shed is in the garden.
3. Mr Brook ☐ computer shop is in 240 Holburne Road.
4. The Brook ☐ flat is small.
5. The girl ☐ room is a problem.
6. Sam ☐ flat is in Wendover Road.
7. His parent ☐ name is Spencer; they are divorced.
8. Sam ☐ family is very European.

forty-nine 49

3 Check-in | Language | Story | Wordwise | Check-out

Barker's story

> **READING SKILLS**
>
> Before you read, look at the pictures in the story. What can you see in the pictures? The pictures can help you with the story.
>
> *Example:* In picture one I can see Barker and the Taylors.

A Hello. I'm Barker. My people are the Taylors – Richard, Sue and Lisa, Ben and Jade. I help the Taylor family. I love the Taylors!

5 Every morning at 7:30 I wake up Lisa and wash her face. Then she washes her face again and makes my breakfast. After that, she makes her breakfast. Then her brother Ben and her sister Jade make their
10 breakfast.

B At twenty past eight Lisa and Ben ride their bikes to school. Then I wake up Susan and we go to the Jazz Café. It's her café, but I help when people come in. I'm very nice to the people.

15

I also like to be outside in our garden. Sometimes cats come into our garden, but I always bark and then they run away.

C On Saturdays I take Lisa to the park.
20 I bring Lisa a ball and she throws it. Sometimes she gets lost in the park. Then she calls my name and I find Lisa.

On Sundays I usually take my people in our car. There are always a lot of cars.
25 Sometimes there are dogs in the cars, too. I bark at them and they bark at me. It's great fun!

50 fifty

4

D My people like picnics. I like picnics, too, because there's no table. Sometimes Jade puts her drink next to me and it falls over. Silly girl!

5

E In the evening my people often watch TV. Then we play a game. I watch TV, too, and they throw shoes at me. I take the shoes to Lisa's bedroom. I like shoes!

At nine o'clock I take Lisa to bed. She's nice to me, so she can always sleep in my bed. I've got a very nice bed. I usually fall asleep quickly after my busy day.

READING SKILLS

When you read a text, always ask these questions first. They can help.

- Who is in the story?   → Make a list.
- Where are they?   → They are in … .
- What happens when?   → At 7.30 Barker wakes up Lisa … .
                              Then … .
                              After that … .

★ 1 Say why or why not

1. Is this a nice story?   2. Is Barker a nice dog?   3. Are Barker's days fun?

Example: 1. The story is nice because it is fun. (or: … isn't nice because … .)

→ WB 31, 1–3

fifty-one **51**

1 Small words

VOCABULARY SKILLS

Viele Vokabeln lernst du besser im Zusammenhang. Bei Ausdrücken wie *at two o'clock* kannst du dir so die dazugehörige Präposition (z.B. *at, to, on, in, …*) besser merken. Schreibe Sätze mit diesen Vokabeln.

Example: be good at: **I'm good at** football.

to be good at: …	at ten o'clock: …	to wake up: …
to be at home: …	in the morning: …	to get up: …
to be married to: …	in the evening: …	to go to bed: …

2 Collect words

1. Collect words for your day:
   Example: I get up, I go to, …

2. Collect words for the park:
   Example: I often take the dog for a walk, …

3. Collect words for free time:
   Example: I never play football, …

4. Collect words for school:
   Example: My school is big, …

5. Collect words for your family:
   Example: I have got a sister, …

3 Find the pairs

to tell	a good film
to meet	the dog for a walk
to open	to bed
to make	the guitar
to take	breakfast
to watch	your homework
to ride	a bike
to do	a joke
to play	a phone call
to eat	a book
to go	in the morning
to get up	a friend

4 Make rhymes

What is the rhyme word?

Great school – very ☐.
Hey, look,
you've got my ☐.
Come on, let's play
every ☐.

5 Sounds: [θ] and [ð]

Listen and write these words in two lists:

Thursday, bathroom, brother, mother, this, then, thirty, thanks, three, those

[ð]	[θ]
brother	Thursday
…	…

6 Barker's day

Put in the right words from this unit.

The Taylors are Barker's [1]. Every morning at 7:30 am he [2] up Lisa. She makes Barker's [3]. On Saturdays Lisa [4] a ball for Barker in the park. Sometimes Barker gets [5] but Lisa [6] his name and finds Barker. Barker [7] at dogs and [8] cats. At 9 pm Barker takes Lisa to [9]. He usually falls [10] quickly after his busy day.

WB 32, 1–3

Check-out **3**

1 What time is it? → G 20

a) *Say the time.*
b) *Write the time.*

2 Tom's Sunday → G 23

Start like this: On Sundays Tom gets up at … .

> do homework
> go to bed
> eat dinner
> get up
> watch TV
> make breakfast

3 The right verb → G 21–23

Put the verbs in the right form.

1. We usually (meet) our friends in Greenwich on Saturdays.
2. He never (do) his homework at the weekend.
3. She often (watch) TV in the evenings.
4. I sometimes (call) my grandma on Sundays.
5. He usually (help) his sister with her homework.

4 Put in *this, that, these* or *those* → G 24

1. ☐ café over there is nice.
2. ☐ crisps here are great.
3. Is ☐ card here your card?
4. ☐ drums over there are Terry's.
5. ☐ apple here is great!
6. ☐ boys over there are nice.
7. ☐ teacher over there is nice.
8. ☐ CD here is bad.

→ WB 33, 1–3

NOW YOU CAN

✔ Tell the time in English. → Sage, wie viel Uhr es ist.
✔ Make a phone call. → Spiele ein Telefongespräch.
✔ Talk about what you do every day. → Nenne fünf Dinge, die du jeden Tag machst.
✔ Talk about your free time. → Nenne vier Dinge, die du in deiner Freizeit machst.
✔ Meet your friends. → Verabrede dich mit einem Freund. Spiele einen Dialog.

fifty-three **53**

Revision 1 Units 1 - 3

GRAMMAR SKILLS   A B C

Versuche erst einmal, jede Wiederholungsübung ohne Nachschlagen zu bearbeiten.

Wenn du aber doch Hilfe brauchst, schau bei den entsprechenden Abschnitten in der **Grammar** nach.

1 The mouse house → G1, G13

| they | I | their (3x) | her |
| his (2x) | he | she | our | it | my | you |

What's missing?

Tom and ⒈ brother Tim have got a big bed in ⒉ room. ⒊ often play in the garden with ⒋ sister, Tess. ⒌ mum is often in the kitchen, but Grandad Thomas is sometimes in the garden, too. ⒍ usually watches TV in the living room with Grandma Tilly. Grandma likes ⒎ family. ⒏ often says, "⒐ 've got all ⒑ pictures."
Tom says, "⑾ like ⑿ picture!"
Tom's father's picture is good, too. ⒀ is on page 27 in this book. "Can ⒁ find ⒂ picture?" Tom asks.

2 Who has got it? → G 14 – 16

Emma can't find her new CD. Put in the correct form of **has/hasn't got** (●) or **have/haven't got** (■) or ask a question with **have/has got** (▲).

Emma: Nasreen, I ■ my old CD with music but I ■ my new CD. ▲ you my new CD?
Nasreen: Oh, Emma, I ■ your CD! Ask Mum. There are a lot of CDs in the kitchen. Maybe she ● your CD there.
Emma: ▲ Mum? No, she ● books and stories on CDs, but not music CDs.
Nasreen: Is it in the shop? Dad ● a lot of CDs there.
Emma: No, they're all computer CDs. He ● music CDs in the shop. Mum and Dad ■ all their music CDs in the living room, but they ■ my CD there.
Nasreen: Well, then, it's in our room. Go and look again.
Emma: Oh, OK. (later) Hey, Nasreen, I ■ my new CD! It's in my school bag!

3 Don't do it! → G 17

Emma is in trouble again. Take Nasreen's role and tell Emma what not to do.

| Don't | + | put
make
forget
use
take | + | your magazines on my chair!
your shoes under my bed!
your dirty T-shirts in the wardrobe.
a mess in the room.
your books.
my pens.
my new T-shirt! |

54 fifty-four

Revision 1

4 What can they do? → G 18–19

Put these words in the right order and write the sentences.
The sentences tell you who can or can't do what and where.

1. Terry • play • can • the drums • in his shed
2. in Sam's room • play • new computer games • can • Sam and Terry
3. take • Terry • Sam's old games • can • to his shed
4. Lisa • on her mobile • can • call • from her room • Terry
5. She • in her room • play • football • can't
6. can't • in the garden • You • watch • TV
7. can't • Emma • have • her own room
8. Barker • Lisa and Ben • take • can • to the park
9. ride • can • in the park • Jade • her bike
10. Emma • songs • sing • in her room • can

5 Terry's friends → G 21–23

Say what they often / usually / … do. Then write the sentences in your exercise book.

1 play / often   2 sleep / usually   3 go / never   4 play / sometimes   5 chase / always

6 Tiger's day → G 21–23

Put in the correct verb forms.

Tiger (be) … the Jacksons' cat. He (sleep) … on Terry's shed in their garden.
Sometimes Tiger (go) … into the shed, but Terry never (like) … that.
Tiger (sleep) … on the shed every morning. One Saturday morning at 11:30
Terry (open) … the door of the shed and (go) … out. He (go) … to the house.
Tiger (get up) … and (look) … at the door. Terry and Mrs Jackson (be) …
in the house. Now Tiger (can / go) … into the shed. He (look) … at Terry's drums.
But drums (be) … boring. You (can / not / eat) … them. What (be) … that?
There (be) … a mouse behind the drums. Tiger (chase) … the mouse, and it
(run away) … into a corner but Tiger (see) … it. He (get up) … on a chair.
He (wash) … his face and (watch) … the corner. Then Terry (come) … in!
"Tiger!" he (shout) … . "No cats in my shed!"

Link-up C   In town

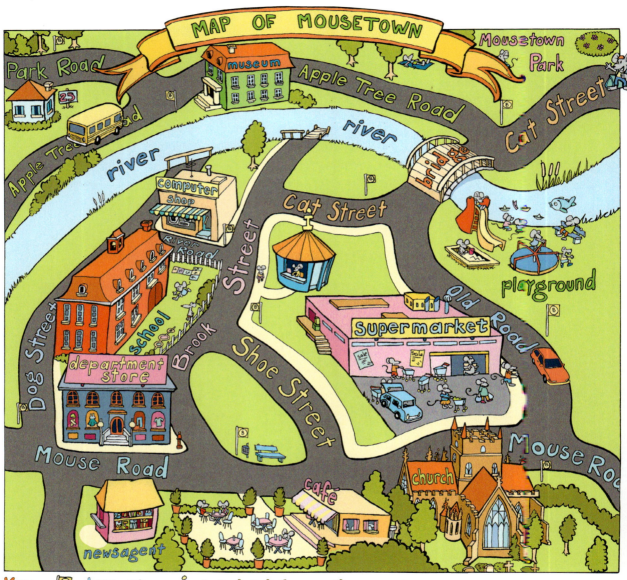

Key: 🚩 bus stop; ℹ tourist information centre

1 Listening: Places in Mousetown

a) *Listen to the words for places on the map. Say the words.*

b) *Now look at the map and the key. What is where?*

   Example: The church is **in Mouse Road**.
   The church is **near / opposite / next to / between** … .

`in … Road`   `opposite`   `next to`   `between`   `near`

→ WB 35, 1

Link-up C

2 A game: Where am I?

Your partner is at a place in Mousetown. Ask questions. Can you find the place?

Examples:

A: Is it near the river?
B: No, it isn't.

A: Is it opposite the playground?
B: Yes, it is.

A: Is it the supermarket?
B: Yes, it is. Now it's your turn.   Go on, please.

Is it the supermarket?

3 Listening: Tom in town

Listen to Tom and answer the questions.

1. What's on the left? Is it the playground or the school?
2. What can you see on the left?
3. What's on the right? Is it the church or the department store?
4. Where are you?
5. What's on the left?

4 How can I get to . . . ?

Look at the map of Mousetown. You are in Dog Street and the school is on your right. How can you get to these places? Ask your partner.

Examples:

A: Excuse me. How can I get to the computer shop?
B: Go down Dog Street. Turn right into River Road. The computer shop is on River Road.
A: Thank you.

B: Excuse me. How can I get to Cat Street?
A: Go down Dog Street. Turn right into River Road. Then turn left into Brook Street. Cross Brook Street. Go straight on. Turn right into Cat Street.
B: Can you repeat that, please?
A: Walk down Dog Street …

1. Excuse me. How can I get to the supermarket?
2. the playground?
3. the tourist information centre?
4. the church?

→ WB 35, 2

5 Link-up quiz

What are these places in Mousetown?

1. It is near the supermarket. There are a lot of children there.
2. It is near the river. It is in Apple Tree Road. There are pictures in it.
3. It is in Dog Street. The children go there every morning.

fifty-seven 57

| Check-in | Language | Story | Wordwise | Check-out |

Unit 4 Greenwich project week

A World Time starts on the Meridian Line at the Royal Observatory. The time line is 'Greenwich Mean Time' or GMT. You can stand over the line with a foot in the east and a foot in the west. When it is 12 o'clock in Greenwich, it is one o'clock in the afternoon in Germany.

B The Greenwich Foot Tunnel goes under the Thames from the north to the south of the river. It is always open. You cannot go by bike or by car. You can go on foot, but it is spooky in the tunnel. Are there ghosts there?

1 In Greenwich

Match the six texts to the six pictures.

Example: Text A goes with picture 1 / 2 / 3 … .
→ WB 36, 1

Can you find Greenwich, too?

2 What is it?

Example: You can listen to stories there. – It's the Cutty Sark.

1. It's a train without a driver.
2. This famous ship is a museum now.
3. The Meridian Line is there.
4. It is under the river and spooky.
5. You can play games there.
6. It is near the river and it has got shops.
→ WB 36, 2

3 Project: Your town (Part 1)

Collect pictures of places in your town.
Look in newspapers, magazines, books and in the Internet.

Check-in **4**

C The DLR (Docklands Light Railway) is a train. It goes from Greenwich to the centre of London. It has not got a driver!

E The Cutty Sark is an English ship and is about 150 years old. It is now a museum near the River Thames. You can listen to stories about life on the sea there.

F In Greenwich Park there is a great playground. A lot of young people come here on skateboards or on skates, and you can play football here, too.

D Church Street is near the River Thames. It has got a lot of interesting shops. You can find things from all round the world here.

5

6

4

A lot of my friends use the tunnel.

4 Listening: A day in Greenwich

a) *Which sights are in the text? Listen and write the sights.*

Cutty Sark • Foot Tunnel • Greenwich Park • Royal Observatory • Church Street • Meridian Line • DLR

b) *What can they do? Put the sights in the right order.*

1. **First** they can walk through the tunnel.
2. **Then** they … .
3. **After that** … .
4. **Then** … .

5 Real talk: At the tourist information centre

A: Excuse me. I'm a visitor here. Where can I go and what can I do in Greenwich?
B: You can go to ☐ . There you can … .
A: Thank you. That's a good idea.
B: You're welcome.

Church Street
Greenwich Park
the Royal Observatory
the Cutty Sark Museum

USEFUL PHRASES

A: Excuse me …
   Where can I go in …?
   What can I do in …?
B: You can visit/see/go to …
A: Thank you.
B: You're welcome.

fifty-nine **59**

4 | Check-in | **Language 1** | Story | Wordwise | Check-out

🔊 A Greenwich project

It is project week at Thomas Tallis School. This year the project is about Greenwich.

Mr Brown: I've got a lot of maps and brochures for our project on Greenwich.
Terry: Mr Brown, have you got a transport map?
Mr Brown: Yes, here you are. This map shows the Underground, buses and the DLR.
5   Terry: Which bus takes us to the Cutty Sark?
Emma: Ugh, the bus. Maybe we can go by Underground. It's fast!
Sam: No, let's go by DLR. It's got a ghost driver!
Emma: No, that's scary!
Terry: Hey! I've got an idea. My dad takes people round London by taxi.
10   He takes them everywhere. Maybe he can take us, too.
Lisa: Cool! Let's ask Terry's dad.
Terry: OK. I can call him after school.

1 Correct the sentences

1. The buses have got ghost drivers.
2. It is football week at Thomas Tallis School.
3. Mr Brown has got maps of Bristol.
4. Terry can call his father in the classroom.
5. Lisa's dad drives a taxi.
6. The friends are in a park.
7. The transport map shows the Underground, the DLR and taxis.

2 Outside the school

Terry: Where's the Cutty Sark? I can't find … on the map.
Lisa: Maybe I can help. Show … the map, Terry.
Emma: Look, your dad is here, Terry. You can ask … .
Mr Jackson: Hey, kids. Is there a problem?
Terry: Hi, Dad. Can you help … . We can't find the Cutty Sark on the map.
Mr Jackson: Of course I can help … . I'm a taxi driver! Here it is. You've got a lot of brochures. Can I see … ?
Terry: Here. Can we go now?
Mr Jackson: OK, but call your mum and tell … first.

GRAMMAR		
I	–	me
you	–	you
he	–	him
she	–	her
it	–	it
we	–	us
you	–	you
they	–	them

→ WB 37, 1   → G 25

Asking the way

Language 1

4

3 Find the right order

1. takes • Dad • them • in his taxi
2. phone • her • I • can • at two o'clock
3. the map • me • give • you • can • please?
4. ask • let's • for the map • him
5. us • the DLR • to the Cutty Sark • takes
6. all the sights • shows • the brochure • you

4 Real talk: Asking the way

a) *Act the situation.*

A: Excuse me. Can you help me?
B: Yes, of course.
A: How can I get to the Cutty Sark, please?
B: Hm – go straight down this street.
A: Can you repeat that, please?
B: Go straight down this street.
A: Oh … Thank you.
B: You're welcome. Bye!

USEFUL PHRASES

A: Excuse me, please.
　 Can you help me?/Can I ask you a question?
B: Yes, of course.
A: How can I get to … ?/Where is … ?/
　 What's the way to … ?
B: Go straight down … ./Turn left./Turn right.
A: Can you repeat that, please?/Excuse me?
　 Thank you.
B: You're welcome.

b) *You are at the Cutty Sark. Help a tourist to find Blackheath Park. Look at the London map in your book.*

5 Finish the sentences from the brochure

by bus • by Underground • by DLR • by taxi • by car • by bike • on foot

→ WB 37, 2

Greenwich

1. You can get from Blackheath to Greenwich [1]. Go through the park.
2. Visit the sights in Greenwich [2]. It leaves from the tourist information centre.
3. You can use the Greenwich tunnel [3], but you can't go through it [4].
4. It's 20 minutes from London to Greenwich [5] or [6].
5. Of course you can go everywhere [7], but NOT through the park!

6 Your turn: Transport

Ask your partner.
Where can you go by bike?

Example: I can go to the park by bike.

by bus? • by train? • on foot?

7 Project: Your town (Part 2)

What transport is there in your town?

In my town … .
We've got … .
You can go by … .
I often go by … .

sixty-one **61**

At the Cutty Sark

Terry's dad drives the kids to the Cutty Sark, so they can find information for their **p**roject.

1 A great time

Answer with **Yes, they do.** or **No, they don't.**

1. Do the kids go to the Cutty Sark?
2. Do the kids ask Mr Jackson questions?
3. Do the kids like burgers?
4. Do the kids know how long the ship is?

GRAMMAR
Do I / you / we / they play … ?
Yes, I / you / we / they do.
No, I / you / we / they don't.

→ G 26–27

Do and don't   Language 2   4

2 Do you play in the park?

Example: Do you play computer games? – **Yes, I do. / No, I don't.**
Do you and your friends play computer games? – **Yes, we do. / No, we don't.**

| Do you and your friends
Do you
Do you and your parents | go
live
play
visit
like
… | with your friends?
with your parents?
your friends at the weekend?
in an interesting town?
old towns?
to museums?
in the park?
… | Yes, I do.
No, I don't.
Yes, we do.
No, we don't. |

→ WB 38,1–2   → G 27

3 Terry and his friends

Terry likes his friends a lot but … .

Say how Terry and his friends are different.

Example: They **don't** like the same films.

1
like • same films

2
play • same music

3
read • same magazines

4
eat • same things

5
like • same games

6
do • same things

→ G 26

4 Your turn: What do you like?

a) *Ask your partner questions.*
What does your partner like?
What doesn't your partner like?

b) *Tell the class about you and your partner.*

Example: We play the same games.

→ WB 38,3

5 Project: Your town (Part 3)

Where can visitors go in your town? Make a list. Then make a tourist map.

sixty-three **63**

4 | Check-in | Language 3 | Story | Wordwise | Check-out

⦿ The ghost driver

The four friends are in the DLR. Sam likes the DLR because it has got a ghost driver.

Terry: This is cool. Tell us about the ghost driver, Sam.
Sam: Well, …
Emma: Oh, no. Please don't.
Terry: Does he scare people?
Sam: Yes, of course he does! He drives the train without his head.
Lisa: Stop it. Don't scare Emma. She doesn't like ghost stories.
Terry: Oh, Emma. Don't be scared! Where is the ghost driver, Sam? Can we see him?
Sam: Of course you can't see him.
Lisa: Why not?
Terry: He doesn't like girls.
Lisa: Be quiet, Terry. Does he walk through the train, Sam?

Sam: No, he doesn't.
Lisa: But he drives the DLR, right?
Sam: Well, yes and no.
Emma: Yes and no?
Sam: Yes, he does, but he's not a person. He's a computer programme.

1 True or false?

1. The DLR has really got a ghost.
2. Sam knows all about the driver.
3. Sam likes the train.
4. Emma isn't scared.
5. The friends are on the Underground.
6. The DLR has got a computer programme.
7. Terry is scared.
8. A person drives the DLR.

2 Scary story

Example: **Does** Sam **like** the DLR?
– **Yes, he does**.

1. Does Sam tell them about the ghost?
2. Does Emma like ghost stories?
3. Does the ghost walk through the train?
4. Does a person drive the DLR?
5. Does a computer drive the DLR?

→ WB 39, 1–2

> Does a ghost live here?

GRAMMAR
Does he / she / it play … ?
Yes, he / she / it does.
No, he / she / it doesn't.

→ G 28

3 Ask your partner

Write six questions. Then ask your partner the questions.

Example: **Does** Terry **drive** a taxi?
– **No, he doesn't**.

| Does | Sam / Mr Jackson / Terry / Lisa / Emma / Tom | like the DLR? / drive a taxi? / know about Greenwich? / visit the Cutty Sark? / go to Church Street? / have a map of London? |

→ WB 39, 3

64 sixty-four

Does and doesn't Language 3 4

4 How can you get there?

Example: **A: Does** the DLR **go** to Greenwich Park?
B: No, it **doesn't**.

5 Wrong names

Who does what on Saturdays?

Example: That isn't Sam. He **doesn't** take Barker for walks in the park. It's … .

Sam?	Lisa?	Lisa's mum?	Jade?	Terry's dad?	Tiger?
take for a walk	play	drive	use	work	bark

6 Your turn: Family transport

Finish the questions and then answer them.

1. ☐ your family use the train every day?
2. ☐ your mum or dad drive you to school?
3. ☐ your family ride bikes?
4. ☐ your family take the bus?

7 Project: Your town (Part 4)

Look at your pictures and sentences in parts 1 to 3 of your project.
Make a poster and present it to your class.

sixty-five **65**

4 | Check-in | Language 4 | Story | Wordwise | Check-out

The Greenwich quiz

Greenwich Project Week always ends with a quiz.
The best teams win a prize. The friends do the quiz and win a prize.
Now you can do the quiz, too.

Mr Brown's Greenwich quiz

1. What does GMT mean?
2. a) What does DLR mean?
   b) Who drives it?
   c) What colour is it?
3. a) What is the name of the big ship in Greenwich?
   b) How long is it?
4. Where can you walk under the Thames?
5. Are there buses in Church Street?
6. Where do you find things from all round the world?
7. When does the Greenwich Foot Tunnel close?
8. Where can you find a great playground in Greenwich?

1 Question words

Write and answer the questions.

Example: What does Mr Jackson drive? – He drives a taxi.

| What / Where / When / How / Why / Who | + | do / does | + | the friends get to the Cutty Sark? the friends do at the end of the project? Sam like the DLR? the Foot Tunnel close? people in Greenwich listen to stories about life on the sea? Terry call after school? |

GRAMMAR

who? – wer?   where? – wo?
what? – was?   how?   – wie?
when? – wann?   why?   – warum?

→ WB 40, 1–2   → G 29

2 Project: Your town (Part 5)

Can you make a quiz about your town? Write five questions.

3 Your turn: Where do you live?

What questions can you ask a friend?

Example: A: Where do you live? – B: I live in … .

Where?
live
do your homework
…

When?
get up
go to bed
…

How?
get to school
spell your name
…

What?
do after school
watch on TV
…

→ WB 40, 3

66 sixty-six

Questions with question words   Language 5   4

1 Listening: The prize

LISTENING SKILLS

a) *When you listen to a text, always ask these questions first. They can help!*

- **Who** is there?
- **Where** are they?
- **When** is it?

b) **What** *happens? Now listen to the text again and answer the questions.*

1. What is the prize?
2. Does Mr Jackson like the prize?
3. Why does Terry like the prize?
4. What can't Mr Jackson do?
5. What can Terry do after dinner?

2 A song: A jolly fine pirate

I'm a jolly, jolly, jolly fine pirate
and my name is Grumpy Greg.
My left hand has three fingers
and I've got a wooden leg.
But I'm a jolly, jolly, jolly fine pirate
and my parrot's name is Peg.

I'm a jolly, jolly, jolly fine pirate
and I'm master of my ship.
My ears are full of rings and things.
There's a scar above my lip.
But I'm a jolly, jolly, jolly fine pirate
with a cutlass at my hip.

Words: Sheila McBride

3 Revision: Jade, Ben and Barker → G 23

Put in the right verb form. Use the simple present.

Example: Jade **is** five years old. (be)

1. Jade ☐1 (be) five years old. Sometimes she ☐2 (ride) her bike to Greenwich Park with her brother.
2. He ☐3 (help) her to cross the big roads.
3. Ben ☐4 (be) 16 and he ☐5 (like) football.

4 Revision: Finish the sentences with your ideas

→ G 22

Example: Lisa often takes Barker to the park.

1. Lisa often … .
2. Sam's grandma never … .
3. Lisa and Emma always … .
4. Terry and his friends sometimes … .
5. Barker always … .
6. Sam often … .

Tiger sometimes plays with me!

sixty-seven **67**

4 | Check-in | Language | Story | Wordwise | Check-out

◎ Terry's dream

A Terry is in his shed. He has got a book about the Cutty Sark with him. The book is the prize from the Greenwich quiz. It is very interesting. Terry reads and reads it.
5 It is nine o'clock. And then …

z*z*z*z*z*z*z

B Everything is quiet. It is a beautiful day. Captain Terry is at the wheel of the Cutty Sark. Sam brings him his diary. He writes:
10 'Monday: From Shanghai to London. We have got the tea and a TREASURE MAP of the Chocolate Islands. The ship and sea are quiet. No problems.'

C Suddenly there is a big bang.
"What's that?" shouts Captain Terry. 15
"I don't know!" says Sam.
Captain Terry can't believe his eyes. A big, black ship!
Sam shouts, "Oh no, Terry, call for help!"
Terry asks, "Where's my mobile? I can't find 20
my mobile!"
It is too late. Lisa, the awful pirate, is there.
"You're lucky, Captain, I don't want your tea," says Lisa. "You can sail to London with that. I only want your treasure map." 25
"No, no, no! We don't have a treasure map, Lisa. There is only tea on this ship," says Captain Terry.

D Now Emma is there. "You're in big trouble, Captain! Give us the treasure map 30
or you can walk the plank!" shouts Emma.
"Lisa! You're a pain! And you too, Emma!" shouts Terry.
Terry is angry. "Lisa, it's *my* ship and *my* map." 35
"Give Lisa the map!" says Emma.
"Never!" shouts Captain Terry

68 sixty-eight

Story 4

E   The pirate and the captain fight. Terry is big, but Lisa is fast. She runs all round Captain Terry.

Then she wins the fight. Captain Terry walks to the plank.
"You win, Lisa and Emma. Goodbye, Sam," says Terry.
Captain Terry falls into the water. He is wet, but it is funny. There is something next to Terry's face … .

F   Tiger is on Terry's desk.
"Meow!"
"Oh – oh – it's you, Tiger. Yuh, you silly cat. You always wake me up!"

1 Right or wrong?

Which sentences are wrong?
Correct the wrong sentences.

Example: Sam is the ship's captain.
            That's wrong. Terry is the ship's captain.

1. Lisa and Emma are pirates.
2. Sam walks the plank.
3. Tiger is in Terry's dream.
4. Lisa wins the fight with Captain Terry.
5. Lisa and Emma want the tea.
6. Terry's book is very good.
7. The treasure map is of the Cake Islands.
8. Terry wakes Tiger up.

2 Find the right order

Example: 1. Terry reads a book about the Cutty Sark.
            2. …

- Suddenly the awful pirate, Lisa, is on the ship.
- Captain Terry is at the wheel of his ship.
- Tiger wakes Terry up.
- Lisa says, "I want your treasure map."
- Lisa and Terry have a big fight.
- Terry reads a book about the Cutty Sark.
- Lisa wins the fight, and Terry walks the plank.
- Captain Terry writes in his diary.
- Terry does not want to give Lisa the map.
- Terry falls into the water.

→ WB 41, 1–2

∗ 3 A quiz about the friends

Make questions with **Who**.

Example: Who is captain of the Cutty Sark? – That's Terry.
            Who are the awful pirates? – That's Lisa and Emma.

captain of the Cutty Sark • awful pirates • has got a book • fights with Terry • works on the Cutty Sark • brings the diary • wins the fight • pains • fast • has got a map

→ WB 41, 3

sixty-nine 69

1 Example sentences

VOCABULARY SKILLS   A **3** C

Wenn du ein neues Wort lernst, schreibe immer einen ganzen Beispielsatz. Auf diese Weise kannst du dir das Wort leichter merken. Du kannst auch einen kurzen Dialog mit dem Wort schreiben. Dann kannst du diesen Dialog mit deinem Partner üben. Nachher vergesst ihr beide das Wort nicht mehr so schnell!

a) *Example*: spooky: I like really spooky films.
ghost: There are ghosts in Greenwich.

`train` `run` `pirate` `interesting` `river` `…`

b) A: Do you like spooky films?
B: Yes, I do.
A: I do, too. My favourite film is about ghosts in Greenwich.
B: Is it very spooky?
A: Yes, it is.

2 Cars, buses, trains

a) What can you drive?
You can drive … .
b) What can you take?
c) What can you ride?
d) How do you get to school?

car • bus • ship • taxi • bike • train • skateboard • …

3 Sounds: [w] and [v]

Listen. Find the word with the wrong sound.

[w] / [v]
1. way • word • very • with
2. why • white • video • when
3. walk • TV • wash • weekend
4. very • of • evening • window

4 A game: Word game

Play this game in class.

A finds a word and writes it down – driver.
B starts with the last letter and makes a new word – repeat.
C starts with the last letter and writes a new word – taxi …   Then D … .

This is a great game!

5 People and things

a) Find words about you. Make a list.
b) Find a thing you like or do not like. Find words about your thing and make a list.
c) Can your partner say what you like?
Can your partner say what you don't like?

lucky • cool • boring • big • slow • small • beautiful • great • sweet • quiet • loud • fast • nice • scary • happy • funny • interesting

→ WB 42, 1–4

70 seventy

Check-out **4**

1 Find the pronouns → G 25

Example: No problem, Emma. I can get you in ten minutes.

1. When does the bus leave? Emma goes by bus. Ask ☐.
2. Hey – We're lucky. My dad can take ☐ on a tour of the sights!
3. The Cutty Sark is great. I like ☐ because it's so beautiful.
4. I can find the tunnel. It's easy! Please give ☐ the map.
5. OK, Terry. I can help ☐ with your transport project today.
6. Mr Jackson knows the way. Ask ☐.
7. Lisa is always funny on the bus. I like ☐.
8. Mr Jackson drives the friends all round town. He takes ☐ everywhere.

2 Questions → G 27, 28

Ask your partner questions.

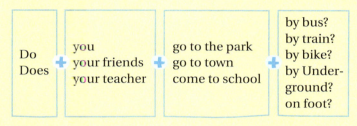
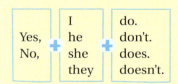

3 The friends and transport → G 22–23

What transport do the friends use?

Example: Sam often rides his bike.

✗ = never   ✓ = sometimes   ✓✓ = often

	bike	walk	train	bus
Sam	✓✓	✓	✓	✓✓
Lisa	✓✓	✓✓	✓	✗
Terry	✓	✗	✓	✓
Emma	✗	✓✓	✓	✓✓
Ben	✓	✗	✓✓	✓
Nasreen	✗	✓✓	✓✓	✓
Jade	✓✓	✓✓	✗	✗

→ WB 43, 1–3

NOW YOU CAN

- ✓ Ask and answer questions.
- ✓ Talk about Greenwich.
- ✓ Talk about your town.
- ✓ Help visitors in your town.

→ Notiere fünf Fragen und stelle sie deinem Partner.
→ Schreibe fünf Sätze über Greenwich.
→ Schreibe fünf Sätze über deine Stadt.
→ Spiele einen Dialog mit deinem Partner.

| 5 | Check-in | Language | Story | Wordwise | Check-out |

Unit 5 Shopping for a birthday

What size is my T-shirt? It's extra large.

TIP
Sizes
S = small   L = large
M = medium XL = extra large

1 Different shops

Match the photos with the words.

Photo 1 is a … .   *Go on, please.*

newsagent • sports shop • CD shop • supermarket • department store

2 What can you buy there?

Example: You can buy newspapers, crisps, and chocolate at the newsagent.

in the sports shop • in the supermarket • at the newsagent • in the CD shop • in the department store

Check-in 5

3 British money

There are 100 pence (p) in a pound (£). Say the prices.

1 p	one p (= penny)	35 p
25 p	twenty-five p (= pence)	£ 5.50
£ 1.00	a / one pound	£ 17.80
£ 1.50	one (pound) fifty	75 p
£ 2.00	two pounds	£ 1.99
£ 3.80	three (pounds) eighty	£ 27

→ WB 46, 1

4 How much is it?

Examples:

A: How much **is** the T-shirt?   A: How much **are** the crisps?
B: **It's** five pounds.   B: **They're** thirty-four p.

5 Real talk: Shopping

Read the dialogue. Act out new dialogues with your partner.

A: Assistant: Can I help you?
B: Customer: Yes, have you got crisps?
A: Assistant: Yes, we have. They're here – next to the chocolate.
B: Customer: How much are they?
A: Assistant: They're 35 p.
B: Customer: Thank you. Bye.

→ WB 46, 2

USEFUL PHRASES

Excuse me, please.
Can I help you?
Have you got … ?
Yes, we have. / No we haven't.
Where is … ? / Where are … ?
How much is … ? / How much are … ?
It's … / They're …
Thank you. / Great, thanks.
You're welcome.

6 Listening: Different shops

Where are the friends?

1. Lisa is in the … .   Go on, please.

7 Your turn: Shopping in your town

*In groups talk about shops in your town.
What are your favourite shops?
What can you buy there? Make a poster.*

→ WB 46, 3

seventy-three 73

5 | Check-in | **Language 1** | Story | Wordwise | Check-out

🔊 Sam's party

```
     Sam:     Dad, do you know what 3rd March is?
     Dad:     Hm, let's see … no school? Greenwich Day?
              Oh, I know! It's your birthday. What would you
              like to do for your birthday? Would you like to
  5           have a party?
     Sam:     I'd like to invite my friends to Angelo's Pizza
              Place at the end of the street.
     Dad:     Sam, I'd like to say yes, but it's too expensive.
              You can invite your friends here.
 10  Sam:     I don't want a party in the flat, and my friends don't want to come
              here. They want to go to pizza places or the cinema.
     Grandma: Sam, you can do a lot of great things here. You can play computer
              games, watch DVDs and you can have lots of great food and drinks.
     Sam:     OK … but I'd like a really big birthday cake, too.
 15  Grandma: OK, Sam. No problem. We can make it together. But I want to go to
              the shops now.
     Sam:     I want to work on my computer. I'd like to make the invitations for
              my party. I want to invite Terry, Lisa, Emma, Phil, Tracy, Susan …
```

PARTY

Dear friends,

Please come to my birthday party at my flat on Friday at 5:00. I live at 39 Wendover Road. See you then!

Sam   RSVP

1 Make sentences

Example: Sam would like to invite his friends to a pizza place.

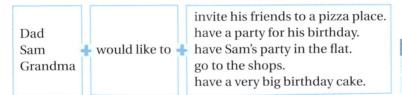

| Dad
Sam
Grandma | + would like to + | invite his friends to a pizza place.
have a party for his birthday.
have Sam's party in the flat.
go to the shops.
have a very big birthday cake. |

GRAMMAR

long form	short from
I would like	I'd like

→ G 31

2 What they want

Example: 1. Ted **wants to** go to the sports shop. Sue **doesn't want to** … .

Let's do our homework!

No, it's boring!

1 Ted – Sue

2 Fiona – Fred

3 Nina – Susan

4 Grandma – Sam

5 Alice – Rob

6 Sam – Dad

74 seventy-four

Months and ordinal numbers Language 1 5

3 The months of the year

a) *Listen and say the months.*

September • May • August • December • June • January • March • July • October • February • April • November

b) *Now write the months in the right order.*

c) *Now sing the months song.*

→ WB 47,1

GRAMMAR			
1st	first	16th	sixteenth
2nd	second	17th	seventeenth
3rd	third	18th	eighteenth
4th	fourth	19th	nineteenth
5th	fifth	20th	twentieth
6th	sixth	21st	twenty-first
7th	seventh	22nd	twenty-second
8th	eighth	23rd	twenty-third
9th	ninth	…	
10th	tenth	30th	thirtieth
11th	eleventh	40th	fortieth
12th	twelfth	50th	fiftieth
13th	thirteenth	60th	sixtieth
14th	fourteenth	…	
15th	fifteenth	100th	hundredth

→ G 30, G 32

4 A month quiz

Make a quiz for your partner.

A: It has got only three letters.   – B: That's May.
A: It's the month with Christmas. – B: That's … .

5 Birthdays

a) *Look at Sam's birthday list and say when the birthdays are.*

Example: His mum's birthday is on the **twenty-first of May**.

Mum — 21st May
Dad — 10th December
Grandma — 15th September
Terry — 6th November
Lisa — 22nd July
Emma — 3rd January

TIP
You write: 21st May
You say: the twenty-first of May

b) *Ask pupils in your class: "When is your birthday?" Then make a class birthday calendar.*

→ WB 47, 2–3

6 Real talk: Invitations and plans

Act short dialogues with your partner.

USEFUL PHRASES

Would you like to ☐ ?
Let's ☐ .

Yes, I would.
Oh yes, that's a good idea!
Oh, thanks for the invitation.
Sorry, I haven't got time then.
Sorry, I'd like to but I can't.

come to my party on …?
go to the cinema on …?
play … at the weekend?
go shopping on …?
…?

→ WB 47,4

7 Your turn: Your birthday

a) *What would you like to do on your birthday? Make a plan.*

b) *Look at Sam's invitation. Then make your own birthday invitation.*

seventy-five 75

5 | Check-in | **Language 2** | Story | Wordwise | Check-out

◉ A present for Sam

Lisa, Emma and Terry are shopping in town. They are looking for Sam's present now.

I'm taking this T-shirt for Sam.

No, you aren't. It's too expensive.

Yes, I am. I'm looking for a great card.

We're leaving. Are you still reading the cards?

Let's go to the department store. We can take the bus.

Wait for me!

Come on. We're late! The bus is leaving.

At the moment Emma and Lisa are looking at T-shirts in the sports shop. The name of the shop is All Sports. But they are not buying a T-shirt. They are too expensive.

The friends go to the newsagent's. Emma is reading the cards. But Terry and Lisa are not looking at the cards. They are leaving. They want to find a present first.

Emma and Lisa are running to the bus stop. They want to go to the department store. Where is Terry? He is not running. Is he going, too?

1 What is happening?

Finish these sentences with information from the pictures and text.

1. The three friends are looking for … .
2. They are not buying a … .
3. Emma is reading the … .
4. She is looking for a … .
5. But Terry and Lisa are leaving the … .
6. The two girls are running to the … .

→ WB 48,1

GRAMMAR		
I	am	looking
You	are	buying
He / She / It	is	listening
We	are	shopping
They	are	leaving

→ G 3

2 In a department store

Lisa is in a department store. Terry calls her.

Example:

Terry: Hi, Lisa. Where are you?
Lisa: I'm in the department store.
I'm ⟦looking for⟧ a ⟦sweatshirt⟧ now.

sweatshirt • bags • a computer game • a magazine • TV • a present for my …

playing • buying • looking for • trying on • looking at • watching

→ WB 48,2

76 seventy-six

What's happening?   Language 2   5

3   New forms

Write these sentences with the right forms.

1. Wow! You (buy) a lot of things in this shop.
2. I (look) for a special present.
3. The bus (leave) now.
4. They (run) to the bus stop.
5. She (put) the things in her bag now.
6. The department store (close) now.

GRAMMAR
buy + ing → buying
dance + ing → dancing
run + n + ing → running

→ G 34

4   In town

Example: Lisa and Emma aren't playing football in the sports shop.

| Lisa and Emma
The shop assistant
Terry | **+** | isn't
aren't | **+** | playing football in the sports shop.
playing a computer game.
buying a TV.
talking on a mobile.
writing an e-mail. |

→ WB 48, 3   → G 33

5   What are they doing?

a) *Look at the pictures on page 76. Ask and answer questions about the pictures.*

Examples:

Lisa and Emma – look for Sam now?   → **Are** Lisa and Emma **looking** for Sam now?
     – No, they **aren't**.

the bus – leave now?   → **Is** the bus **leaving** now?
     – Yes, it **is**.

1. Emma • buy a T-shirt for Sam?
2. the girls • look at books?
3. Terry • buy shoes?
4. Terry and Lisa • leave the store?
5. Emma • still read the cards?
6. the friends • go to the CD shop?

→ G 35

b) *Make more questions about the pictures for your partner.*

→ WB 49, 4

6   A game: What are you doing?

What are you doing? Can the others guess?

A: What am I doing?
B: Are you playing basketball?
A: No, I'm not.
C: Are you dancing?
A: Yes, I am.

→ WB 49, 5

seventy-seven   **77**

Shopping for Sam's party

Sam: OK, Dad. Here's my shopping list with all the things for my party. I want ten bags of flour, and five boxes of eggs …
Dad: Sam, that's too much.
5   Sam: But, Dad. There's not much flour here and I want to make a very big chocolate cake! How many eggs do I need?
Dad: We need six eggs. That's one small box of eggs, Sam.
Sam: And how much sugar?
10 Dad: About 100 grams, so one packet is plenty of sugar. And, Sam, we only need a little flour, and a few candles.
Sam: OK, but then I want 15 bars of chocolate, 20 packets of crisps …
15 Dad: Sam, that's a lot of food! Do you want to invite a quarter of your school?

Sam's new list

flour — one bag
eggs — one box
sugar — one packet
milk — 3 bottles
chocolate — 15 bars
crisps — 20 packets
lemonade — 5 bottles
sweets — 10 packets
candles — 2 boxes

1 Sam's shopping list

What do Sam's dad and Sam want to buy? Look at Sam's list on this page.

Example: They want to buy a packet of sugar.

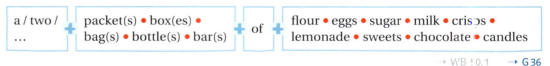

a / two / … + packet(s) • box(es) • bag(s) • bottle(s) • bar(s) + of + flour • eggs • sugar • milk • crisps • lemonade • sweets • chocolate • candles

→ WB 50,1   → G 36

2 Much or many

1. Sam, how ☐ candles have you got on the cake?
2. Lisa, how ☐ flour do we need for the cake?
3. Grandma, how ☐ eggs are in a box?
4. Dad, how ☐ invitations have we got?
5. Terry, how ☐ time have you got this afternoon?
6. Emma, how ☐ fun is this computer game?

→ WB 50, 2

You can count eggs, but you can't count sugar!

GRAMMAR
How many eggs?   – Not many eggs
How much sugar? – Not much sugar

→ G 37

3 Finish the sentences with the words

1. It's time for lunch. I can make **a few** … .
2. I can't do this. I need **a little** … .
3. I can't buy this. I've only got **a few** … .
4. Our teacher is nice. We've only got **a little** … .
5. Do you like music? Let's listen to **a few** … .
6. I'd like a small party – with just **a few** … .

GRAMMAR
a few eggs   **a few** pencils
a little sugar   **a little** time

→ G 37

friends • sandwiches • help • CDs • pounds • homework

→ WB 50, 3 – 51, 4

78 seventy-eight

Much and many Language 4 5

1 Listening: A recipe for chocolate crispies

a) *Emma wants to make chocolate crispies for the party.*
What do you usually eat at parties?

b) *Are the sentences right or wrong? Say why.*

1. Emma has got a problem.
2. Nasreen likes chocolate crispies.
3. There is chocolate in the cupboard.
4. Mrs Brook buys chocolate every week.
5. Nasreen always takes the chocolate.
6. Mr Brook can help the girls.
7. Mr Brook can buy chocolate at the newsagent.
8. Nasreen wants to buy the chocolate.
9. Mr Brook is very nice.

You need: 125 grams of plain chocolate
• 4 tablespoons of rice crispies (or cornflakes) • a few raisins

What you do: Break the chocolate into small pieces. Melt it in a bowl over hot water. Put in the rice crispies (cornflakes) and the raisins, and mix until everything is covered with chocolate. Put spoonfuls into paper cases. When the chocolate is hard again, the chocolate crispies are ready!

c) *Make your own chocolate crispies.*

2 Listening: Up and down

a) *In questions your voice goes up.*
In sentences your voice usually goes down.
Read and listen.

Is he a good pupil? ↗
Yes, he's very good. ↘

Here's a present. ↘
Oh, is it for me? ↗

b) *Listen. Which voices go up? Which voices go down? Say the sentences.*

1. Sam's birthday is on 3rd March.
2. Is it your birthday today?
3. My party starts at five o'clock.
4. I've got lots of nice food.
5. Have you got a big cake?
6. Can I come to your party?

3 Revision: Do or does? → G 28

Example: (**you like**) crisps?
Do you like crisps?

1. (he work) at the supermarket?
2. (he go) shopping in Greenwich?
3. (she eat) a lot of chocolate?
4. (we need) a lot of sugar for the cake?
5. (you have) your shopping list?
6. (they play) basketball on Mondays?

4 Revision: Sentences with 's → G 12

Example: Sam has got a big cake.
Sam's cake is big.

1. Terry has got a great shed.
2. Emma has got a funny sister.
3. Lisa has got a nice dog.
4. Mrs Carter has got a new car.
5. Sam has got a blue bike.
6. Emma has got a good computer.

seventy-nine 79

5 | Check-in | Language | Story | Wordwise | Check-out

◎ Happy Birthday, Sam

> **READING SKILLS**
> The title of a story can give you ideas. Talk about what can happen. These words can help you.
>
> cake | party | date | friends | games | …

A It is lunchtime and Terry, Lisa and Emma are in the cafeteria at school. They have got invitations to a disco at school, but there is a problem. The disco is today and Sam's
5 birthday party is today, too. The three friends really want to go to the disco. What can they do?
"Let's tell him we want to go to the disco," says Terry.
10 "We can't do that," says Lisa.
"Shh!" Emma says, "Here's Sam."
Sam sits with his friends.

Invitation
For
Years 7 and 8
School Disco
At Thomas Tallis School
Friday, 3rd March
7:30 pm

B "Hi," says Sam. "Don't forget my party today. And don't be late!"
15 "But *you're* always late," Lisa says and they all smile.
An invitation to the disco is on the table.
"What's this?" Sam asks.
"It's … it's only a disco, Sam," Emma says.
20 She gives Sam the invitation and he reads it.
"A disco on my birthday!" he says. "We can listen to music at my party, too. And I've got a great cake."

C After lunch Emma, Lisa and Terry go to
25 the playground. They are not happy. Sam is still in the cafeteria. He calls his grandma on his mobile. Emma comes back but Sam does not see her. She listens to Sam.
"But, Grandma, I want to go to the disco. My
30 friends want to go, too. … OK. You're right."
Sam wants to go to the disco, too. Emma has got an idea. She runs to the playground and tells Terry and Lisa.

80 eighty

Story 5

D Sam's friends all come to his party at five
o'clock. They sing a birthday song and give
him his present. What is it? He opens the
box. It's an alarm clock!
Sam and his friends have a good time at his
party. They listen to music, play computer
games and eat Sam's great birthday cake.

E Two hours later Sam's new alarm clock
rings.
"What's that?" asks Sam.
"It's your new alarm clock," answers Terry.
Lisa says, "OK, Sam. Let's go!"
"Go where?" asks Sam.
"Your second birthday present is outside,"
says Emma.
Sam's dad is outside in his car.
"It's seven o'clock, and it's time for the
school disco," says Sam's dad.

READING SKILLS

Headings can help you to understand a story better. Match the headings to the parts (A – E) in the story. The heading for part A is ....   *Go on, please.*

A great birthday party • Here's Sam! • The phone call • Another birthday present •
Three friends and an invitation to the disco

1 Questions

Answer these questions about the story.

1. Why aren't the three friends happy?
2. What does Sam see in the cafeteria?
3. When is the school disco?
4. Why does Sam call his grandma?
5. What are Sam's two birthday presents?
6. Who is waiting in the car outside?
7. Where do the four friends go at the end of the story?

* 2 When?

*Here are five times or dates from the story. Make questions with **when**.*

Example: at 7:30
          When does the disco start?

1. at lunchtime
2. on Friday, 3rd March
3. after lunch
4. at 5:00
5. at 7:00

→ WB 52, 1

3 A song: It's your day

Let's sing a song. For you – for you! Happy birthday, Happy birthday to you!
Party time! It's your day. Fun and music – that's OK.
Music: K.H. Böttcher; Lyrics: Böttcher / McBride

→ WB 52, 2

eighty-one **81**

5 Check-in Language Story Wordwise Check-out

1 Use a dictionary

VOCABULARY SKILLS

Wenn du auf ein neues Wort triffst, kannst du das Wort in der englisch-deutschen Wortliste auf den Seiten 195 – 206 nachschlagen. Hier sind alle Wörter aus dem Buch alphabetisch geordnet. Wenn du z. B. das Wort *money* nicht kennst, musst du zuerst unter *m*, dann unter *mo* und weiter unter *mon* nachsehen.

a) *Revision: Say the alphabet in English.*
b) *Put the words on the right in the right order: apple, buy …*
c) *Now find the words in the word list in your book. Who can find them all first?*

- party
- buy
- egg
- recipe
- money
- apple
- candle
- joke
- try on
- pizza
- expensive
- shop

2 Birthday ideas

Look at the ideas for the word **birthday** *on the right. Write ideas for these words. Use the word list.*

1. dance
2. present
3. chocolate
4. supermarket
5. department store

B ig party
I nvite friends
R ap
T hank you
H elp my parents
D raw a map
A re you happy?
Y es, we are

3 Be polite!

Look at Tom's tip on the right. Then say which sentences are polite.

1. I want to buy those CDs.
2. I'd like to meet her.
3. We'd like to have two pizzas, please.
4. We want to buy new shoes.
5. Listen, I want to see your exercise book.
6. I'd like to have a party.

TIP
I'd like to … = polite!
I want … = not so polite!

4 Sounds: [ət] and [əv]

[ət]	[əv]	[ət] - [əv]
Is Lisa **at** home? I'm **at** Thomas Tallis. Let's play **at** Sam's house.	Today is the first **of** April. We've got a lot **of** sweets. That's the end **of** the story.	Our house is **at** the end **of** the street. Who is that man **at** the bus stop?

→ WB 53, 1–3

82 eighty-two

Check-out 5

1 What are the customer's questions? → G 29

1. Customer: … ? – Assistant: The bag is £15.75.
2. Customer: … ? – Assistant: The pencils are next to the pencil cases.
3. Customer: … ? – Assistant: Let's see. It's a large T-shirt.
4. Customer: … ? – Assistant: The crisps are 40 p.
5. Customer: … ? – Assistant: Sorry. We don't sell magazines.

2 At school → G 33

Example: A: Can you help me? – B: No. (I / do / my homework). → No. **I'm doing** my homework.

1. A: Can I use your ruler, please? B: Yes, (I / not use / it / right now).
2. A: Terry? He's in the school shop. B: Again! (What / he / buy / today)?
3. A: Mrs Carter is late this morning. B: No, she isn't. Look, (she / come / now).
4. A: Aren't Lisa and Terry friends? B: No. (They / not talk / today).
5. A: This isn't the right exercise. B: Oh no! (we / do / the wrong homework)?
6. A: Do you want to play football? B: No. (I / eat / my sandwich).

3 What aren't they doing? → G 33

What are they doing? What aren't they doing?

1 eat • sleep   2 draw • write   3 play • dance

4 Put in the right words → G 37

[a little] [a few] [much] [many]

Mrs Taylor: What do we need from the shops? How [1] flour have we still got?
Lisa: There is only [2] flour here. And there isn't [3] sugar.
Mrs Taylor: And how [4] eggs have we got? I want to make a small cake so I only need [5] eggs.
Lisa: We don't need eggs. But there's only [6] cheese. It's not [7] for a big family!
Mrs Taylor: OK. I need flour, sugar and cheese. Oh, and [8] bags of crisps, too. There aren't [9] in the cupboard.

→ WB 54, 1 – 3

NOW YOU CAN

✓ Say the date in English. → Nenne drei Daten, die dir wichtig sind.
✓ Say what you would like to do. → Nenne drei Dinge, die du gerne tun würdest.
✓ Talk about your birthday. → Sage, wann du Geburtstag hast und was du dir zum Geburtstag wünschst.
✓ Write an invitation. → Schreibe eine Einladung zu einer Party.
✓ Go shopping. → Spiele einen Einkaufsdialog.

Revision 2   Units 4 - 5

> **GRAMMAR SKILLS** A B C
>
> Versuche erst einmal, jede Wiederholungsübung ohne Nachschlagen zu bearbeiten.
>
> Wenn du aber doch Hilfe brauchst, schau bei den entsprechenden Abschnitten in der **Grammar** nach.

1 At Sam's party   → G 25

It's six o'clock and Sam's friends are having a good time at his party.

Sam: Where's Lisa, Emma? I can't see … .
Emma: She's in the kitchen. Look, your grandma's talking to … . They're next to the cake.
Sam: Oh, yes, I can see … now.
Emma: That cake is great! I really like … .
Sam: Thanks. Look, Lisa and Terry are coming.
Lisa: Hi, Sam, we're coming to talk to … .
Terry: Your grandma is giving … lots of cake. We can't eat … all!
Grandma: Hey, Where's Terry? I've got cake for … !
Sam: Oh, Grandma!

2 Make a quiz   → G 26, 28, 29

a) Write sentences about these people, Barker and Tom.
What they do or don't do/like or don't like.

1  football

2 drums

3  guitar

4  computer games

5  Tiger

6  music CDs

7 chocolate

8 apples

b) Then make different sentences and make a quiz with 8 questions for your partner. Don't show them to your partner!

Example: Lisa plays football. Quiz question 1: What does Lisa play / like?
Does Lisa play the drums?

c) Now give your questions to your partner. You write the answers to your partner's questions.

84 eighty-four

Revision 2

3 Saturday → G 31

a) Mr Brook asks Mrs Brook, Nasreen and Emma what they would like to do on Saturday.
Write dialogues and use **would like to** and **want to**.

Example:

Mr Brook: What would you like to do, Farah?
Mrs Brook: I want to work in the flat. Then …

Things to do	Mrs Brook	Nasreen	Emma
work in the flat	✓	✓	
watch TV		✓	
go shopping at the supermarket	✓		✓
go shopping in London		✓	
go to the park			✓
listen to music			✓
read a magazine	✓		

b) Act the dialogues with your partner.

4 Sam's party → G 33 – 35

1. Sam is (make) … invitations on the computer.
   He is (invite) … all his friends to his birthday party.
2. Sam's dad is at the supermarket. He's (buy) … eggs.
3. What's Sam (do) … now? – He's (make) … a cake.
4. They're all at the party. They're (eat) … the cake.
5. Now it's seven o'clock and they're (go) … to the school disco.
6. It's great. They're all (dance) … .
7. The music stops. What's (happen) …?
8. All the people at the disco are (sing) … "Happy Birthday" to Sam!

PARTY
Dear friends,
Please come to my birthday party at my flat on Friday at 5:00. I live at 39 Wendover Road. See you then!
Sam   RSVP

5 Terry's Saturday → G 33 – 35

Examples:

It's nine o'clock. What is Terry doing?
– He's getting up.

It's 9:30. Is Terry playing the drums?
– No, he isn't, he's … .

It's 9:40. What is Terry doing?
– …

9:00 am	get up late
9:15 – 9:40	have breakfast
9:40 – 10:30	help Dad in the garden
10:30	go to the park
10:40 – 11:15	talk to Emma and Sam in the park
11:30 – 12:30 pm	play drums in the shed
12:30 – 1:00	have lunch
1:00 – 1:30	clean the kitchen with Mum
1:30 – 2:15	play computer game
2:15	go to the park again
2:30 – 4:15	play football with Lisa
4:20	go home for tea
5:30 – 6:00	watch TV
6:00 – 7:00	do homework
7:00 – 8:30	watch a video

eighty-five 85

| 6 | Check-in | Language | Story | Wordwise | Check-out |

Unit 6 At the farm park

Come to the Cotswold Farm Park. Fun for all the family!

The Cotswold Farm Park is a great place to visit. We are open in both spring and summer. We have got horses, sheep, geese, pigs and much, much more. You can do a lot of fun things on the farm. Then stay at the Cotswold Hostel for a night. It is near the farm and the food there is great.

Our baby lambs are born in spring (20th March to 3rd May). They're everybody's favourite! Come and see.

At the Tractor School children can drive our mini red tractors. They are really fast and a lot of fun!

Meet the baby animals at the Pets Corner. You can feed the kids with a bottle. Or buy a bag of animal snacks in the Gift Shop. Be careful! The goats like to eat the bags too. They're always hungry!

> **TIP**
> kids = children and young goats

Milk does not come from a supermarket! Visit the Milking Barn and watch the farmers milk the cows every evening. Try it too, but not with real cows. We have got a special cow for you.

Opening times:
10:30 am to 5:00 pm

Tickets:
children   £3.50
adults   £4.95
family ticket   £15.50

> **TIP**
> am = morning + night
> pm = afternoon + evening

Do you want to see all of the farm? Then go on the Farm Safari Ride.
→ G 38

You can buy lots of great things at the Gift Shop:
postcards, books, posters, farm cheese, super sweatshirts and cool pullovers.

86 eighty-six

Check-in 6

1 At the farm park

1. What can you see at the farm park?
2. What can you do at the Pets Corner?
3. When is the farm park open?
4. What can you buy in the Gift Shop?
5. How much is a family ticket?
6. What can you drive on the farm?

2 Plural forms

*Make a list of plurals with the words.
Look at the text on page 86. It can help you.*

apple • cow • goose • dog • cat • farm • man •
mouse • pig • sheep • lamb • horse • tractor •
snack • child • animal • woman • shop • chicken

→ WB 56, 1

GRAMMAR	
one	two, three
child	children
goose	geese
mouse	mice
sheep	sheep
man	men
woman	women

→ G 39

3 Seasons

a) *Look at the pictures and the jumbled words. Do you know the four seasons?*

ginrsp   mumser   nutuma   rentiw

b) *What can you do in summer?*

   Example: In summer I can ride my bike and play in the park.

→ WB 56, 2

4 Listening: A school trip

1. When does the bus leave?
2. Who has got a new alarm clock?
3. Where does Year 7 always sleep?
4. Can Barker go to the farm park, too?
5. When do the farmers milk the cows?
6. Where can you buy animal snacks?

→ WB 56, 3

5 Your turn: An animal poster

*Write lists of animals and make a poster of
your favourite animals. Find pictures of the
animals and write sentences about them.*

pets	farm animals	?
cat	goose	...
...	...	...

eighty-seven 87

6 | Check-in | Language 1 | Story | Wordwise | Check-out

🔊 Not that pullover!

It is Saturday afternoon. Sam and Terry are in Sam's room. Sam is packing his bag for the trip to the Cotswold Farm Park.

Sam: No school uniform. Great! I'm packing my favourite clothes. And I'm wearing these sunglasses and my new trainers.
Terry: Wow! Great.
Sam: I want to take my new sweatshirt. But I can't find it!
Terry: What's this in the wardrobe? A pullover? Ugh!
Sam: I know, it's not cool. Grandma likes it. Quick! She's coming. Put it behind the wardrobe.
Grandma: Sam, I can't find your pullover downstairs. It can be very cold on a farm in spring. Is it in your wardrobe?
Sam: No! No! It's not in my wardrobe.
Grandma: Sam, why are you wearing sunglasses? It's not sunny. It's raining! And you can't wear those new trainers. You need good farm shoes. Pack these wellies.
Sam: Oh, Grandma. Wellies aren't cool!
Terry: Oh, it's 1:30. We haven't got much time. The bus is waiting for us at the school.
Sam: See you, Grandma.
Terry: Bye, Mrs Spencer.
Grandma: OK, Sam. Have fun. Bye. Oh! What's this behind the wardrobe?

1 True or false?

Say true or false. Then correct the false sentences.

1. Sam and Terry are at school.
2. Sam is packing his school uniform.
3. It is raining.
4. Grandma likes Sam's pullover.
5. The pullover is behind the wardrobe.
6. It is eleven o'clock and Barker is waiting.

2 Clothes

a) What clothes words do you know?

b) What are the friends wearing now?

   Example: Terry is wearing jeans, trainers, … .   Go on, please.

c) What are you wearing?
   What is your teacher wearing?

→ WB 57,1

88 eighty-eight

Clothes and weather   Language 1   6

3 **What's the weather like today?**

1. Saturday morning

Lisa is taking Barker for a walk. It's raining. Barker and Lisa are very wet.

2. Saturday afternoon

Sam and Terry are playing football. Both boys are wearing caps. It's sunny and warm.

3. Saturday evening

Emma and Nasreen are waiting for the bus. It's cold and very windy.

a) *What is the weather like in the three pictures?* In picture 1, it's … .

b) *Look out of the window. What is the weather like today?*

→ WB 57, 2

4 **Write sentences**

Example: It's sunny today. We can … .

| It's sunny today.
It's warm.
It's raining.
It's wet.
It's very cold.
It's really windy. | ＋ | We can
We can't
Let's | ＋ | go to the cinema.
play basketball outside.
read magazines.
play computer games.
ride our bikes.
… . |

5 **Poems**

COMMUNICATION SKILLS

a) Listen and say the poems with the CD.
b) Now say the poems without the CD.

The windy shed

Oh, the wind!
The wind is in my shed.
It's dancing round my head.
And now my nose is really red.

nose

Barker's summer

Oh look! I see the sun!
And Barker wants to swim and run.
It's summer now!
Let's go have fun.
It's summer now!
Let's go and run!

6 **Your turn: Your favourite season**

Draw your favourite season. What is the weather like? What clothes do you wear in your favourite season?

eighty-nine **89**

At the Cotswold Hostel

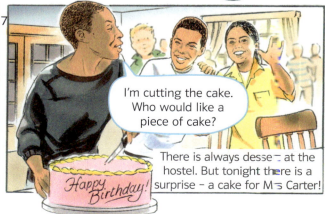

Simple present and present progressive — Language 2 — 6

1 At the hostel

Match the sentences with the pictures.

Example: "We're in the yellow room!" – That's picture number … . *Go on, please.*

1. "We're in the yellow room!"
2. "That's a big box!"
3. "Let's sing a different song."
4. "What a great surprise! Thank you."
5. "Umm … I love cheese."
6. "There's the hostel!"
7. "Sam, can I play your game?"

2 Finish the sentences

Example: At home Lisa **usually reads** in her room.
But **now** she **is reading** on the bus.

1. At home Terry always sings in the bathroom.
   Now he (**sing**) on the bus.
2. At home Mrs Carter never eats cake.
   But this evening she (**eat**) a lot of cake!
3. At home Emma often talks to Lisa on the phone.
   But this evening she (**talk**) to Lisa in the hostel.
4. At home Sam never drinks milk.
   But now at breakfast at the hostel he (**drink**) milk.

→ WB 58, 1–2

> **GRAMMAR**
>
> He **never / usually / often / always** works at home. (simple present)
>
> He **is working this weekend / now / this morning / this …** at home. (present progressive)

→ G 40

3 The friends on a school trip

What do their families usually do on Saturday mornings?
What are the friends' families doing this Saturday morning?

Example: 1. Jade **usually listens** to the radio on Saturday mornings.
This Saturday morning Jade **is using** Lisa's Discman.

1. Jade usually listen to • the radio • on Saturday mornings.
   This Saturday morning • Jade • use • Lisa's Discman.
2. Nasreen usually sleep • on Saturday mornings.
   This Saturday morning • Nasreen • work • in the shop.
3. Ben usually read • comics • on Saturday mornings.
   This Saturday morning • Ben • take • Barker for a walk.
4. Mrs Jackson usually go shopping • on Saturday mornings.
   This Saturday morning • Mrs Jackson • clean • Terry's shed.
5. Tiger usually sleep • in the kitchen • on Saturday mornings.
   This Saturday morning • Tiger • sleep • on Terry's bed.
6. Grandma usually make • breakfast • on Saturday mornings.
   This Saturday morning • Grandma • play • computer games.

→ WB 58, 3 – 59, 5

4 Your turn: Saturday mornings

What do you usually do on Saturday mornings? Write four sentences.

ninety-one **91**

6 Check-in | Language 3 | Story | Wordwise | Check-out

Breakfast at the hostel

It is Sunday morning. Year 7 is eating breakfast at the hostel. Mrs Carter is talking about the day.

Mrs Carter: We must be at the farm park at nine o'clock. It's raining so you must take your wellies.
Sam: Must we take food?
5 Mrs Carter: No, Sam, you needn't take food. I've got sandwiches for the class in the bus.
Sam: OK, Mrs Carter, but I've got my favourite crisps in my bag.
10 Lisa: Oh, Sam. You're always hungry.
Mrs Carter: That's OK, Sam … We must be back at the hostel at five o'clock for tea.
Emma: Can we have some scones for tea, Mrs Carter?
15
Terry: Oh, not scones! I want chocolate cake for tea.
Emma: I love scones. We must have scones!

1 At breakfast

1. When must they be at the farm park in the morning?
2. Why must the pupils take wellies to the farm park?
3. Why needn't they take food to the farm park?
4. What has Sam got in his bag?
5. When must they be back at the hostel for tea?

I usually eat breakfast in bed.

→ WB 60, 1

2 Must or needn't?

Example: Sam needn't bring food.

The class Sam Emma Mrs Carter	must needn't	take their wellies. have some scones for tea. be at the farm at nine o'clock. talk about the day. bring food.

GRAMMAR
You **needn't** bring food.
We **must** have scones!

→ WB 60, 2   → G 41

3 Your turn: Class trips

Where do you go on class trips? What must you take?

Example: We go to … . We must take … .

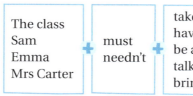

What food?   What clothes?
….

92 ninety-two

Needn't and must   Language 4   6

1 Listening: At the farm park

a) *Listen to the text. Then answer the questions.*

1. Who is Mrs Smith?
2. What is Mrs Smith telling the pupils?
3. Can the pupils go to the Tractor School?
4. Are the farmers milking the cows now?
5. When do the farmers milk the cows?
6. What is in the barn behind Mrs Smith?
7. How many kids are in the Pets Corner?
8. Can you give crisps to the animals?
9. Where can you buy animal snacks?
10. Can you buy bottles of milk in the shop?

b) *What are your favourite animals at the farm park? Write sentences.*

Example: I like the cows because they are big and nice.

2 Revision: What's fun?   → G 27–28

a) *Write six questions about different hobbies.*

b) *Ask three friends the questions.*

c) *Tell the class about your answers.*

Questions	Tina	Peter	Anna
1. Do you listen to English music?	Yes	No	No
2. Do you play football?	Yes	Yes	No
… .	…	…	…

play computer games

watch a lot of TV

collect comics

play the guitar

read books

…

→ WB 61, 1

3 Revision: Present progressive   → G 33, 35

a) *What are the friends doing in the park? Write sentences.*

b) *Ask your partner questions about the picture.*

Example:

A: Is Terry playing basketball?
B: Yes, he is.
B: Is Lisa eating crisps?
A: No, she isn't. She … .
A: Are Lisa and Terry … .

→ WB 61, 2

ninety-three **93**

6   Check-in   Language   Story   Wordwise   Check-out

◎ Pet pig Polly

A The four friends are in the Cotswold Farm Park. They know a lot about the farm from Mrs Smith, and now they want to see everything. Terry and Sam want to drive the
5 tractors and Lisa wants to feed the kids. But Emma is not very happy. She does not like the farm because she does not like animals. Suddenly Emma hears something. Oink! Oh, no! There is a little pig standing next to her.
10 Emma shouts, "Help!"
Terry laughs, "Oh, Emma, it's only a little pig."
Mrs Smith says, "Her name is Polly. She's very funny – she thinks she's a dog, and so she always wants to play with children!"
15

B The friends go to see the kids next. Lisa has got a little bottle of milk and wants to feed a kid. Suddenly Polly is there. She wants some milk from Emma. The friends laugh – Polly likes Emma, but Emma doesn't
20 like pigs!
Then the friends go to the tractor school. They all want to drive a tractor. Emma drives a tractor, too, and she is really fast. Now suddenly the friends are all laughing. The
25 little pig Polly is running behind Emma's tractor. She really likes Emma a lot. Emma laughs, too, and now she thinks Polly is cute.

C After the tractor school, they want to see
30 the cows. Suddenly there is a big black dog behind Emma, and she is scared.
But Polly is there again. She runs around the dog; he is scared and runs away.
"Thanks, Polly," she says and pats little Polly
35 on the head.
Terry and Sam want to play with the little pig, but Polly only wants to play with Emma.
"Silly pig!" the boys shout.
"You're scaring her!" says Emma. "Go away,
40 you two!"
"OK, OK, we're going," they say.
"Have fun with your pet pig!" shouts Terry.

Story 6

D Emma and Polly walk to a small field and Emma sits down on the grass. Lisa, Terry
45 and Sam see her. Terry and Sam say "sorry" to Emma. They want to be nice to Polly now. Emma says, "That's OK."
Then Lisa says, "Oh, it's twelve o'clock. It's time for lunch!"
50 "I'm really hungry," says Terry.
They all want to eat their sandwiches in the field together.

E Emma opens her lunch bag and then
55 suddenly stops. They all look at her. Emma looks in her bag, and then she looks at Polly.
"Emma, what's wrong?" asks Lisa. "Are you OK?"
"I … can't … eat this!" answers Emma.
60 Then she takes a big sandwich out of her bag – a *ham* sandwich. All the friends laugh.
"Here you are, Emma," laughs Terry. "Have my *cheese* sandwich!"

1 The right names

Write the right names.

Example: ☐ wants to feed the kids. → **Lisa** wants to feed the kids.

1. ☐ does not like the farm.
2. ☐ thinks she is a dog.
3. ☐ is Emma's new friend.
4. ☐ drives the tractor really fast.
5. ☐ shouts, "Help!"
6. ☐ is really hungry.
7. ☐ has got a ham sandwich.
8. ☐ gives Emma a cheese sandwich.

2 The story

Answer the questions about the story.

1. Who tells the friends about the farm?
2. What doesn't Emma like?
3. Who is Polly?
4. What happens at the tractor school?
5. What scares Emma?
6. How does Polly help Emma?
7. Who scares Polly?
8. Where do the friends eat lunch?
9. What has Emma got for lunch?
10. What is the problem?
11. How does Terry help?
12. What does Emma eat?

→ WB 62, 1

ninety-five **95**

6 | Check-in | Language | Story | Wordwise | Check-out

1 Words and things

VOCABULARY SKILLS   A B C

Wenn du ein neues Wort lernst, nimm – wenn möglich – den entsprechenden Gegenstand oder ein Bild davon in die Hand und sprich das Wort mehrmals vor dich hin. Überlege dir dann einen ganzen Satz mit diesem Wort.

Examples: This is my favourite **car**.   I love my **skateboard**!

2 Mind map

a) Draw a mind map with the word **clothes**.

b) Draw a mind map with the word **farm**.

3 Tom's shopping

Here is a picture of Tom's kitchen. What can you see in Tom's kitchen? Make a list.

Example: I can see a bottle of milk, some cheese, … .

4 Sounds: [ɪ] and [i:]

Listen and say.

[ɪ]	[i:]
it • visit • pig • Italy • crisp • kid	easy • eat • sheep • geese • evening
→ The kids visit the pigs on the farm.	→ The sheep and the geese eat in the evening.

5 Weather

a) Talk about the weather in the pictures.   *Example:* It is warm in Greece.

Greece    Italy    Turkey    Russia

b) What other weather words do you know? Make a mind map.

→ WB 63, 1–4

Check-out 6

1 Simple present or present progressive? → G 40

Put in the right forms.

Don't forget. They drive on the left in Britain!

Example: 1. Sam's cousins and their parents often **go** on trips.

1. Sam's cousins and their parents often **(go)** on trips. 2. This Saturday they **(go)** to the Cotswolds. 3. Sam's uncle usually **(drive)**, but today he **(read)** the map and Sam's aunt **(drive)**. 4. Phil, Tracy and Susan always **(sit)** behind their parents. 5. Tracy usually **(sleep)** and Phil often **(play)** his computer games. What is Susan doing now? 6. She **(tell)** jokes. 7. She always **(tell)** jokes.

2 Plurals: Regular and irregular → G 39

Write the words in the box in the plural.

Example: bottle → bottles

child	picture	desk	island	shop	cake
cat	sheep	bottle	pound	woman	teacher
goose	mouse	sandwich	pencil case	man	

3 Must and needn't → G 41

a) *Example:* It's late. You **must pack** your bag.   b) *Example:* We **needn't take** food to the farm.

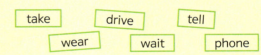

be · clean · wear · listen · tell · send · pack

take · drive · tell · wear · wait · phone

1. It's late. You ☐ your bag.
2. Oh no! It's raining. I ☐ my wellies.
3. Hurry! We ☐ at the bus stop at 2:00.
4. This room is really dirty. We ☐ it!
5. Terry, you ☐ jokes on the bus.
6. I ☐ a postcard to Grandma.
7. You ☐ to your teacher in the lesson.

1. We ☐ food to the farm.
2. Great! I ☐ my uniform today.
3. Dad, you ☐ us to school. We can walk.
4. Terry, you ☐ your old jokes.
5. Lisa, you ☐ for us. You can go to the shop without us.
6. You ☐ your mum. She is not at home.

→ WB 64, 1–2

NOW YOU CAN

✓ Talk about your clothes.   → Beschreibe, was du heute trägst.
✓ Talk about the weather.   → Wie ist das Wetter heute? Sprich darüber.
✓ Say the names of animals.   → Nenne drei Tiere, die Milch geben. Nenne zwei Tiere, die Eier legen.
✓ Write about a farm park.   → Schreibe drei Sachen auf, die man im Cotswold Farm Park machen kann.

ninety-seven 97

Unit 7 The school year

September

The Thames Festival Lantern Procession is at the end of September. Every pupil in Years 7 and 8 at Thomas Tallis makes his or her own lantern.

The school year is full of big events. They are all in our school planner. The school year always starts in September and the first big event is the Thames Festival Lantern Procession.

March

Every March, there is a big school disco. The pupils organize the disco and sell tickets. You can hear plenty of cool songs there!

May

Year 7 always goes on a school trip to a farm in May. They see all kinds of farm animals - even kid goats. Remember your wellies!

June

Pupils, teachers and parents help at the summer fair. Half of the money we collect is for charities and the other half is for school projects. You can buy or sell things at different stalls and you can play games, too.

July

A lot of pupils act in the school play. This year's play is *Turn again, Whittington!* It is a really funny play about Dick Whittington, a boy with a cat.

June

Sports day is great! We can invite our friends and families to school. It is on the third Saturday in June. And there's no homework the next Monday!

1 When are the events?

Example: The Thames Festival Lantern Procession is in … .
Sports day is on … .

→ WB 65, 1

98 ninety-eight

Check-in 7

2 The year at Thomas Tallis

Look at the pictures of events at Thomas Tallis on page 98.
Match the events with the sentences.

Example: 1. Pupils do different sports, and their friends and parents watch them. That's sports day in June.

1. Pupils do different sports, and their friends and parents watch them.
2. You can feed a lot of animals there.
3. Years 7 and 8 walk near the river with lanterns.
4. You can meet new friends, dance and listen to great music.
5. This helps charities and school projects.
6. Pupils do a play for parents, teachers and friends.

3 Listening: Thames Festival Lantern Procession

In the autumn the Year 7 pupils always talk about the Lantern Procession.
Listen and answer the questions.

1. Do the pupils meet at school?
2. Do the pupils wear their uniforms?
3. Is the Lantern Procession long?
4. Must the pupils bring food?
5. When can the pupils meet their parents?
6. Can they listen to music after the procession?

→ WB 65, 2

4 Questions

Ask your partner questions about the events at Thomas Tallis School.

Example: A: When is the school disco?
B: It's in March.
B: Where does Year 7 go in May?
A: They go to a farm.

When? Where? Why?
What? Who?

5 Your turn: Your school year

a) *Write about your school year.*
b) *Then compare your school year with the school year at Thomas Tallis.*

Our school year sometimes starts in ... .
We haven't got a ... in September.
We've got a ... in ... .
Our sports day / school play is in ... .
...

→ WB 65, 3

7 | Check-in | Language 1 | Story | Wordwise | Check-out

◎ Sports day at Thomas Tallis

Sports day is always a lot of fun. You can do the long jump, run a race, or play cricket on the big field. After the races and games there is plenty of ice-cream, water and juice for all the pupils. But not everybody is doing sports. A lot of parents are watching the events – it's all very exciting. Oh look! Year 7 is running a race now and Emma is winning!

1 What a day!

Look at the picture and read the text about sports day. Then answer the questions.

1. What can you do at sports day?
2. What can you eat at sports day?
3. Who is winning the Year 7 girls' race?
4. Can you find Jade in the picture?

2 A game: Do you know?

Look at the picture of sports day for one minute.
A: *You can look at your book. Ask your partner questions about the picture.*
B: *Close your book. Answer your partner's questions about sports day.*

Examples: A: Are the boys running a race?   B: No, they aren't. The girls are … .
           A: Is Sam drinking?   B: … .

100 one hundred

Revision: conjunctions and prepositions — Language 1 — 7

3 Good style with conjunctions

You can connect sentences. This makes your text better.
*Put the two sentences together. Use **but**, **so**, **or**.*

Example: Mrs Carter brings ice-cream. The pupils are happy.
Mrs Carter brings ice-cream **so** the pupils are happy.

1. Terry is eating an ice-cream. He can't do the long jump.
2. Sam, do you want an ice-cream? Do you want some water?
3. Jade is at sports day. She can't do a sport.
4. Do you want to watch the race? Do you want to play cricket?
5. Emma often wins the races. She never wins at cricket.
6. The parents think sports day is fun. They always go to it.

→ WB 66, 1

4 More about sports day

Make sentences with the conjunctions.

Example: The girls are running a race **and** Emma is winning.

1. The girls are running a race **and** …
2. Sports day is in summer **so** …
3. Mrs Brook is at sports day **but** …
4. This afternoon Sam can play cricket **or** …
5. Jade is at sports day **and** …
6. It is very hot **so** …

a) Mr Brook is in the computer shop.
b) Emma is winning.
c) Lisa is playing ball with her.
d) the weather is often good.
e) the pupils are sitting under the trees.
f) he can do the long jump.

→ WB 66, 2   → G 42

5 After sports day

Put prepositions in the sentences.
*Use **with**, **without**, **next to**, **on**, **in**, **at**.*

1. The four friends are still ☐ school.
2. The four friends are sitting ☐ a sofa.
3. Emma is sitting ☐ Lisa.
4. They are all ☐ the same sports class.
5. Terry never goes to sports day ☐ his cap.
6. Lisa wants to go home ☐ Emma.

→ WB 66, 3

6 Your turn: Sports

a) What is your favourite sport? Why do you like it?
   When do you play it? Where do you play it?
   Make a poster.

b) Tell your class about it.
   You can bring something with you.

My favourite sport is swimming. It's great because … .

one hundred and one **101**

| 7 | Check-in | **Language 2** | Story | Wordwise | Check-out |

A summer fair at Thomas Tallis

1 What can you do there?

Look at the picture. What can you do at the summer fair? Make a list.

Example: You can buy … .   Go on, please.

eat   look at   buy   pla.
listen to   try on   …

2 Real talk: Different stalls

Choose a stall. Make a poster with prices. Buy and sell things with the other groups.

A: Hello. Can I help you?
B: Yes, how much are your …, please?
A: They're … .
B: OK. Can I have …, please?
A: Yes, of course. Here you are.
   That's …, please.

Revision: place and time

Language 2

7

3 Place and time

*Look at these words. Are they about **place** or **time**? Make two lists.*

Place
at home
in the shed
…

Time
at three o'clock
on 15th June
…

at three o'clock • in the shed • on the Cutty Sark • on 15th June • outside • today • at home • next week • tonight • now • at school • at the stall • in two hours • near the house • at the summer fair

→ WB 67, 1–2   → G 43

4 Word order

Put the words in the sentences in the right order.

Example: is selling • Year 7 • this afternoon • cake • at the fair
Year 7 is selling cake at the fair this afternoon.

1. CDs • this afternoon • is listening to • A pupil • at the music stall
2. at the fair • Mrs Carter • wants to be • at eight o'clock
3. must stay • today • Barker • at home
4. is selling • Year 8 • at the fair • drinks • this afternoon
5. at Thomas Tallis • today • can play • Jade • football
6. are working a lot • All the pupils • this week • at school

GRAMMAR
Place before time!

→ WB 67, 3   → G 43

5 A game: A school quiz

Thomas Tallis quiz

Ask your partner questions about events at Thomas Tallis School. You can look at page 98. Don't forget the right word order.

Example: Is there a disco at Thomas Tallis in March?
Go on, please.

Yes, there is.   No, there isn't. It's in … .

6 Your turn: Your dream school year

What do you like about the Thomas Tallis school year?
What would you like to have in your school year? Make a list. Tell the class about your ideas.

Example: I think the summer fair is great.
I would like to have a summer fair at my school.

one hundred and three **103**

Behind the scenes

The opening night of the school play *Turn again, Whittington* is in one week. Everybody is working hard. The pupils in Years 9 and 10 are the actors and actresses, but the younger pupils may help with the play, too. They work behind the scenes – Sam and Emma are painting the scenery.

What are Lisa and Terry doing? They are building trees. They need a lot of trees for the play – that's hard work! Terry is tired. Oh, not another tree, he thinks. They're really boring! Lisa loves this but I don't. I know! I can scare Lisa. I can stand behind this tree and then … .

1 Listening: True or false?

Listen to the text about the play. Are the sentences true or false?

1. The friends are not busy now.
2. Lisa and Emma are painting the scenery.
3. Terry does not like making trees.
4. The actors come and practise their text.
5. Terry doesn't want to be an actor.
6. Sam wants to be an actor.

→ WB 69, 1

2 A song: Turn again, Whittington

Turn again, Whittington,
Lord Mayor of London!
Turn again, Whittington,
Lord Mayor of London!

3 Your turn: Plays at your school?

You want to do a play at your school? What do you need to do for the play?

Example: You need to make posters.
You need to paint scenery.

→ WB 69, 2

104 one hundred and four

Revision: simple present or present progressive and word order

1 Revision: Do or doing? → G 40

Use the simple present or the present progressive.

Example: Emma usually ☐ in class. – She ☐ the scenery for the play now. (**paint**)
Emma usually **paints** in class. – She **is painting** the scenery for the play now.

1. The pupils ☐ in the park on Saturdays. – This afternoon they ☐ a race. (**run**)
2. The parents always ☐ fun at sports day. – They ☐ a lot of fun today. (**have**)
3. Sam ☐ a bottle of water at the moment. – He never ☐ water at home. (**drink**)
4. Terry often ☐ sports after school. – He ☐ the long jump now. (**do**)
5. Now Sam ☐ Emma with the play. – Sam sometimes ☐ Emma with German. (**help**)
6. Lisa usually ☐ breakfast at home. – Today she ☐ breakfast at the summer fair. (**eat**)
7. Mrs Carter never ☐ football. – This afternoon at sports day she ☐ football. (**play**)

→ WB 70, 1

2 Revision: What's different? → G 40

What do the friends often do on Saturday afternoons? What are they doing now?

Example: 1. Terry often plays … . Today he is … .

1. often / play / today / build
2. sometimes / write e-mails / at the moment / run
3. always / take for a walk / now / throw

→ WB 70, 2

3 Revision: At lunch → G 41

What are the friends saying at lunch? Put the parts of the sentences in the right order.

Example: Terry: tell • I • a funny joke • must • you
Terry: I must tell you a funny joke.

1. Lisa: needn't • your old jokes • tell • you
2. Sam: can • Lisa's brother • I • see
3. Lisa: my brother • talk to • I • needn't
4. Sam: can't • my mobile • find • I
5. Lisa: in your bag • it • be • must
6. Sam: my bag • I • find • can't
7. Lisa: you • your bag • look for • must

one hundred and five **105**

7 | Check-in | Language | Story | Wordwise | Check-out

Two great actors!

A Opening night is in one week. Everybody at school is talking about the play, and the four friends are happy with their scenery.
"My people look real, don't they?" Sam asks his friends.
"Look! One woman has got your face, Lisa!"
"Ha, ha – very funny, Sam!" says Lisa.
"Next year I want a real part in the play," says Terry.
"But Terry, the real parts are for Years 9 and 10. You can't have a part. You're only in Year 7 now,"
Lisa tells him. "Oh, look. There's Mrs Carter."
"Mrs Carter … Mrs Carter!" shouts Terry.
"Oh, hello. I'm thinking about the play. An actor is ill and … well, maybe you can all help," Mrs Carter says. "Can you come to my classroom after school? Then I can tell you about the part. I must go to the library now. See you later."

B "A real part! Wow!" Terry shouts. "And Mrs Carter wants *me*!"
"We can *all* go, Terry," Sam tells him. "And I want the part."
"You? But you're not an actor. I play in the Samba Band," says Terry, "so … ."
"So what!" says Sam in an angry voice.
"So I know how to be on a stage and … and …," says Terry.
Sam and Terry are both angry, and Emma and Lisa think the boys are silly.
"Don't be silly, you two," says Emma. "The parts are not for Year 7 pupils."
Sam and Terry look at the girls.
"You've got no idea!" they both shout.

C In the afternoon Sam and Terry talk to Mrs Carter in her classroom. Mrs Carter is really happy.
"Thank you, Sam and Terry. You're a great help. You can go now."
Sam must go to the computer club and Terry wants to go home.

D Terry is walking home from school and sees Lisa.
"Hey, Lisa!" Terry calls and runs after her.
"I'm really excited about the play, and our scenery is so good …," says Lisa.
"Scenery! That's for children," says Terry. "I'm an actor now. A real actor with a real part in a real play."
"What?" She cannot believe her ears.
"Sorry, I must go. See you later," shouts Terry and runs home.

106 one hundred and six

Story   7

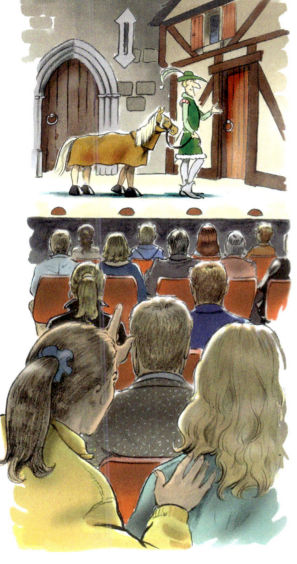

E   After school Sam sees Emma at the computer club.
"Emma. Guess what!" shouts Sam.
Emma is playing a game. She isn't listening to Sam at the moment.
"I've got a part in the play."
"What are you talking about?"
"The play. I'm an actor now."
"I don't believe you."
"It's true."
"OK, what part?"
"It's a secret. I can't tell you. You must wait for opening night. Hey, can I play that game, too?"
"No, Sam, wait. You can play the next game."

F   Finally it is the opening night of the play. Lisa and Emma are sitting in the audience. The curtain goes up and Lisa whispers, "Wow! Look at our scenery!"
"But where are Terry and Sam?" asks Emma.
"I don't think they're in the play. It's just a big joke," Lisa answers. "Oh, no! Look at that horse on the stage. It's so funny!"
The girls laugh a lot. They think the play is very, very good.

Later, when the play is over, all the actors are on the stage and everybody claps. Suddenly Terry and Sam are on the stage, too. Terry is carrying the horse's head and Sam is carrying the horse's tail. The boys wave to Emma and Lisa.
"They *are* good actors," Emma says.
"Well, they make a good horse," Lisa says and laughs.

1 The right order

Put the sentences in the right order.

a) Sam goes to the computer club.
b) Terry and Sam are a great horse!
c) The curtain goes up.
d) Terry tells Lisa about his part.
e) The friends are happy with the scenery.
f) The boys are both angry.
g) The friends see Mrs Carter in the hall.

▸ WB 71, 1

2 A great play

Answer the questions about the story.

1. When is opening night?
2. Why does Mrs Carter need a new actor?
3. Who wants the part in the school play?
4. What does Sam tell Emma?
5. Who has got a part in the school play?
6. What are Sam and Terry in the play?
7. Are Sam and Terry good actors?

▸ WB 71, 2

one hundred and seven   **107**

7 | Check-in | Language | Story | Wordwise | Check-out

1 Words with two meanings

VOCABULARY SKILLS A B C

Manchmal hörst oder liest du ein englisches Wort, das mehrere Bedeutungen im Deutschen hat, z.B. *letter* = „Buchstabe" oder „Brief". Nur wenn du den ganzen Satz hörst oder liest, kannst du erkennen, was das Wort bedeutet.

Beispiel:
There are 26 letters in the alphabet.
My friend sends me a letter every week.

Falls eine Bedeutung nicht passt, versuche es mit der anderen Bedeutung.

Look at the underlined words in the sentences. What do they mean in German?

1. She is in Year 7.
2. There are twelve months in a year.
3. Let's play cards.
4. This is a birthday card.
5. All your answers are right!
6. Turn right into River Road.

Here's a bag of sweets for you.

Tom, you're really sweet!

2 What do you think?

a) *Sort the phrases and make two lists.*

☺	☹
That's great!	That's awful!
...	...

You're cool!
You're an idiot!
I think it's great!
That's a good answer.
You've got no idea.

That's not very nice! Very nice. No, thank you. That's awful! That's OK.
That's right. I don't think that's right. That's wrong! Yes! No! ...

b) *Write short dialogues with the phrases.*

   Example: Do you want an apple? – No, thank you.

3 Sounds: [v] and [w]

[v]	[w]	[v] – [w]
I love the new video.	I don't want to go without you.	Where is my invitation?
His bag is very expensive.	Emma always wins the race!	Wear your favourite pullover.
David is seventeen.	Today is really wet and windy.	It's very warm in the library.
She lives above the shop.	Which boy is working?	I'm waiting for my visitors.

→ WB 72, 1–3

108 one hundred and eight

Check-out 7

1 In the library → G 10

Put prepositions in the sentences.
*Use **without, in, next to, on, under**.*

Example: Terry and Lisa are **in** the library.

1. Terry is sitting ☐ Lisa in the library.
2. There are books ☐ the table.
3. I cannot see Terry's and Lisa's bags.
   They must be ☐ the table.
4. You can't have a library ☐ books!
5. Mrs Carter is often ☐ the library.
6. Terry has got a great book!
   There are a lot of interesting things ☐ it.

2 What does Terry say? → G 42

*Put in the right conjunctions. Use **but, and, so**.*

1. I like cats ☐ I don't like dogs.
2. Next year I want to be in the play
   ☐ I want to go to sports day.
3. At 3:30 I must play my drums ☐
   I can't go to the park.
4. This morning I want to go to Emma's
   shop ☐ this afternoon I want to play
   computer games with Sam.
5. It's raining ☐ I can't play basketball.
6. Today I must clean my room ☐
   I needn't clean my shed.

3 Where and when? → G 43

Say where and when you do things.

Example: I do sports … .
          I do sports in the park after school.

1. I do my homework … .
2. I see my friends … .
3. I have breakfast … .
4. I listen to music … .
5. I have lunch … .
6. I eat dinner … .
7. I sometimes watch TV … .
8. I often meet my friends … .

4 A Thomas Tallis quiz

Can you answer Tom's questions?

1. What is the name of the school play?	5. When is sports day?
2. What can you do at the summer fair?	6. Who is a horse in the play?
3. What is in the school planner?	7. Can you play cricket at sports day?
4. Where is the Lantern Procession?	8. When does the school year start?

→ WB 73, 1

NOW YOU CAN

✓ Talk about events at an English school.
✓ Talk about your school year.

→ Nenne vier Ereignisse, die an einer englischen Schule stattfinden können.
→ Nenne drei Ereignisse, die an deiner Schule stattfinden. Erzähle, was man dort tun kann.

one hundred and nine **109**

Passing on information

COMMUNICATION SKILLS

Du weißt bereits, dass du nicht immer jedes einzelne Wort aus dem Deutschen in eine andere Sprache übertragen kannst. Zum Beispiel: „Wie heißt du?" heißt im Englischen *"What's your name?"* Deshalb ist es wichtig, dass du dich an feststehende Redewendungen erinnerst. Es gibt auch in jeder Sprache verschiedene Möglichkeiten, etwas zu sagen. Auf die Frage *"What's your name?"* kannst du im Englischen nicht nur *"My name's Kristin."* sondern auch *"I'm Kristin."* antworten. Wie würdest du auf Deutsch antworten?

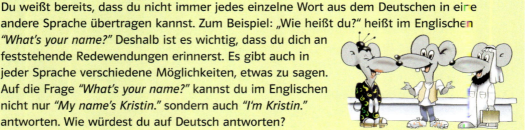

Unit 1   An English School

Du findest eine englische Schule im Internet. Dein Vater ist neugierig und stellt einige Fragen über die Schule. Beantworte sie auf Deutsch.

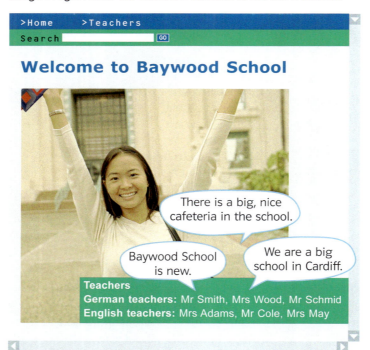

Wie heißt die Schule?
Wo ist die Schule?
Unterrichten Deutschlehrer an der Schule?
Ist die Schule groß?
Ist die Schule alt?
Gibt es eine Cafeteria?

Unit 2   Martin and Anja

Martin, ein Junge aus Großbritannien, ist bei euch zu Hause zu Besuch. Deine kleine Schwester Anja stellt ihm ganz viele Fragen, aber Martin spricht kein Deutsch. Hilf ihnen.

a) Überlege, wie Anjas Fragen auf Englisch lauten, und wie man Martins Antworten auf Deutsch sagen würde.

Passing on information P

b) *Stelle dann einen Dialog zusammen mit Anjas Fragen, Martins Antworten und deinen Kommentaren.*

Wie heißt du?
Wie alt bist du?
Woher kommst du?
Wo liegt das?
Was ist deine Lieblingssportart?

My name's Martin.
I'm twelve.
I'm from Greenwich.
Greenwich is in London.
It's football. Football is cool.

Unit 3 An e-mail from Simone

a) *Simone, eine englische Schülerin, hat in einer E-Mail etwas über sich geschrieben. Deine Mutter stellt dir einige Fragen über Simone. Was kannst du ihr erzählen?*

Hi!
My name's Simone. I'm twelve and I'm from Cardiff. I have guitar lessons on Thursdays, but I'm not in the school band. I collect pictures and posters of dogs for my room. My mum and I go swimming every Saturday morning, and then we go shopping in town. On Sundays we go out in the car or my uncle and aunt and my two cousins come to our house. I play computer games with my cousins.

Wie alt ist Simone?
Woher kommt sie?
Spielt sie ein Instrument?
Hat sie noch andere Hobbys?
Treibt sie Sport?
Was macht sie sonntags?

b) *Schreibe eine E-Mail an Simone und teile ihr mit wie alt du bist, woher du kommst, welche Hobbys du hast usw.*

Unit 4 Where's the museum?

Du bist in der Stadt unterwegs. Ein amerikanischer Tourist spricht dich an: "Excuse me, how can I get to the city museum?" Du kennst das Museum, weißt aber den Weg nicht genau und sprichst deshalb eine Dame an. Sie weiß den Weg, spricht aber kein Englisch. Sage dem Amerikaner, wie er zum Museum kommt:

American: Excuse me, how can I get to the city museum?
     You: Oh, I don't know the way from here. We can ask this person.
          (An die Person) Entschuldigen Sie, …?
  Person: Ja, kein Problem. Gehen Sie zuerst geradeaus. Dann ist rechts eine alte Kirche.
     You: First go … . Then …
  Person: Biegen Sie an der Kirche rechts ab. Dann gehen Sie wieder geradeaus. Das Museum ist auf der linken Seite neben einer großen neuen Schule.
     You: …
American: That's great. Thanks.
     You: That's OK. *(An die Person)* Vielen Dank!

Alle neuen Wörter findest du im *Dictionary* ganz hinten im Buch.

one hundred and eleven **111**

P Passing on information

Unit 5 Bluewater

COMMUNICATION SKILLS

Häufig willst du Informationen weitergeben, kennst aber im Englischen nicht jedes Wort. Überlege dann, ob du nicht ein anderes Wort mit ähnlicher Bedeutung oder ein Beispiel kennst.

In einer deutschen Zeitung erschien ein kurzer Artikel über "Bluewater", ein riesiges Einkaufszentrum, 25 km von Greenwich. Eine englische Schülerin aus Greenwich möchte wissen, was darin steht. Hilf ihr!

Riesen-Shoppingcenter "Bluewater"

Sie möchten ein neues Kleid für eine Party, einen Kuchen und zwei DVDs kaufen. Wo bekommen Sie all dies? Mit zwei großen Warenhäusern, Filialen von vielen bekannten Ladenketten und über 300 anderen Geschäften haben Sie im Einkaufszentrum "Bluewater" die Qual der Wahl. "Bluewater", etwa 30 km südöstlich vom Londoner Zentrum gelegen, ermöglicht 11 Stunden langes Einkaufen täglich von 10 Uhr morgens bis 21 Uhr abends. (Sonntags ist es 6 Stunden geöffnet.)

Aber diese Zeit werden Sie benötigen! In „Bluewater" befinden sich ja mehr Geschäfte als in einer durchschnittlichen Kleinstadt. Sie können den ganzen Tag dort verbringen.

Aber keine Sorge! Mit fast 50 Cafés, Schnellimbissen und Restaurants können Sie sich an fast jeder Ecke ausruhen – und für weitere Einkäufe neue Kraft sammeln!

1. I can see "300". Do 300 people work at Bluewater?
2. Where is Bluewater? Does it say?
3. When does it open in the mornings?
4. Does it close at six in the evening?
5. Is it open on Sundays?
6. It's very big. Are there only shops there?
7. What does it say about DVDs in line 2?

Unit 6 Fisher's Farm Park

Finde fünf Informationen in dieser Broschüre, die für einen Besuch bei Fisher's Farm Park wichtig sind und die du z.B. deinen Eltern oder Großeltern auf Deutsch weitergeben kannst. Denke an

- Dinge, die man machen oder
- sehen kann;
- Öffnungszeiten;
- Eintrittspreise;
- Essen.

COMMUNICATION SKILLS

In einer Broschüre stehen oft mehr Informationen als du brauchst. Daher ist es nicht so schlimm, wenn du nicht jedes einzelne Wort verstehst.

Passing on information P

Fisher's Farm Park

On the farm and in the barns children and adults can see happy animals. You can say hello to the goats and lambs. Come and meet our new animals: **Dorothy** our white cow, **Cassie** our pony and **Velvet** our new horse.

There are playgrounds for children of different age groups. Walk through the trees to the mini-farm tractors, and race ring!

The **Ghost House** in the trees is a favourite place for all the children.

The Farm Show in the Barn Theatre is about 20 minutes: the farm workers show you a lot of lambs, pigs, rabbits, horses and goats. It is fun!

The Food Barn: there is room for 180 people. There is hot food from 11am to 3pm every day. The menus include hot and cold snacks and drinks, lunches and cakes. **The Tuck Shop** has popcorn, ice-cream, and hot and cold drinks.

Fisher's Farm Park is open from 10am to 5pm every day of the year.

Adult: £9.25
Child: £8.75   **Child under 3:** free

Boo!

Unit 7 A card from Martin

COMMUNICATION SKILLS

Wichtig ist, dass du den Inhalt sinngemäß übersetzt. Dabei kann das eine oder andere Wort gelegentlich weggelassen werden.
Formen wie *present progressive*, die es im Deutschen nicht gibt, kannst du mit Adverbien wie „gerade" oder „eben" übertragen.
Vergiss nicht, dass die Wortstellung im Englischen oft anders ist als im Deutschen.

Du bekommst eine Karte von Martin aus England. Deine kleine Schwester Anja möchte wissen, was er schreibt.

Hi,
I'm in Greenwich: we're here for two days and it's really interesting here.
We're staying with my aunt and uncle. Mum and Dad are in London today and my cousins are showing me the Cutty Sark. It's a great ship and we're having a good time.
How about you? Are you all OK?
Love to you and the family,

Martin

Alle neuen Wörter findest du im *Dictionary* ganz hinten im Buch.

A project   Poems and chants

A diamond poem: School

School
Busy, loud
Speaking, listening, learning,
Teacher, classroom, evening, homework,
Watching TV, eating, playing
Quiet, tired
Home

My letter poem: A

I am an "**A**"
Born in **August**,
Sometimes **angry**,
I don't like **alarm clocks** or **awful aunts**.
I like **animals**
and **Arsenal**,
And in **autumn**
I eat a lot of **apples**.
But being **alone**
Is not **always** fun.
I am an "**A**".

GROUP SKILLS

- Jeder in der Gruppe soll bei dem Projekt eine Aufgabe übernehmen. Entscheidet, wer was machen soll. Es gibt viele verschiedene Aufgaben: das Gedicht soll schön geschrieben und schön gestaltet werden, einer kann vorstellen, wer was lesen wird, und ihr könnt die Gedichte sogar zu zweit oder zu dritt vortragen. Überlegt euch auch, ob die Klasse an einigen Stellen mitmachen soll.
- Macht eine Liste von Themen, die ihr interessant findet, und die ihr gut kennt. Dann einigt euch auf ein Thema.
- Wo findet ihr weitere Informationen, Bilder und andere Dinge zu eurem Thema? Sucht in eurem Englischbuch, in anderen Büchern, in Zeitschriften, in eurer Bibliothek oder im Internet. Entscheidet, wer wo suchen soll.
- Schaut euch dann alles, was ihr gefunden habt, gemeinsam an. Macht Listen und *mind maps*.

Step 1: Prepare your project

1. Make groups of four to six pupils.
2. Read and act the four poems. Which poems do you like? Why?

Step 2: Collect ideas for your project

1. In this project you write and present your own poems or chants. Find an idea for your poem or chant.
2. Choose a kind of poem or chant.
3. Collect words, pictures, music or other things you need for your poem or chant.

Step 3: Write your poem or chant

1. Write two or three poems in your group.
2. Use the dictionary in this book to help you. Ask your teacher for help.
3. Now read your poems again. Are you happy with them? Can you make them better?

A project E

An action poem: Pirate, pirate

Say the poem and do the actions, too.

Pirate big	(stand up)
Pirate small	(crouch down)
Pirate, dance!	(dance)
Pirate, fall!	(fall over)
Pirate, walk the plank!	(walk and jump)
Pirate, jump in!	(fall over)
The sea is cold	(be cold)
Swim, pirate, swim!	(swim fast)

A chant: Cats and dogs

You need two groups for this chant, group A and group B.

A: Dogs
B: Cats
A: Dogs
B: Cats
A: We like dogs – they're very, very nice!
B: We like cats – they find lots of mice!
A: Woof!
B: Meow!
A: Woof!
B: Meow!
A & B: Dogs and cats.

Step 4: Present your poem or chant

1. *How are you going to present your poems and chants? You can make a poster, use your computer, say them as a rap, say them with music, act them, …*
2. *Decide who will read which poem or chant and practise reading them to the other people in your group.*
3. *Now have a poem party and perform your poems and chants to your class.*

PRESENTATION SKILLS

- Übt das Gedicht vor einem Spiegel zu Hause und vor eurer Gruppe in der Schule. Fragt eure Gruppenmitglieder oder euren Lehrer/eure Lehrerin, ob eure Aussprache so in Ordnung ist.
- Habt ihr alles, was ihr braucht? Überlegt euch, ob ihr Bilder, Plakate, Masken, Kostüme, Musik, Instrumente oder andere Dinge benötigt.
- Wenn ihr euer Gedicht vortragt, lest nicht nur vom Blatt ab, sondern versucht auch, eure Zuhörer anzuschauen.
- Sprecht langsam und deutlich und laut genug, so dass man euch auch ganz hinten im Klassenzimmer gut verstehen kann.

Step 5: How good is your poem?

1. *Now talk to your teacher and the other pupils in your class.*
   Which three poems are the best?
2. *Which poems do you like? Which poems don't you like? Why?*

USEFUL PHRASES

I like the poem / chant about …
The poem about … is good because …
It makes me feel …
I like / don't like the topic / the pictures / the actions / the music / …
I think … is good.
I don't think … is very good.

Alle neuen Wörter findest du im Dictionary ganz hinten im Buch.

E A story

A story Reading skills

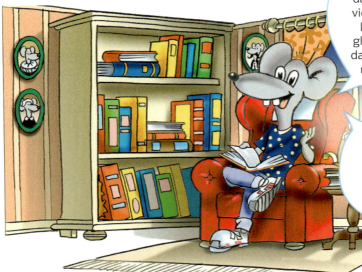

Magst du Geschichten? Ich lese für mein Leben gern! Man kann dabei so viel lernen und man begegnet vielen interessanten Typen. Eine meiner Lieblingsgeschichten kannst du auch gleich lesen. Es geht um … . Aber nein, das will ich dir nicht verraten – ich kann nur versprechen, dass es ganz schön spannend wird.

Kennst du eigentlich schon die neun Tricks, die einem das Lesen leichter machen? Nein? Mein Großvater Thomas Tiny hat sie mir verraten, als ich noch ein winziger Mäuserich war. Welche Tricks? Na gut, weil du es bist, verrate ich sie dir auch:

READING SKILLS

VOR DEM LESEN:

Trick Nr. 1: Stelle dich innerlich darauf ein, dass du gleich eine Geschichte lesen wirst. Suche dir einen bequemen und angenehmen Leseort, wo du nicht gestört wirst. Entspanne dich und freue dich auf ein spannendes Leseerlebnis.

Trick Nr. 2: Schau dir den Umschlag des Buchs an. Dann lies auch den Titel der Geschichte. Überlege, worum es in der Geschichte gehen könnte. Schau dir auch die Bilder an. Vielleicht hast du ja eine ähnliche Geschichte schon einmal gelesen?

Oh, there's a BIG BLACK CAT on the ship! And there's a big black cat in this library, too. Where is she?

116 one hundred and sixteen

A story E

READING SKILLS

WÄHREND DU LIEST:

Trick Nr. 3: Nimm dir nicht zu viel auf einmal vor. Wenn du häufiger ein kurzes Stück liest, macht das Lesen mehr Spaß und strengt nicht so sehr an.

Trick Nr. 4: Bemühe dich immer die Hauptgedanken der Geschichte zu verstehen. Ignoriere unbekannte Wörter, wenn sie nicht wirklich wichtig für das Verstehen sind. Wichtige unbekannte Wörter kannst du in deinem Wörterverzeichnis nachschlagen.

Trick Nr. 5: Versuche immer, dir das Gelesene bildlich vorzustellen. Denke dich in die Situation hinein. Was siehst du? Was riechst du? Was hörst du? Wie findest du die Menschen, denen du begegnest? Frage dich, ob du etwas Ähnliches schon einmal erlebt hast.

Trick Nr. 6: Mache während des Lesens immer mal wieder eine Pause und fasse für dich den Abschnitt, den du gerade gelesen hast, in eigenen Worten zusammen.

READING SKILLS

NACH DEM LESEN:

Trick Nr. 7: Nachdem du mit dem Lesen fertig bist, fasse alles, was du gelesen hast, noch einmal zusammen. Frage dich immer
- wer
- wo
- was
- mit wem
- wann
- warum erlebt hat.

Trick Nr. 8: Vielleicht hast du das Gefühl nicht alles richtig verstanden zu haben und du möchtest den Abschnitt ein zweites Mal lesen. Finde heraus ob du beim zweiten Lesedurchgang mehr verstehst.

Trick Nr. 9: Überlege, wie dir das Gelesene gefallen hat und was es für dich persönlich bedeutet. Was hast du Neues erfahren und was hast du aus dem Gelesenen gelernt?

Also dann viel Spaß beim Schmökern. PS: Wenn du jetzt häufiger längere englische Geschichten liest, ist es eine gute Idee ein Lesetagebuch zu führen. Ganz hinten in deinem Workbook findest du hierfür einige Tipps.

one hundred and seventeen **117**

E — A story

🔊 A story Paul and Jason on a ship to China

"Paul! Jason! Stay with the group, please," says Mrs Sanderson, their teacher. When Paul's and Jason's class go to the Old Ships Festival in Greenwich, they visit the Cutty Sark. All the old ships are sitting at anchor on the River Thames. When the pupils go on board the Cutty Sark, an old man takes their tickets. He is wearing clothes like in the old days. Paul and Jason are last, as usual.

"He looks just like an old sea captain," says Paul.
"He's even got a patch on one eye," says Jason. "And his white beard looks real. Ha, ha!"

When the old man takes their tickets he winks at Paul and Jason with his good eye, and whispers, "Pssst! We lift the anchor at two o'clock, boys! Then we sail to China!" Paul and Jason think he is very funny.

"Welcome on board the Cutty Sark," says the guide, a small woman with a very loud voice.
"The Cutty Sark is a museum now, but it was once the fastest ship in the world. It sailed all the way from London to China and brought tea back to Britain. Later, we can go downstairs and you can see the hold, where they stored the tea from China. Tea was very special in those days, and very expensive."

The guide takes them to see the cabins where the crew used to sleep.
"Now, stay together class," Mrs Sanderson says. Mrs Sanderson is a new teacher – this is her first school trip and she is a little scared.

The crew's cabins are very small: twelve men to one cabin. "Look at this little bed," says Lucy. "How can a man sleep in that?" Lucy always asks a lot of questions.
"That bed is for a young boy – a cabin boy," the guide tells Lucy. "Young boys of eleven or twelve went to sea in the old days. Cabin boys were part of the crew. They worked very hard on the ship for the captain."
"We're lucky we don't live in those days," laughs Jason.

118 one hundred and eighteen

A story E

Then the class goes to see Captain Moodie's cabin. "Look", Paul says to Jason, "that old ticket collector is following us."

50 The captain's cabin is very nice. There's a big bed with curtains you can close. There's a funny old clock on the table, and on the captain's desk there's an old map. It shows the fastest way to sail from London to China.

55 The guide shows the class a very old telescope. "It's for finding land," she says. "Without the captain's telescope and the map, this ship can't sail anywhere."
　　The class likes the captain's cabin. There
60 are old papers on his desk and his books are still in the cupboard.
　"Captain Moodie even had a cat," the guide says.
　"A cat on a ship? What for?" asks Paul.
65 "To catch mice, silly," says Lucy.
　"That's right," says the guide. "Mice and rats. They eat everything on board, even the tea."
　"What colour was Captain Moodie's cat?" Lucy asks.
70　　The guide tells them that it was a black cat and it only had one ear.
　"Only one ear? Poor thing! How did that happen?" the class wants to know.

"No one knows," the guide says. "Maybe it was in a fight." 75
"Wow! What was the cat's name?" Lucy asks.
"Hmm. Good question", the guide says, "I'm sorry – I really don't know. But I can find out and tell you later. Now let's go downstairs to the ship's hold. That's where they stored 80 the tea. I'm sorry we can't sail on the Cutty Sark, but we can watch a video about sailing down the river to the North Sea and then to China!"

The class all leave the captain's cabin. But 85 Paul and Jason are looking at the old map of the way to China and the cool telescope. "Come on, you guys," Lucy tells them. "Don't you want to see the video?"
"We're coming," they say, but the boys stay 90 in the captain's cabin. It's fun to look at the captain's things and think what it was like to go to sea.

Just then a cat comes out from behind the curtain on the captain's bed. "Hey, look, 95 Paul, a cat!" says Jason. "How did a cat get in here?" But Paul is not listening. He is staring at the cat, and he is very excited.
"Look, it's black – and it's only got one ear – just like Captain Moodie's cat!" 100

Alle neuen Wörter findest du im *Dictionary* ganz hinten im Buch.

one hundred and nineteen **119**

E A story

The ticket collector with the patch on his eye is suddenly in the cabin. The boys think it's because they must stay with the group. But he doesn't speak to them, he only speaks to the cat.

"Oh, there you are!" he says. "Are you hungry? Well, you know I haven't got any food for you, because I want you to catch some of those mice. I don't want them to run around this ship. Come on, let's go and find some mice, Blackjack."

"Excuse me …" says Paul, "is that your cat?"

"Yes", says the old man. "I got him last time this ship was in China."

"But … that was over a hundred years ago!" says Paul. "Ha, ha! Blackjack must be a very old cat!" The boys laugh, but the old man is not laughing.

"How did Blackjack lose his ear?" Paul asks.

"In a fight with a rat. In China. They've got very big, bad rats there, you know."

Just then, the funny old clock starts to chime. Ding! Ding!

"Aha! It's two o'clock, lads," says the old man. "It's time to lift anchor and sail! Where is all my crew? Where are the other cabin boys?"

The boys think the ticket collector is a very good actor. They laugh and walk to the cabin door. But the old man is still not laughing.

"Where do you think you are going?" says the old man. His eye without the patch is watching them, and the old man looks scary.

"We must go and find our class now, but thanks a lot, you were really funny and this ship is a great museum!" says Jason.

The old man looks very angry. "What are you talking about? My ship is not a museum! It's the fastest ship in the world! Come on, the river is high! Let's lift anchor, boys! It's time to sail!"

"Sail? Where to?" the boys ask.

"China, of course!" says the captain. "What kind of cabin boys are you! Must I do everything here myself?" And he runs out of the cabin.

The boys are not laughing now. "W-what was all that about?" asks Paul.

"H-he's no ticket collector!" says Jason.

"W-who is he then?"

"He's … Captain Moodie!"

"But how, Jason? Captain Moodie lived over a hundred years ago!"

A story E

155 The boys look at each other. They are very scared now.
"He must be … a Ghost Captain!"
Paul and Jason run outside quickly. They want to go back to their class and
160 Mrs Sanderson. They must stop the Ghost Captain. But they can't see him. Suddenly, Paul says. "I don't feel so good …"
"What do you mean? How do you feel?"
Paul's face is a little green. "Er … seasick."
165 Jason runs to the window. "Oh no!" he says. "It looks like Greenwich is getting smaller …"
"If I feel seasick and Greenwich is getting smaller," says Paul, "It can mean only one
170 thing …"
"Oh no! The ship's sailing!" they both shout. And they are right. It's true.
The old ship is sailing down the River Thames!

175 Suddenly they see the Ghost Captain. "You can't do this," the boys say. "We're telling Mrs Sanderson!"
"Mrs Sanderson?" says the Ghost Captain. "There is no Mrs Sanderson here. There are
180 no women on my ship!" He runs back to the ship's wheel.

Now they are sailing faster down the Thames. They can already see the Thames Barrier.
185 "Ha ha, boys! China, here we come!" the Ghost Captain shouts to the wind. "But we need to find our way before we get out to sea!"

Just then, the class comes up from the hold.
190 They see the ship is sailing!
"Wow, Mrs Sanderson!" they say. "This is a really cool surprise! A trip on the Cutty Sark! This is much better than the video!"
But Mrs Sanderson does not think it is a cool
195 surprise. She cannot understand what is happening. The Thames Barrier is now far behind them. London looks like a little town far away.
The guide does not know what to do. "But – the Cutty Sark can't sail!" she says again 200 and again. "The anchor was down! I saw it with my own two eyes."
Mrs Sanderson calls the school on her mobile. "Headteacher? … Yes, it's me, Mrs Sanderson … the school trip with class 7B, 205 yes. … On the Cutty Sark, that's right. … No, everything's not OK … . I'm sorry … . I think we're on our way to China! Help!"

Lucy sees Paul and Jason. "What's happening?" 210
"It's the Ghost Captain!" they tell her.
"Who?" Lucy asks.
"The ticket collector … a black cat … Blackjack … one ear … just like Captain Moodie's … he thinks we're his cabin boys! 215 He's lifted anchor!"
Lucy looks at Paul and Jason. "What are you talking about?" she says. "I don't understand a thing!"
"Lucy, we have to stop the Ghost Captain," 220 says Paul.
Lucy does not know what to think. "So where is this 'Ghost Captain' now?" she asks them.

Alle neuen Wörter findest du im *Dictionary* ganz hinten im Buch.

E A story

225 "We don't know …" the boys tell her.
"What can we do?"
"Well", says Lucy, "remember the guide said you can't sail the ship without two things."
"The map to find your way!" Paul shouts
230 "… and the telescope to find land!" says Jason. "Come on – back to the cabin! We must get them before he does!"

Police boats are now on both sides of the old ship. "Stop now!" the police are shouting
235 through a megaphone. "Police. Stop right now!" There is another boat full of reporters. They are taking pictures of class 7B on the Cutty Sark. There are TV cameras, too. The pupils on board the Cutty Sark are
240 taking pictures of the police boats and waving at the TV cameras.

Paul, Jason and Lucy run to the captain's cabin. The door is closed. When they open it, they see the map of the way to China and
245 the telescope are still on the desk. "Phew – they are still here!" says Paul.
"Let's take them so he can't get them," says Lucy. They take the telescope and the map and run out – straight into the guide and
250 Mrs Sanderson.
"Stop! Where are you going with the map and the telescope? They're stealing the ship's things!" says the guide.

The police come on board and stop the old ship. Later, back in Greenwich, there 255 are a lot of questions to answer. Who lifted the ship's anchor? Who was standing at the ship's wheel? Why were the boys taking the captain's map and the telescope? Paul and Jason try to explain, but it's not easy. 260
"It was the ticket collector …," they start to say.
"You mean the nice old man with the eye patch and the funny old clothes?" says Mrs Sanderson. 265
"Yes, he's a real captain! He's Captain Moodie …. You can ask him yourselves!"
"Old Mr Dudley?" says the guide.
"That's silly!"
"Where is this ticket collector?" the 270 policeman asks.
"He always goes home for lunch," says the guide.
"We think he lifted the anchor!" the boys explain. "He wanted to take the ship to 275 China!"
"I don't understand," says the policeman. "Who is this Captain Moodie?"
"I'm sorry," the guide says. "Captain Moodie was the ship's captain a very long time ago. 280 In 1870!"
"He still is the captain," the boys say.
"A Ghost Captain!"

122 one hundred and twenty-two

A story E

It's no good No one believes the boys' ghost
285 story. And you can understand why! Only
Paul and Jason know it's true.
"Who else was in the captain's cabin when
you saw this 'ghost'?" the policeman asks.
"Only Blackjack," the boys answer.
290 "Who is Blackjack?" asks the policeman.
"Another pupil in your class?"
"Blackjack's not a pupil," the boys say.
"He's the captain's cat. He was in a fight with
a big rat when the ship was in China … ."
295 "That's right!" says the guide. "Blackjack was
the name of Captain Moodie's cat! I found
that information in my book! And Blackjack
lost his ear in a fight with a rat! But – how did
you boys know that?"

300 The Cutty Sark is a museum in Greenwich
again, now, so you can visit it if you go there.
Nobody understands how the museum ship
sailed down the Thames on the day of class
7B's visit. And nobody really knows where
305 Blackjack the cat suddenly came from, or
where he went. Is the boys' story true? Lucy
doesn't know, and Mrs Sanderson doesn't
want to take class 7B on another school trip.
Only Paul and Jason know that something
310 very strange happened on the Cutty Sark
with Captain Moodie that day.

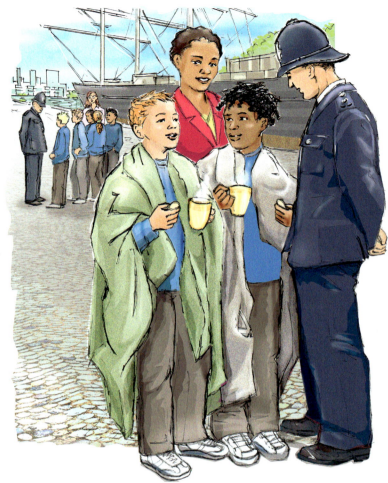

The end

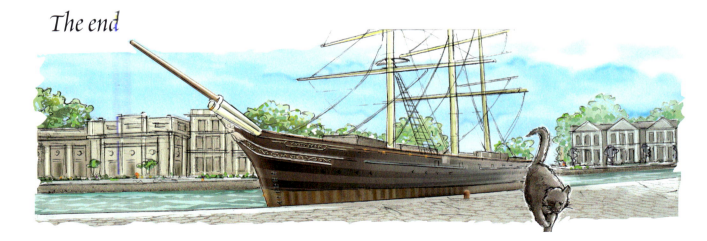

Alle neuen Wörter findest du im *Dictionary* ganz hinten im Buch.

one hundred and twenty-three **123**

E — A play

🔊 A play Turn again, Whittington!

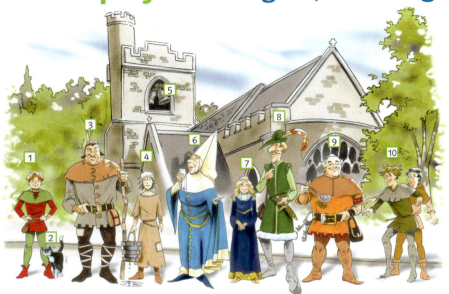

1 Dick Whittington
2 Blacky (his cat)
3 Barny Forge
4 Sissy Forge, his daughter
5 The bells of Bow Church
6 Lady Anne Fitzwarren
7 Alice Fitzwarren, her daughter
8 George Buckingham
9 Stouty Burke
10 two pickpockets
11 two storytellers

Storyteller 1: Dear friends, please come and see our play. The place is London, not today. But 1380, let us say. It tells of Dick and of his cat. He gets a lot of gold for that, and soon he wears the Lord Mayor's hat.

Scene One

Storyteller 2: We are in the country near London. A man with a horse stops near a small,
5   old house.
  Sissy Forge: Good morning, good morning. What can I do for you?
Buckingham: Can you tell me the way to London, please?
       Sissy: Yes, I can. But it isn't easy to find. My friend, Dick, can show you the way. Dick! Dick!
10   Dick: I'm coming! What's wrong, Sissy? Can I help you?
      Sissy: Dick, can you show this man the road to London? He doesn't know the way.
       Dick: Yes, of course. Come with me, please. *(they walk together)*
       Dick: They say there's gold in the streets of London and all of the houses are big and new, there – is that true?
15 Buckingham: Well, there are some big, new houses, but there is no gold in the streets – just a lot of rubbish. But London is beautiful.
       Dick: Here we are, now. Go over the river, and the road to London is behind those trees.
Buckingham: Thank you, Dick! *(throws him a piece of gold)* That's for your help.
       Dick: Wow! A piece of gold! Thank you! Bye! *(whistling)*
20 Barny Forge: Hey, Dick! What are you doing? Why aren't you working? Why aren't you feeding the pigs and the sheep? You sleep in my kitchen, eat my food, and then you don't work? I don't want you here. Go and pack your things and leave!
       Dick: But, but – where can I go, Mr Forge? I haven't got a mother or a father now.
     Barny: That's not my problem, Dick – that's your problem!
25   Dick: Oh no! What can I do? *(has an idea)* I know – I can go to London.

124 one hundred and twenty-four

Scene Two

Storyteller 2: Dick walks for two days. Finally, he arrives in London. He is tired and hungry. He takes out his piece of gold, but suddenly …
Dick: Hey – watch out!
Pickpocket 1: Sorry!
Pickpocket 2: We're in a hurry.
Dick: Wait! Where's my piece of gold? Give it back!
Pickpockets: We haven't got your piece of gold!
Stouty Burke: What's wrong? Who has got a piece of gold?
Dick: They've got it. But it's my piece of gold.
Pickpocket 2: We're poor boys. We haven't got a piece of gold.
Stouty Burke: Show me your hands.
Pickpocket 1: See! He's right!
Stouty Burke: *(to the second pickpocket)* Now your pockets. Aha! That's funny. You say you haven't got a piece of gold? What's this then? *(gives the coin to Dick)* Here you are, boy.
Pickpocket 1: We're sorry.
Pickpocket 2: Yes, but we're poor and we're hungry.
Stouty Burke: Well, OK – here's an apple for you.
Pickpockets: Thank you very much. Bye.
Dick: How can I thank you?
Stouty Burke: Well, I work for a very rich family, the Fitzwarrens. You can come and help me in the kitchen. Tonight I'm cooking dinner for the Lord Mayor of London.
Dick: The Lord who?
Stouty Burke: The Lord Mayor of London. He's a very rich and a very good man.
Dick: Oh! Then I want to be Lord Mayor of London one day, too!
Stouty Burke: What? You? With only one piece of gold? *(laughs)* Come on!
Dick: I've only got one piece of gold today, but I'm young and I can work hard.

Scene Three

Storyteller 2: Dick helps in the kitchen all day and in the evening he is very tired. He wants to sleep, and the cook shows him his bed, in the kitchen. But there are lots of mice, and Dick can't sleep. The next morning he is very tired, but he gets up and works in the kitchen again. He hears a noise.
Blacky: Meow! Meow!
Dick: Oh, it's a little black cat! Hello! What's your name?
Blacky: Meow! Meow! Meow!
Dick: Hey! Where are you going? Are you hungry?
Blacky: Purr! Purr!
Dick: What's that in your mouth? Oh, it's a big mouse. Clever cat. You can stay here and help us in the kitchen. But I can't call you 'Cat'. What about 'Blacky'?
Blacky: Purr! Purr!

Alle neuen Wörter findest du im *Dictionary* ganz hinten im Buch.

E A play

Scene Four

70 Storyteller 2: One day Stouty Burke goes home to his family. A new cook comes. He doesn't like Dick and he doesn't like cats. Dick is very unhappy. He leaves the house. The next morning Dick and Blacky are sleeping in a field near a big church. It's six o'clock, and the bells are ringing. Dick wakes up.
75 Dick: Listen, Blacky! The bells are talking to us. What are they saying?
Bells: Turn again, Whittington, Lord Mayor of London! Turn again, Whittington, Lord Mayor of London! Turn again, Whittington, Lord Mayor of London!
Dick: Come on, Blacky! I want to be Lord Mayor of London one day, and a Lord Mayor doesn't run away from problems! Let's go back and tell Lady Anne about
80 the cook. Maybe she can help us.

Scene Five

Storyteller 2: Dick and Blacky go back to the Fitzwarren's house. Lady Anne is in the living room with her brother, George, and Alice. Suddenly, she screams.

85 Lady Anne: *(standing on a chair)* Ah! Ah! There's a mouse! It wants the cake!
Buckingham: Oh, Anne! It's only a mouse. I've got hundreds of mice on my ship.
Alice: Please, Uncle George. Catch it!
90 Dick: Just a minute! We can help. Catch it, Blacky! Good cat! Bring it here!
Lady Anne: Oh! Thank you, Dick. And thank you, Blacky.
Blacky: Purr! Purr!
Buckingham: Dick? I know you. You helped me. You showed
95 me the road to London.
Dick: Yes, that's right.
Buckingham: You've got a very fast cat! Can I buy your cat for my ship? Here are three pieces of gold for her.
Blacky: Meow! Meow! Meow!
100 Dick: Sorry, Sir, but Blacky is my friend. I can't sell her to you.
Buckingham: Well, can I borrow her? There are a lot of mice on my ship. They eat the silk. You can have a gold coin for every ten mice she catches.
Blacky: Purr! Purr!!
Dick: Well, Blacky likes the idea. But please bring her back to me.
105 Buckingham: OK, Dick. Now let's all eat this cake.

Scene Six

Storyteller 2: Stouty Burke comes back to the house, and Dick is very happy. Alice likes Dick, and sometimes she goes to the market with Dick and the cook. One day, they see a big black and gold coach with two black horses.

110	Dick:	Wow! A gold coach! I want to ride in a gold coach, too.
	Stouty:	That isn't for people like you and me, Dick. That's the Lord Mayor's coach.
115	Dick:	Then I want to be Lord Mayor one day, too.
	Alice:	You? But you can't read or write, Dick.
	Dick:	Yes, but I can learn. A, B, C … Hey! Watch out!
120	Alice:	*(Dick pushes Alice away.)* Arrgh!
	Stouty:	Are you OK, my dear?
	Alice:	Yes, I'm OK now. But these coaches are scary!
	Stouty:	Can you get up?
125	Alice:	Yes. Thank you, Dick. You saved my life!

Scene Seven

	Storyteller 2:	Stouty and Dick bring Alice to her mother. Lady Anne has got a visitor.
	Lady Anne	Come in! Ah, hello children! Hello, Stouty.
	Buckingham:	Alice! What …?
130	Alice	Hello, Uncle George! Mum, a fast coach came down the road. I didn't see it, but Dick pushed me away from it and saved my life.
	Lady Anne	Oh, my poor Alice. Dick, how can we thank you?
	Alice	I've got an idea, Mum. Dick wants to learn to read and write. Can we help him?
	Lady Anne	Is that right, Dick?
135	Dick	Yes, it is, Lady Anne.
	Lady Anne	Well, OK, we can help you. But first my brother wants to speak to you.
	Buckingham:	Hello, young man. *(gives him a bag and a box)* Here's your cat. Blacky caught a lot of mice. And I can sell my silk now for a lot of money. Your pieces of gold are in this bag.
140	Dick:	Blacky! Hello!
	Blacky:	Purr! Purr! Purr!!
	Dick:	*(looks in the bag)* Wow – there are a lot of pieces of gold in here.
	Buckingham:	Yes, you are a rich young man.

Scene Eight

	Storyteller 1	Dick uses his pieces of gold well, and in a few years he is very, very rich.
145		He becomes Lord Mayor of London, and uses his gold to help people.
	Dick:	I don't want children in London to be poor or hungry. *(gives gold to children)*
	Storyteller 2:	And this is where our story ends, of Dick and Blacky and their friends, Of how a boy whose luck is down, becomes Lord Mayor of London Town.

Alle neuen Wörter findest du im *Dictionary* ganz hinten im Buch.

A calendar   Around the year

In Britain there are lots of special days. You know some of them, like Christmas and Easter, in Germany, too. But people do different things on these days in Britain. Other days, like Guy Fawkes Day, are not special days in Germany. Some days, like Red Nose Day, are new, and others, like Valentine's Day, are very old. Here you can read and learn about some special days in Britain.

Valentine's Day – February

On 14th February, Valentine's Day, in Britain you write a card to a girl or boy that you love. You often write a poem in the card, but you do not write your name. The person must guess who the card is from. Sometimes people give flowers or other presents, too.

Think of M,
Think of E.
Put them together
And think of ME!

HAPPY VALENTINE'S DAY!

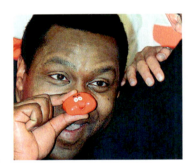

Red Nose Day – March

On this day lots of people in Britain wear a red nose and do something funny for charity. Many schools in Britain organize events for Red Nose Day. The pupils do funny things – they sing, dance or tell jokes – and ask for money for charity. Famous people collect money, too. They want to make people laugh and to help poor or ill people in Britain and in other countries, too. Red Nose Day is a British idea, but you can find it in other countries, even in Germany.

Guy Fawkes Day – November

5th November, 1605: Guy Fawkes and some friends try to blow up Parliament and kill King James I, but the King's men find them. Three months later, Parliament and the King are OK, and Guy Fawkes and his friends are dead.
Today, children make 'guys' and carry them through the streets. On 5th November they put the 'guys' on fires. There are a lot of fireworks.

1 From February to November

Read the texts. Then do the exercises.

a) Make a Valentine's Day card for a card shop. You can draw a picture, write a poem …

b) Do you know Red Nose Day? What do people do on Red Nose Day, and why?

c) What happens in Britain on November 5th?

A calendar E

Christmas – 25th December

2 Christmas

a) *What do you know about Christmas in Britain?*

b) *What is the same and what is different about Christmas in Britain and Germany?*

Christmas Eve (24th December): Young children put stockings under the chimney or on their beds. Their parents tell them that in the night Father Christmas comes down the chimney and puts small presents into the stockings. Children often leave a glass of milk for Father Christmas and a carrot for Rudolph, Father Christmas's reindeer next to the chimney.

Christmas Day (25th December): In the morning the children's stockings are full of small toys, sweets and fruit. All of the family open their other presents under the Christmas tree. Christmas dinner is always on 25th December, usually at lunchtime. Some families pull crackers and wear paper hats. For Christmas dinner there is usually a turkey and Christmas pudding.

Other British Christmas traditions: People in Britain write lots of Christmas cards. They often put them on the wall in the living room. Sometimes people go carol-singing. They visit friends and neighbours and sing Christmas songs. People give them money for charity.

3 A song: We wish you a Merry Christmas (trad.)

We wish you a Merry Christmas, we wish you a Merry Christmas,
We wish you a Merry Christmas and a Happy New Year.
Chorus: Good tidings we bring to you and your kin.
We wish you a Merry Christmas and a Happy New Year.

4 Your special days

a) *Which special days do you know? Make a calendar with these days.*

b) *What do you and your friends and family do on these days?*

5 Special days in Britain

*Work in groups. Find out more about a special day in Britain.
You can use books or the Internet. Write five sentences and draw some pictures.*

Alle neuen Wörter findest du im *Dictionary* ganz hinten im Buch.

Grammar

Die Regeln, nach denen eine Sprache funktioniert, heißen Grammatik (auf Englisch: *grammar*). Auf den folgenden Seiten sind die wichtigsten Regeln der englischen Sprache zusammengestellt. Die Grammatik kann dir helfen,

- wenn du **Hausaufgaben machst.**
- wenn du dich **auf einen Test oder eine Klassenarbeit vorbereitest.**
- wenn du **etwas nicht ganz verstanden hast.**
- wenn du **etwas wiederholen möchtest.**

In diesem Bild herrscht völliges Durcheinander. Wenn man sich im Straßenverkehr nicht an die Regeln hält, kracht es. Wenn man sich in einer Sprache nicht an die Regeln hält, versteht niemand, was eigentlich gemeint ist. Das kann böse Folgen haben.

Jedes Kapitel hat eine dicke Überschrift, die angibt, um welches Thema es geht. Danach folgen ein kurzer Merksatz und Beispiele und Übersichten. Sie zeigen dir, wozu du diese Formen brauchst und wie diese Formen gebildet werden.

Sachen, die du dir merken solltest, sind **blau** hervorgehoben. Tom gibt dir hin und wieder nützliche Tipps.

 Bei diesem Zeichen stehen weitere Hinweise, die du dir merken solltest.

 Vorsicht, Falle! Bei diesem Zeichen wird auf besondere Schwierigkeiten hingewiesen.

→ p. 16,2   Dieser Verweis sagt dir, wo du die zugehörige Übung im Buch findest (hier: page 16, exercise 2/Seite 16, Übung 2)

Wenn du einmal einen Begriff nicht mehr weißt, kannst du auf Seite 159 nachschlagen. Dort findest du eine Übersicht mit den wichtigsten grammatischen Begriffen.

Du kannst dir die Regeln gut merken, wenn du die Übersichten in deinen *Folder* einträgst, Karteikarten anlegst oder ein Grammatik-Poster machst. Das kann dir auch helfen, Beispielsätze und Merksätze auswendig zu lernen.

130 one hundred and thirty

Unit 1

G1 Personalpronomen
Personal pronouns → p. 16,2

Die Personalpronomen werden auch **persönliche FÜRwörter** genannt, weil sie **FÜR** Personen, **FÜR** Tiere oder **FÜR** Gegenstände stehen.

I	ich	I'm a mouse.
you	du/Sie	You're twelve.
he	er	He's from Istanbul.
she	sie	She's my teacher.
it	es	It's a big school.
we	wir	We're in the right classroom.
you	ihr/Sie	You're friends.
they	sie	They're new here.

I wird immer groß geschrieben, nicht nur am Satzanfang.

 You kann **du**, **Sie** oder **ihr** heißen.

 He steht immer für eine männliche Person!
She steht immer für eine weibliche Person!
Für Tiere, deren Namen man kennt, verwendet man *he* oder *she*!

 Für Sachen wird im Englischen immer *it* verwendet!
Auch für Tiere, deren Namen man nicht kennt, verwendet man *it*!

G2 Das Verb *to be*: Langformen
The long forms of the verb 'to be' → p. 16,3

Das Verb *to be* brauchst du, wenn du Aussagen zu Personen oder Gegenständen machen willst. Genau wie das deutsche Verb „**sein**" (bin, bist, sind, seid) ändert sich das englische Verb *to be* auch jeweils nach der Person. *To be* kann in Lang- oder Kurzformen auftreten. Die Langform verwendet man meist beim Schreiben.

I	**am**	ich bin	I	**am**	new here.
you	**are**	du bist/Sie sind	You	**are**	late, Sam.
he	**is**	er ist	He	**is**	eleven.
she	**is**	sie ist	She	**is**	from Bristol.
it	**is**	es ist	It	**is**	a big school.
we	**are**	wir sind	We	**are**	at Thomas Tallis.
you	**are**	ihr seid/Sie sind	You	**are**	here.
they	**are**	sie sind	They	**are**	my friends.

In geschriebenen Texten, z. B. in einem Brief, benutzt du diese Langformen des Verbs.

G 3 Das Verb *to be*: Kurzformen
The short forms of the verb 'to be'

→ p. 16,2–3

Wenn man Englisch spricht, wird oft eine Silbe verschluckt. So kann man schneller und flüssiger sprechen. Diese Kurzform verwendet man auch, wenn man Gespräche aufschreibt oder an Freunde schreibt.

I	**'m**	ich bin	I**'m**	new in Greenwich.	
you	**'re**	du bist / Sie sind	You**'re**	late, Sam.	
he	**'s**	er ist	He**'s**	eleven.	
she	**'s**	sie ist	She**'s**	from Bristol.	
it	**'s**	es ist	It**'s**	a big school.	
we	**'re**	wir sind	We**'re**	at Thomas Tallis.	
you	**'re**	ihr seid / Sie sind	You**'re**	here.	
they	**'re**	sie sind	They**'re**	my friends.	

I'm one. He's three. We're at Thomas Tallis.

 Beim Schreiben setzt man einen Apostroph ('), um zu zeigen, dass ein Buchstabe weggefallen ist.

G 4 Die Verneinung des Verbs *to be*
The negative of the verb 'to be'

→ p. 17,5

Wenn du die Formen von *to be* verneinen willst, fügst du nach *am*, *is* und *are* einfach **not** ein.

I	**am not** / **'m not**	ich bin nicht	I**'m not** new in Greenwich.	
you	**are not** / **aren't**	du bist nicht / Sie sind nicht	You **aren't** late, Sam.	
he / she / it	**is not** / **isn't**	er/sie/es ist nicht	He / She **isn't** eleven. It **isn't** a big school.	
we	**are not** / **aren't**	wir sind nicht	We **aren't** at Thomas Tallis.	
you	**are not** / **aren't**	ihr seid / Sie sind nicht	You **aren't** here.	
they	**are not** / **aren't**	sie sind nicht	They **aren't** my friends.	

 Manchmal findet man auch die Kurzformen *you're not*, *she's not*, *he's not*, *it's not*, *we're not*, *they're not*.

 Die einzige Kurzform von *I am not* ist *I'm not*.

132 one hundred and thirty-two

G 5 Das Verb *to be* in Fragen und Kurzantworten
Questions and short answers with 'to be'
→ p. 17,6

Wenn du eine Frage mit den Formen von *to be* bilden willst, stellst du einfach das Verb an den Satzanfang. Das funktioniert genauso wie im Deutschen.		
Am I ... ?	*Bin ich ...?*	**Am** I late?
Are you ... ?	*Bist du ...?/Sind Sie ...?*	**Are** you from Greenwich?
Is he/she/it ... ?	*Ist er/sie/es ...?*	**Is** he/she at Thomas Tallis?
		Is it in your bag?
Are we ... ?	*Sind wir ...?*	**Are** we late?
Are you ... ?	*Seid ihr ...?/Sind Sie ...?*	**Are** you new in Greenwich?
Are they ... ?	*Sind sie ...?*	**Are** they in your tutor group?

Wenn du auf eine Frage antwortest, können *yes* oder *no* allein manchmal etwas unhöflich klingen. Deshalb antwortet man meistens mit einem verkürzten Satz, einer **Kurzantwort**, die höflicher klingt.

Am I late?	Yes, **you are.**	No, **you aren't.**
Are you from Greenwich?	Yes, **I am.**	No, **I'm not.**
Is he at Thomas Tallis?	Yes, **he is.**	No, **he isn't.**
Is she from Bristol?	Yes, **she is.**	No, **she isn't.**
Is it in your bag?	Yes, **it is.**	No, **it isn't.**
Are we late?	Yes, **you are.**	No, **you aren't.**
Are you new in Greenwich?	Yes, **we are.**	No, **we aren't.**
Are they in your group?	Yes, **they are.**	No, **they aren't.**

G 6 Der unbestimmte Artikel *a/an*
The indefinite article 'a/an'
→ p. 18,2

Der unbestimmte Artikel (unbestimmte Begleiter), deutsch „ein" oder „eine", heißt im Englischen *a* oder *an*. Vor einem Konsonanten (Mitlaut) wie in den Wörtern *ball*, *pencil* sagst du **a**.
Vor einem Vokal (Selbstlaut a, e, i, o, u) wie in *apple*, *old* sagst du **an**.

a [ə]			**an** [ən]	
This is	a	bag.	And this is	an	apple.
Here's	a	pencil.	And here's	an	exercise book.
Is that	a	pencil case?	– Yes, it's	an	old pencil case.

 Es heißt *a unit*, obwohl das Wort mit dem geschriebenen Vokal ‚u' beginnt. Die Aussprache ['juːnɪt] entscheidet, nicht die Schreibung.

G 7 Der bestimmte Artikel *the*
The definite article 'the'

→ p. 18,3

Der bestimmte Artikel (bestimmte Begleiter), deutsch „der", „die" oder „das", heißt im Englischen ***the***. Vor einem Konsonanten (Mitlaut) wie in den Wörtern *ball, pencil* sagst du [ðə]. Vor einem Vokal wie in *apple, old* sagst du [ði].

	the [ðə]			**the** [ði]	
This is	the	bag.	And this is	the	apple.
Here's	the	pencil.	And here's	the	exercise book.
Is that	the	pencil case?	– Yes, it's	the	old pencil case.

 Bei *unit* [ˈjuːnɪt] heißt es [ðə]. Die Aussprache entscheidet, nicht die Schreibung. (vergleiche **G 6** *a/an*)

G 8 Die Mehrzahlformen/Pluralformen
Plural forms

→ p. 19,5–6

Du kannst den Plural (Mehrzahl) der meisten englischen Substantive (Hauptwörter) bilden, indem du ein **s** direkt an die Singularform (Einzahlform) anhängst.
-es schreibt man, wenn das Wort bereits mit einem Zischlaut [s, z, ʃ, tʃ, ʒ, dʒ] endet, wie *box – boxes* oder *sandwich – sandwiches*.

Singular (Einzahl)	**Plural** (Mehrzahl)
a book	five books
a dog	two dogs
a sandwich	five sandwich**es**

Die Aussprache des Plural-*s*

Nach den stimmlosen Konsonanten [p, t, k, f, θ] wird das Plural-*s* stimmlos (scharf) ausgesprochen **[s]**.	Nach Vokalen und nach stimmhaften Konsonanten [b, d, g, l, m, n, ð, v] wird das Plural-*s* stimmhaft (weich) ausgesprochen **[z]**.	Nach Zischlauten [s, z, ʃ, tʃ, ʒ, dʒ] wird die Pluralendung **[ɪz]** gesprochen und *(e)s* geschrieben.
[s]	**[z]**	**[ɪz]**
five book**s** [ks]	five tree**s** [iːz]	two exerci**ses** [zɪz]
three group**s** [ps]	two dog**s** [gz]	three sandwi**ches** [dʒɪz]
two unit**s** [ts]	four friend**s** [dz]	ten pa**ges** [dʒɪz]

 Wenn ein Wort mit einem Zischlaut endet und mit *-e* am Ende geschrieben wird (z. B. *pencil case*), hängt man nur ein *-s* an: *pencil cases*. Wenn ein Wort mit einem Zischlaut ohne *-e* endet, hängt man *-es* an (z. B. *sandwiches*). Die Aussprache lautet in beiden Fällen **[ɪz]**.

G 9 There is … / There are …

→ p. 20,1

Wenn du darauf hinweisen möchtest, dass Personen oder Dinge existieren, kannst du das mit **there is** oder **there are** tun. Es entspricht dem deutschen **es gibt …, es ist/sind …**.

There is	a mouse in the classroom.	*Es ist eine Maus im Klassenzimmer.*
There's	an apple on the table.	*Es liegt ein Apfel auf dem Tisch.*
There are	three girls in the tutor group.	*Es gibt drei Mädchen in der Klasse.*
There are	four books in my bag.	*Es sind vier Bücher in meiner Tasche.*

 There is/There's verwendest du, wenn es sich um **eine** Person oder Sache handelt.
There are verwendest du, wenn du über **mehrere** Personen oder Dinge sprichst.
There is … und *There are …* stehen meistens am Anfang des Satzes.
Von *there are* gibt es keine Kurzform.

 There is … und *There are …* geben nicht den Ort an, an dem sich die Person oder die Sache befindet. Du musst immer noch hinzufügen, wo diese sind: *There are two girls here and three boys there.*

G 10 Präpositionen
Prepositions

→ p. 20,2

Die kleinen Wörter wie **in, on, behind** oder **under** heißen **Präpositionen**. Sie sagen uns, wo etwas ist, etwas stattfindet usw.

They are **in** the classroom.	*… im Klassenzimmer.*
There **is** a poster **behind** the door.	*… hinter der Tür.*
The pencil case is **on** the table.	*… auf dem Tisch.*
Tom is **under** the chair.	*… unter dem Stuhl.*

G 11 Fragen mit Fragewörtern
Questions with question words

→ p. 21,6

Fragewörter sind Wörter wie **Who …? What …? Where …?** und **How …?** (Wer …? Was …? Wo …? Wie …?). Fragewörter stehen immer am Anfang der Frage.

Who	are you?	– I'm Tom.	**Wer?**
Where	are the apples?	– In my bag.	**Wo?**
What	's on the table?	– A book.	**Was?**
How	old are you?	– I'm one.	**Wie?**

Merk dir: In *Where?* steckt die Antwort *here*. In *Who?* steckt ein Gesicht.

 **Who** fragt nach Personen.
Where fragt nach einem Ort.

Unit 2

G 12 Der *s*-Genitiv
The s-genitive

→ 30,1–31,3

Wenn du sagen möchtest, dass etwas jemandem gehört oder zugeordnet ist, kannst du das mit dem **s-Genitiv** tun. Er wird bei Personen und auch bei Tieren verwendet.
Dazu hängt man einfach ein **'s** an: **Terry's cat** oder **the girl's name**.

Singular (Einzahl)

The ca**t's** name is Tiger.	[s]	*Der Name **der** Katze …*
Jade is Lisa**'s** sister.	[s]	*Jade ist Lisas Schwester.*
The teache**r's** computer is old.	[z]	*Der Computer **der** Lehrerin …*
Tom is Tes**s's** brother.	[sɪz]	*… der Bruder **von** Tess.*

 Die Aussprache des *'s* folgt den gleichen Regeln wie beim Plural-*s*. (siehe **G8**)

Bei Pluralformen, die ohnehin auf -s enden, hängst du im Genitiv nur einen Apostroph an das -s an: **s'**.

Kein -s am Ende? Gar nicht schwer:
Ein Apostroph und -s muss her.
Ein -s am Ende ist schon da?
Na, dann nur „Apo", ist doch klar!

Plural (Mehrzahl)

The girl**s'** bags are new.	[z]	*Die Taschen **der** Mädchen …*
The Spencer**s'** flat is in Wendover Road.	[z]	*Die Wohnung **der** Familie Spencer …*

The **girl's** bike is new. ⟷ The **girls'** bikes are new.

G13 Die Possessivbegleiter
The possessive determiners

→ p. 31,4

Mit den Possessivbegleitern kannst du ausdrücken, wem etwas gehört oder zu wem jemand gehört.

Is that **your** book, Tom?

Yes, it's **my** new mouse book.

Personal pronouns		*Possessive determiners*	
I	'm from Greenwich.	My	name is Terry.
You	're in Year 7, Terry.	Your	tutor is Mrs Carter.
He	's eleven.	His	friend is eleven, too.
She	's in my tutor group.	Her	name is Lisa.
It	's the Brooks' flat.	Its	rooms are very small.
We	're in Year 7.	Our	classroom is nice.
You	're late, boys!	Your	bags aren't here.
They	're at Thomas Tallis School.	Their	school is in Greenwich.

 *Y*our kann „dein", „euer" oder „Ihr" heißen. Es kommt auf den Zusammenhang an:

- I'm **your** new German teacher, Sam.   Ich bin **dein** …
- I'm **your** tutor, boys and girls.   Ich bin **euer** …
- Is this **your** pen, Mrs Carter?   Ist das **Ihr** …

 *Y*our und *you're*, *its* und *it's*, *their* und *they're* werden gleich ausgesprochen, aber unterschiedlich geschrieben. Die Possessivbegleiter haben keinen Apostroph.

Denk dran:
it's steht für *it is*,
you're steht für *you are*,
they're steht für *they are*.

G Grammar Unit 2

G14 *have got/has got*
→ p. 32,1–2; 33,4

Wenn du sagen möchtest, dass jemand etwas hat oder besitzt, verwendest du das Verb *have got/has got*. Die Kurzform lautet *'ve got / 's got*.
Wenn du sagen willst, dass jemand etwas nicht hat oder nicht besitzt, kannst du **n't** (die verkürzte Form von *not*) direkt an *have/has* anhängen.

I	've got	a small room.		I	haven't got	a computer.
You	've got	nice friends.		You	haven't got	a big room, Emma.
He	's got	a new football.		He	hasn't got	a mobile.
She	's got	a big sister.		She	hasn't got	her English book.
It	's got	three bedrooms.		It	hasn't got	a big garden.
We	've got	a new English teacher.		We	haven't got	a sofa in our classroom.
You	've got	two new folders.		You	haven't got	your bags, girls.
They	've got	five trees.		They	haven't got	a TV in their room.

 n't/not muss immer zwischen *have* und *got* stehen!

I have ~~not~~ got a computer.

 Verwechsle nicht die Kurzformen von *has* und *is*:
She**'s** got a big sister. = She **has** got a big sister.
She**'s** Ben's sister. = She **is** Ben's sister.

Wie beim Verb *to be* verwendet man die Langformen von *have got/has got* eher in der geschriebenen Sprache (die Kurzformen eher beim Sprechen).

I	have got	a small room.		I	have not got	a computer.
You	have got	nice friends.		You	have not got	a big room, Emma.
He	has got	a new football.		He	has not got	a mobile.
She	has got	a big sister.		She	has not got	her English book.
It	has got	three bedrooms.		It	has not got	a big garden.
We	have got	a new English teacher.		We	have not got	a sofa in our classroom.
You	have got	two new folders.		You	have not got	your bags, girls.
They	have got	five trees.		They	have not got	a TV in their room.

138 one hundred and thirty-eight

Unit 2 | Grammar | **G**

G 15 Die Satzstellung in Aussagesätzen
Word order in statements → p. 33,4

Die Satzstellung im englischen Aussagesatz ist: Subjekt – Verb – Objekt
(Merke: **S**traßen**v**erkehrs**o**rdnung). Das **Subjekt** (englisch: *subject*) muss immer **vor** dem Verb stehen, das **Objekt** (englisch: *object*) kommt **nach** dem Verb.

Subject	**V**erb	**O**bject
I	have got	a new CD.
Lisa	has got	a dog.
We	have got	a nice flat.

Im Deutschen kannst du die Stellung von Subjekt und Objekt austauschen, im Englischen nicht!

Lisa hat einen Hund.

Einen Hund hat Lisa.

Lisa has got a dog.
 S   V   O

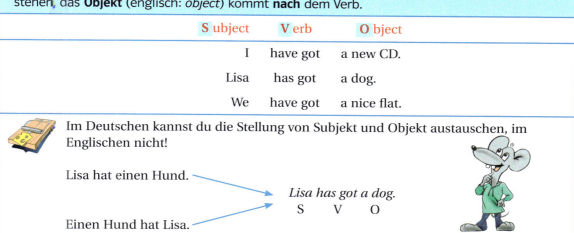

G 16 *have got / has got*: Fragen und Kurzantworten
Questions and short answers → p. 33,5–6

Wenn du Fragen mit **have got / has got** bilden möchtest, musst du den Fragesatz mit **have** oder **has** beginnen.

Terry **has got** a new mobile.	**Has** Terry **got** a new mobile?

Wie bei *to be* kannst du mit *have got / has got* Kurzantworten geben. Dabei wird *got* einfach weggelassen und nur *have* oder *has* wiederholt.

Have I **got** my homework?	– Yes, you have.	– No, you haven't.
Have you **got** a football, Emma?	– Yes, I have.	– No, I haven't.
Has Terry **got** friends?	– Yes, he has.	– No, he hasn't.
Has Mrs Carter **got** a German book?	– Yes, she has.	– No, she hasn't.
Has Terry's shed **got** three chairs?	– Yes, it has.	– No, it hasn't.
Have we **got** homework?	– Yes, you have.	– No, you haven't.
Have you **got** a computer?	– Yes, we have.	– No, we haven't.
Have they **got** a new flat?	– Yes, they have.	– No, they haven't.

one hundred and thirty-nine **139**

G17 Der Imperativ/Die Befehlsform
The imperative

→ p. 34,1

Mit dieser Form kannst du jemanden auffordern, etwas zu tun *(Listen!)* oder nicht zu tun *(Don't go!)*. Wie im Deutschen drückt der Imperativ eine Bitte, eine Warnung oder einen Befehl aus.

 "Oh, be quiet, please." **Open** your books, please. Please **be** quiet. **Help** your brother, please, Lisa.	Den Imperativ (die Befehlsform) bildest du mit der Grundform des Verbs ohne *to*.
Don't play football in here, boys. Please **don't call** Terry now. **Don't write** in your English books.  "Bei Verboten – sei ganz Ohr – setz einfach mal ein **don't** davor." "DON'T!"	Der verneinte Imperativ wird mit **don't** und der Grundform des Verbs gebildet. (Die Langform von *don't* ist *do not*.)

 Der Imperativ hat immer die gleiche Form, egal ob eine oder mehrere Personen angesprochen werden: *Don't play football in here.* – Spiel nicht / Spielt nicht … .

 Wenn man höflich sein will, sollte das Wort *please* nicht fehlen. Es steht oft am Anfang oder am Ende des Satzes.

Unit 2 | Grammar | G

G 18 Das Hilfsverb *can/can't*
The auxiliary 'can'/'can't' → p. 34,3

Ein Hilfsverb ist ein Verb, das nicht allein ohne ein anderes Verb verwendet werden kann. Mit dem Hilfsverb **can** kannst du ausdrücken, dass jemand etwas tun **kann** oder **darf**.
Can bleibt in allen Personen gleich und steht immer mit der Grundform eines anderen Verbs (ohne *to*): He can **see** ....

I	**can see**	Mrs Carter in the playground.
You	**can write**	in English now.
Terry	**can play**	in his shed.
Lisa	**can't do**	her homework.
Chocolate	**can be**	too sweet.
We	**can listen**	to CDs in our room.
You	**can't play**	football here.
They	**can have**	a party.

Can I take you home? — Yes, you can! — No, you can't!

 Im Englischen steht das Verb immer direkt hinter *can*, im Deutschen aber am Satzende. Vergleiche:
Terry **can play** *in his shed.* – Terry **kann** in seinem Schuppen **spielen**.

 Die verneinte Form von *can* [kæn] heißt *can't* [kɑ:nt]. Beim Schreiben wird meistens die Langform *cannot* verwendet. *Cannot* wird immer zusammengeschrieben.

Im Deutschen kann man „können" manchmal allein gebrauchen. Im Englischen dagegen muss in einer Aussage nach *can* immer ein Vollverb folgen:

Meine Mutter kann viele italienische Wörter. – *My mum can say a lot of Italian words.*

G 19 Fragen mit *can*
Questions with 'can' → p. 34,2

Fragesätze mit *can* bildest du indem du *can* an den Satzanfang schiebst.

Can	you	**help**	Jade, please, Lisa?	– Yes, I	**can.**
Can	your friends	**play**	the drums, Terry?	– No, they	**can't.**
Can	I	**play**	in the garden, Mum?	– Yes, you	**can.**

 Bei den Kurzantworten wird die Grundform des anderen Verbs weggelassen und nur *can* oder *can't* wiederholt.

one hundred and forty-one **141**

Unit 3

G 20 Die Uhrzeit → p. 43,3
The time

Im Englischen benutzt du *past* für die ersten 30 Minuten der vollen Stunde.	Nach *half past* zählst du mit *to* zur kommenden Stunde hin.
o'clock / five / ten / quarter / twenty / twenty-five / half — past 3	o'clock / five / ten / quarter / twenty / twenty-five / half — to
2:00 – It's two **o'clock**.	2:35 – It's twenty-five **to** three.
2:05 – It's five **past** two.	2:40 – It's twenty **to** three.
2:10 – It's ten **past** two.	2:45 – It's **quarter to** three.
2:15 – It's **quarter past** two.	2:50 – It's ten **to** three.
2:20 – It's twenty **past** two.	2:55 – It's five **to** three.
2:25 – It's twenty-five **past** two.	3:00 – It's three **o'clock**.
2:30 – It's **half past** two.	

Du kannst die Uhrzeit aber auch ganz einfach ohne **to** und **past** angeben, ähnlich wie im Deutschen: *9:07 – It's nine-oh-seven; 9:48 – It's nine forty-eight.*

 o'clock verwendet man nur bei vollen Stunden: *one o'clock, five o'clock.*

 Bei den Fünferzahlen (5, 10, 15 usw.) wird das Wort *minutes* gewöhnlich weggelassen. Bei anderen Angaben musst du *minutes* hinzufügen: *2:08 – It's eight minutes past two.*

G 21 Die einfache Form der Gegenwart → p. 44,1
The simple present

Wenn du sagen möchtest, dass etwas eine Tatsache ist oder häufig oder regelmäßig geschieht, gebrauchst du das **simple present**. Bei **I, you, we** und **they** hat das *simple present* die gleiche Form wie der Infinitiv (die Grundform des Verbs).

I	**play**	football.	We	**play**	in the band.
You	**play**	basketball at school.	They	**play**	computer games.

 Das *simple present* gebrauchst du auch, um zu erzählen, wie jemand mehrere Dinge nacheinander tut: *First they go to Terry's house. Then they go into the garden. They look at Terry's shed. Tiger is on the shed. …*

G 22 Häufigkeitsadverbien: Satzstellung
Adverbs of frequency: word order

→ p. 44,2–45,4

Wörter wie *always, often, never, sometimes* teilen mit, wie oft oder wie häufig etwas getan wird. Sie heißen deshalb **Häufigkeitsadverbien** *(adverbs of frequency)*. In Aussagesätzen im *simple present* stehen sie vor dem Verb. Im Deutschen stehen sie meist nach dem Verb.

*Always, often, sometimes, never – **vor** das Verb, dann bist du clever!*

I	**sometimes**	eat	crisps.
You	**always**	ride	your bike to school.
Tiger and Terry	**often**	sit	in the shed.
We	**never**	play	basketball.

Ich esse manchmal …
Du fährst immer …
Tiger und Terry sitzen oft …
Wir spielen nie …

Wenn das Verb eine Form von *to be* ist, steht das Häufigkeitsadverb dahinter:

My pen	is	**always**	in my bag.
We	are	**never**	late.

Bei einem mehrteiligen Verb, z.B. *have got* oder *can* + Infinitiv, steht das Häufigkeitsadverb zwischen den beiden Teilen:

I	can	**never**	find	my rubber.
Terry	has	**always**	got	his mobile.

G 23 Das -s in der 3. Person Singular
The -s in the 3rd person singular

→ p. 46,1; 47,4

Bei *he*, *she* und *it* (3. Person Singular) hängst du im *simple present* ein **s** an das Verb an. Beim Schreiben und Sprechen musst du dir einige Besonderheiten merken!
- Nach Zischlauten wie *sh* [ʃ] oder *ch* [tʃ] wird ein **-es** angehängt.
- Die Aussprache der **(e)s**-Laute ist wie beim Plural-**s** (siehe **G 8**).

HE – SHE – IT
Das **s** muss mit!

Emma	**gets up**	at 7 o'clock.	[s]
She	**talks**	to Terry.	[s]
Terry often	**plays**	the drums.	[z]
Lisa sometimes	**swims**	after school.	[z]
School	**finishes**	at 3:20.	[ɪz]
Grandma always	**watches**	TV in the evenings.	[ɪz]

Auch bei *go* und *do* wird beim Schreiben ein **-es** angehängt. *Goes* und *does* werden aber unterschiedlich ausgesprochen!

Emma	**goes**	to dance lessons.	[gəʊz]
She always	**does**	her homework.	[dʌz]

G 24 This/that – these/those

→ p. 48,1

This und **these** kannst du gebrauchen, um über Dinge und Personen zu sprechen, die in deiner Nähe sind. **That** und **those** gebrauchst du, um auf Dinge oder Personen zu weisen, die weiter weg sind. **This** und **that** sind die Singularformen, **these** und **those** sind die Pluralformen.

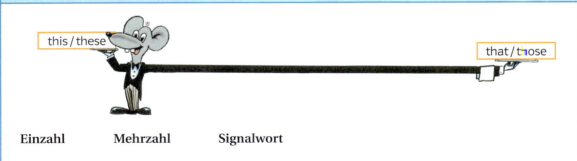

Einzahl	Mehrzahl	Signalwort	
this	these	here	*das / dies(e) hier*
that	those	over there	*das / die dort*

Unit 4

G 25 Die Personalpronomen: die Objektform → p. 60,2
Object pronouns

Du kennst bereits die Personalpronomen in der Subjektform (*I, you, he, she* usw.). Sie sagen, wer oder was etwas tut. Diese Pronomen gibt es auch in der Objektform. Sie sagen auf wen oder was sich eine Handlung bezieht.
Im Englischen gibt es jeweils nur eine Form, z. B. *me*, im Deutschen meistens zwei: mir, mich.

Subjektform		Objektform		
I	Show	me	the way, please.	*mir*
	Can you see	me	in the photo?	*mich*
you	I can tell	you	the way.	*dir/Ihnen*
	We can see	you	in the photo.	*dich/Sie*
he	Terry's here. Talk to	him	now.	*ihm*
	My dad? Let's ask	him.		*ihn*
she	Please show	her	this letter.	*ihr*
	Where is she? I can't find	her.		*sie*
it	Here's a ball. Play with	it.		*ihm*
	Where? I can't see	it.		*es*
we	Please help	us	with the picture.	*uns*
	Can you take	us	to school, Dad?	*uns*
you	I can show	you	the way.	*euch/Ihnen*
	But I can't take	you	there.	*euch/Sie*
they	My parents? Yes, talk to	them.		*ihnen*
	Let's ask	them.		*sie*

G 26 Die einfache Gegenwart: Verneinung
The simple present: negatives

→ c. 62,1; 63,3

Du kennst bereits verschiedene Formen der Verneinung:				Wenn der Satz ein **Hilfsverb** wie *can* oder *have/has* enthält oder eine Form von *to be*, hängst du einfach *not/n't* an.
I	**can't**	find it on the map.		
You	**cannot**	go by bus or car.		
We	**haven't**	got German today.		
They	**aren't**	in their room.		

Wenn nur ein **Vollverb** im Satz steht, das keine Form von *to be* ist, und der Satz kein Hilfsverb enthält, dann setzt du zur Verneinung das Hilfsverb **don't** vor das Verb. *Don't* ist die Kurzform von *do not*.

I	**don't**	like	buses.
You	**don't**	go	to school by taxi.
We	**don't**	know	everything.
They	**don't**	like	the same films.

And I don't like cats!

G 27 Die einfache Gegenwart: Fragen und Kurzantworten
The simple present: questions and short answers

→ f. 62,1–63,2

In einer Frage steht eine Form von *to be*, *have (got)* oder ein Hilfsverb (z. B. *can*) am Anfang. Wenn kein anderes Hilfsverb da ist, verwendest du *do*. Das gleiche Hilfsverb wird dann in der Kurzantwort gebraucht.

Im Englischen brauchst du für Frage und Verneinung meist ein Hilfsverb. Hast du keins – hol dir eins: das **do**-Hilfsverb!

Can	you	read	this?	– Yes, I	**can** .
Are	we		late?	– No, you	**aren't** .
Have	they	**got**	new computers?	– Yes, they	**have** .
Do	you	know	the answer?	– Yes, I	**do** .
Do	you	like	burgers?	– No, I	**don't** .
Do	they	go	to Thomas Tallis?	– Yes, they	**do** .

G 28 Verneinung, Fragen u. Kurzantworten in der 3. Person Singular → p. 64,2
Negatives, questions and short answers in the 3rd person singular

> Wie du weißt, musst du in der 3. Person Singular in der einfachen Gegenwart immer ein **-s** oder **-es** an das Verb anhängen: **he, she, it** – das **s** muss mit! Das gilt natürlich auch für Fragen, Kurzantworten und die Verneinung. Aber hier gehört das **-s** zum Hilfsverb: du benutzt *has* statt *have* oder **does** [dʌz] statt *do*. Die verneinte Form heißt **doesn't** [ˈdʌznt].

Is	he		here?	– No, he **isn't**.
Has	she	**got**	a new computer?	– Yes, she **has**.
Does	Mr Jackson	**know**	the Cutty Sark?	– Yes, he **does**.
Does	she	**like**	burgers?	– No, she **doesn't**.

Das *simple present* im Überblick

Aussage	Verneinung	
I like chocolate.	I don't like burgers.	
You know everything!	You don't know my name.	
He pla**ys** the drums.	He do**es**n't play the guitar.	
She liv**es** in Greenwich.	She do**es**n't live in a house.	
It go**es** round Greenwich.	It do**es**n't go through the park.	
We visit friends.	We don't visit museums.	
You go by DLR.	You don't go by bus.	
They go to school.	They don't go to the park.	
Frage	**Kurzantworten**	
Do I know Terry?	– Yes, you do.	– No, you don't.
Do you drive a taxi?	– Yes, I do.	– No, I don't.
Do**es** Terry play in a shed?	– Yes, he do**es**.	– No, he do**es**n't.
Do**es** she live in a flat?	– Yes, she do**es**.	– No, she do**es**n't.
Do**es** this bus go to the sights?	– Yes, it do**es**.	– No, it do**es**n't.
Do we visit old ships?	– Yes, you do.	– No, you don't.
Do you like cheese?	– Yes, we do.	– No, we don't.
Do they go to Thomas Tallis?	– Yes, they do.	– No, they don't.

G 29 Fragen mit Fragewörtern
Questions with question words

→ p. 66,1

Wenn du nach einer bestimmten Person oder Sache fragen möchtest, setzt du ein **Fragewort** ganz an den Anfang der Frage. Erst danach kommt *do/does*, ein Hilfsverb wie *can* oder *have/has* oder eine Form von *to be*.

Who? Where? What? When? Why? and How?
You can ask these questions now!

Who	are	you?	*Wer bist du?*
What	can	you do in the park?	*Was kannst du im Park machen?*
Where	does	the DLR go?	*Wohin fährt die DLR?*
Where	do	you live?	*Wo wohnt ihr?*
When	does	school start?	*Wann fängt die Schule an?*
Why	have	we got German now?	*Warum haben wir jetzt Deutsch?*
How	do	they get to Church Street?	*Wie kommen sie zur Church Street?*

 Mit *where* kannst du nach dem Ort („Wo?") oder nach der Richtung („Wohin?") fragen.

 Who? und *Where?* solltest du nicht verwechseln! *Who?* fragt nach einer Person, *Where?* fragt nach einem Ort oder einer Richtung (siehe **G 11**).

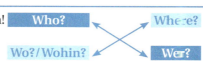

148 one hundred and forty-eight

Unit 5

G 30 Der *of*-Genitiv
The of-genitive

→ p. 74 – 75

> Du kennst bereits den *s*-Genitiv ('s oder s'), mit dem du sagen kannst, dass jemandem etwas gehört. Er wird bei Personen und Tieren verwendet (siehe G 12).
> Um zu sagen, dass etwas zu einer Sache gehört, brauchst du den *of*-Genitiv: *the first page of the book*.

There's a car at the end **of** the street.	It's Terry's dad's taxi.
Friday is the fifth day **of** the week.	It's Sam's birthday.

G 31 *Would like to* und *want to* + Infinitiv
'Would like to' and 'want to' + infinitive

→ p. 74,1

> Wenn du im Englischen einen Wunsch ausdrücken willst, kannst du **would like to** oder **want to** und den **Infinitiv** (die Grundform) eines Verbs verwenden. *I would like to* (ich möchte/ich würde gern) ist viel höflicher als *I want to* (ich will).

> Die Kurzform von *would like to* ist *'d like to*. *Would* ist ein Hilfsverb wie *can*, deshalb verändert sich die Form *would like to* / *'d like to* nie.

I	would like to	visit	Greenwich.
I	'd like to	see	the Cutty Sark.
	Would you like to	go	to Sam's party?
Sam	would like to	have	a party.
He	'd like to	invite	his friends to a pizza place.
He	wouldn't like to	have	a party in the flat.
Sam's grandma	would like to	make	a cake for him.
She	'd like to	make	it with Sam.
We	wouldn't like to	go	to a pizza place.
We	'd like to	have	a pizza now.
	Would you like to	have	a pizza, too?
Terry and Lisa	would like to	have	an invitation to the party.
	Would they like to	go	to the cinema?

> In einer Frage oder einer Verneinung verwendest du die Langform:
> *Would you like to? / I wouldn't like to.*

Want to ist ein Vollverb. Es wird in der einfachen Gegenwart *(simple present)* wie andere Verben gebildet: In der 3. Person Singular musst du ein -s anhängen: (*he – she – it:* das **s** muss mit!). *Want to* hat keine Kurzform.

I	want to	see	the Cutty Sark.		
Sam/He	wants to	invite	his friends to a pizza place.		
Sam's grandma	wants to	make	a very big cake.		
We	want to	watch	DVDs.		
Terry and Lisa	want to	play	computer games.		
Do you	want to	visit	Greenwich?	– Yes, I	do.
Does Grandma	want to	make	a cake?	– Yes, she	does.
Does she	want to	go	to the shops?	– Yes, she	does.
Does Sam	want to	have	a party in the flat?	– No, he	doesn't.
Do they	want to	play	in the park?	– No, they	don't.

 Bei einer Frage oder Verneinung musst du wie bei anderen Verben ***do/don't*** gebrauchen und in der 3. Person Singular entsprechend ***does/doesn't***.

G 32 Das Datum
The date

→ p. 75,3–5

Im Englischen musst du zwischen Schreibung und Aussprache des Datums unterscheiden: Beim Lesen eines Datums fügt man *the* und *of* hinzu.

Man schreibt	Man spricht
21st May	"the twenty-first of May"

 Du kannst das Datum aber auch ganz einfach mit Grundzahlen schreiben: ***22 July*** oder ***July 22***, aber auch dann musst du **"the twenty-second of July"** oder **"July the twenty-second"** sagen.

Merke dir, welche Präpositionen bei welchen Zeitangaben stehen.

Lisa's birthday is **in** July.
My birthday is **on** 20th August.
The party starts **at** 3 o'clock **on** Tuesday.

150 one hundred and fifty

G 33 Die Verlaufsform der Gegenwart
The present progressive

→ p. 76,1; 77,4

Du kennst schon die einfache Form der Gegenwart *(simple present)*. Anders als im Deutschen gibt es im Englischen von allen Zeiten zwei verschiedene Formen, die man zu unterschiedlichen Zwecken verwendet. So gibt es in der Gegenwart neben dem *simple present* noch das **present progressive** (Verlaufsform der Gegenwart).

Die Verlaufsform der Gegenwart *(present progressive)* besteht aus einer
Form von **to be** und einem **Vollverb** + **ing**.
Zum Verneinen fügst du *not* nach der Form von *to be* ein oder verwendest die entsprechende Kurzform *aren't* oder *isn't*.

I	**am** look**ing**	for a CD.
I	**'m** not buy**ing**	a book.
You	**'re** go**ing**	the wrong way!
You	**aren't** eat**ing**	your pizza!
The game	**is** start**ing**.	
Sam	**is** watch**ing**	it.
Emma	**isn't** watch**ing**	TV.
We	**'re** learn**ing**	English.
We	**aren't** mak**ing**	a poster.
You	**are** listen**ing**	to your Discman.
They	**'re** look**ing**	for a present.
They	**aren't** look**ing**	for T-shirts.

Mit dem *present progressive* kannst du ausdrücken, dass jemand gerade dabei ist, etwas zu tun oder etwas gerade tut und noch nicht damit fertig ist:
Terry is eating a sandwich.

 Im Deutschen gibt es die Verlaufsform nicht! Wenn du diese Form im Deutschen wiedergeben möchtest, kannst du Ausdrücke wie **gerade, im Augenblick, im Moment** oder **jetzt** verwenden:
We're buying a T-shirt. – Wir kaufen gerade ein T-Shirt.

 Einige Wörter kommen besonders häufig in Verbindung mit dem *present progressive* vor: **now, right now, just, still**. Diese Wörter können für dich ein **Signal** sein, dass du die Verlaufsform benutzen musst: *I'm just doing my homework.*

G 34 Besonderheiten beim Schreiben der *-ing*-Form
Spelling the -ing form

→ p. 77,3

Steht ein kurzer Vokal (a, e, i, o, u) vor einem Konsonanten (z.B. m, p, t) am Ende des Verbs, verdoppelt sich der Konsonant: *swim* → *swimming*
win + n   He is winning the game.   put + t   She is putting the things in her bag.

Ein Verb mit einem stummen *e* am Ende verliert das *e* vor der *-ing*-Endung.
danc~~e~~   She's danc**ing** on TV.   writ~~e~~   He's writ**ing** a note.

Kurzer Mitlaut wird **verdoppelt**, stummes *-e* wird **abgekoppelt**!

G 35 Die Verlaufsform der Gegenwart: Fragen und Kurzantworten
The present progressive: questions and short answers

→ p. 77,5

Bei Fragen in der Verlaufsform steht die Langform von *to be* am Anfang des Satzes.
Bei Kurzantworten mit *Yes* verwendet man die Langform von *to be* (ohne Verb + *-ing*).
Bei Kurzantworten mit *No* gebrauchst du meistens die Kurzform: *I'm not, he/she/it isn't, we/you/they aren't.*

Are	you	listening	to your discman?	– Yes, I	**am.**
Is	Emma	buying	a computer?	– No, she	**isn't.**
Is	your mobile	working?		– Yes, it	**is.**
Are	we	going	to the shops?	– No, we	**aren't**
Are	you	looking for	a CD?	– Yes, we	**are.**
Are	they	shopping	in town?	– No, they	**aren't.**

Genau wie bei anderen Fragen mit Fragewort (siehe **G29**) kommt zuerst das Fragewort und dann das Hilfsverb. Das Hilfsverb der Verlaufsform ist eine Form von *to be*.

Who	am	I talking to?	
What	are	you listening to	on your discman?
Where	is	Emma shopping?	
When	is	the big game starting?	
How	are	we going to	the shops?
Who	are	you looking for?	
Where	are	they buying	Sam's present?

G 36 Mengenangaben mit *of*
Expressions of quantity with 'of'

→ p. 78,1

Can I have	a bar	**of**	chocolate, please?
Can I have	a packet	**of**	crisps, please?
Here's	a bottle	**of**	lemonade.

Im Englischen werden solche Mengenangaben mit dem Wort *of* gebildet. Im Deutschen fehlt das „von".
Beispiel: eine Flasche Limonade.

G 37 Mengenangaben mit *much/many/a lot of/lots of/a little/a few*
Expressions of quantity with 'much', 'many', 'a lot of', 'lots of', 'a little', 'a few'

→ p. 78,2–3

„Wie viel?" und „Wie viele?" werden immer mit **How much?** und **How many?** übersetzt.

How much benutzt du, um nach Sachen zu fragen, die im Singular stehen und **nicht zählbar** sind, z. B. *sugar, flour, homework*.	**How many** benutzt du, um nach Personen oder Sachen zu fragen, die im Plural stehen und **zählbar** sind, z. B. *girls, eggs*.
How much sugar have we got?	**How many** eggs are there in a box?
How much money does he need?	**How many** girls like football?

In **Aussagen** und **Antworten** gibt man eine genaue Menge an *(two bags)* oder man verwendet vage Ausdrücke wie *a lot of/ lots of/a little*.	In **Aussagen** und **Antworten** gibt man die Anzahl an oder verwendet als vage Angabe einen Ausdruck wie *a lot (of)/ lots (of)/a few*.
We've got **two bags of** sugar.	There are **six** eggs in a box.
He needs **lots of** money.	**A lot of** girls like football.
We only need **a little** flour.	Grandma knows **a few** songs.

In **verneinten** Sätzen wird *not much* oder *not a lot of* gebraucht.	In **verneinten** Sätzen wird *not many* oder *not a lot of* gebraucht.
There is **not much** sugar here.	We do **not** need **many** eggs.
He has **not** got **a lot of** money.	There are **not a lot of** boys in our group.

Hello. This is my shop. I haven't got many things in my shop today. There's a little sugar. And there are a few eggs. But there isn't much cheese. That's not good. I haven't got many customers today. Let's close the shop.

Unit 6

G 38 both → p. 86

Das Wort **both** kann mit und ohne Artikel (*the*) benutzt werden. Es gibt dabei keinen Bedeutungsunterschied.	
Both girls like chocolate.	*Beide Mädchen mögen Schokolade.*
Both the girls like chocolate.	*Beide Mädchen mögen Schokolade.*

 Wenn du *both* mit *the* verwenden möchtest, musst du die Wortfolge beachten! Es heißt im Englischen immer **both the** auch wenn man im Deutschen „die beiden" sagt.

Wenn *both* und *and* zusammen gebraucht werden, ist die deutsche Entsprechung „sowohl … als auch".	
The park is open in **both** spring **and** summer.	*Der Park ist sowohl im Frühjahr als auch im Sommer geöffnet.*

G 39 Der Plural der Substantive (unregelmäßiger Plural) → p. 87,2
The plural of nouns (irregular plural)

Wie du weißt, wird der Plural der meisten englischen Substantive (*nouns*) gebildet, indem man ein **-s** (oder manchmal **-es**) an die Singularform hängt: *one word – five words; one sandwich – two sandwiches.*
Bei einigen der Pluralformen, die auf **s** enden, gibt es bei Schreibung und Aussprache Besonderheiten:

baby country family story	bab**ies** countr**ies** famil**ies** stor**ies**	Wenn ein Substantiv auf einem **Konsonanten + y** endet (z. B. *baby*), so ist die Pluralendung **-ies**. (Steht vor dem *y* jedoch ein Vokal, bleibt das *y*: *boy – boys, day – days*.)
life [-f]	lives [-vz]	Substantive, die auf **-f(e)** enden, haben meist die Pluralendung **-ves**.

154 one hundred and fifty-four

Unit 6 | Grammar | **G**

Es gibt eine kleine Anzahl von unregelmäßigen Pluralformen, die du einzeln lernen musst.
Du findest diese Pluralformen in der *Vocabulary*-Liste immer hinter der Singularform:

foot – feet goose – geese mouse – mice	Bei diesen Wörtern ändert sich der Vokal. One mouse – two mice – three mice …
child – children [tʃaɪld] [ˈtʃɪldrən]	Das Wort *child* bekommt die Endung *-ren* und die Aussprache der ersten Silbe ändert sich.
sheep – sheep	Bei *sheep* und einigen anderen Wörtern, denen du noch begegnen wirst, ändert sich die Pluralform **nicht** und es wird auch kein *-s* angehängt!
person – **people**	Wenn eine Gruppe von Menschen gemeint ist (deutsch: **Leute**), benutzt man das Wort **people**. Eine einzelne Person ist *a person*.

 Weißt du noch, wie man den *s*-Genitiv im Singular und Plural bildet (**G12**)?
Bei den unregelmäßigen Pluralformen, die nicht auf *-s* enden, hängt man nur *'s* an:
the children's room, the geese's food.

G 40 Die einfache Form der Gegenwart und die Verlaufsform → p. 91,2
The simple present forms and present progressive

Look, Tom *is playing* football.   Tom *plays* football.

Wie du schon weißt, gibt es im Englischen zwei Formen der Gegenwart, das *present progressive* und das *simple present*. Diese beiden Formen darfst du nicht verwechseln.

present progressive	simple present
Oh, Terry **is** eating before dinner.	He **sometimes** eats sweets after lunch.
The children **are** having dinner at the hostel **this evening**.	They **always** have a dessert there.
Look, the farmer **is** milking the cows **now**.	He **always** milks them every morning and evening.

one hundred and fifty-five **155**

G | Grammar | Unit 6

Mit dem *present progressive* drückst du aus, dass etwas gerade geschieht und noch nicht zu Ende ist. Sehr oft stehen in Sätzen mit dem *present progressive* **Signalwörter** wie *now*, *just* oder *look*. Häufig wird es auch mit *this morning*, *this afternoon*, *this evening* und *today* verwendet.

Mit dem *simple present* drückst du aus, dass etwas regelmäßig, oft, manchmal oder nie passiert. **Signalwörter sind *usually*, *often*, *always*, *sometimes*, *never*, *every day*, *every year*** usw. *Simple present* verwendest du auch, um auszudrücken, dass etwas eine Tatsache ist. (Tom plays football.)

 Hilfsverben wie *can*, *want* und *has/have* in 'have got' haben keine Verlaufsform *(progressive form)*. *To be* und bestimmte Verben, die Gefühle ausdrücken, wie *to like* oder *want*, werden meist im *simple present* verwendet, sehr selten im *present progressive*.

Merk dir einfach: USA ONE! Das sind die Anfangsbuchstaben von *usually*, *sometimes*, *always*, *often*, *never* und *every*.

G 41 *must – needn't* → p. 92,2

Das Verb **must** ist ein Hilfsverb wie *can*. *Must* bleibt in allen Personen gleich (bei *he*, *she* und *it* bekommt *must* kein *-s*) und steht immer mit der Grundform eines anderen Verbs (ohne *to*). Wie bei *can* gibt es auch von *must* kein *present progressive*.

I	must find	my new sweatshirt.
You	must take	your wellies.
Sam	must wear	his sunglasses.
Emma	must have	scones for tea.
That house	must be	the hostel.
We	must go	– the bus is waiting!
You	must be	back at five o'clock.
The girls	must put	their bags in the orange room.

I must do my homework every day.

Um auszudrücken, dass man etwas nicht machen muss oder nicht zu machen braucht, verwendest du **needn't** (Langform: *need not*).

You	needn't take	your wellies.
Sam	needn't wear	his sunglasses.
We	needn't bring	food!
They	needn't milk	the cows.

156 one hundred and fifty-six

Unit 7

G 42 Die Verknüpfung von Sätzen: *and, or, but, so* → p. 101,3–4
Linking sentences

Tom eats lunch at one o'clock, **but** he doesn't eat at two o'clock.

Mit *and, or, but* und *so* kannst du Sätze oder Satzteile miteinander verbinden.

Year 7 is running a race	**and**	Emma is winning!
You can run a race	**or**	play cricket.
The disco is great,	**but**	you can't invite your family.
Emma is running a race,	**so**	she can't eat an ice-cream now.

I like chocolate, but I love cake.

In den Sätzen, die du miteinander verbindest, verändert sich die Wortstellung (Subjekt – Verb – Objekt) nicht:

Subject	Verb	Object
Emma	*is running*	*a race.*
She	*can't eat*	*an ice-cream.*

Emma is running a race, so she can't eat an ice-cream.
Emma läuft gerade ein Rennen, deshalb kann sie kein Eis essen.

G 43 Die Satzstellung in Aussagesätzen
Word order in statements

→ p. 103, 3–4

Die Satzstellung S – V – O in englischen Aussagesätzen kennst du schon. Wenn du aber in einem Satz gleichzeitig Ortsangaben (z. B. *in the park*) und Zeitangaben (z. B. *after school*) machen möchtest, gilt folgende Regel: **Ort vor Zeit**.

Place before time – that is fine!

Zeit	Subjekt – Verb – Objekt	Ort	Zeit
	You can buy a T-shirt	at the Summer Fair	in June.
In June	you can buy a T-shirt	at the Summer Fair.	
	Lisa plays football	in the park	after school.
After school	Lisa plays football	in the park.	

Orts- und Zeitangaben stehen normalerweise am Ende des Satzes. Dabei gilt immer die Regel: **Ort** vor **Zeit**.
Wenn du aber die Zeitangabe stärker betonen möchtest, kannst du sie auch an den Satzanfang stellen.

Merke:
Ort vor Zeit – das ist gescheit.

Zeit- oder Ortsangaben dürfen **nicht** zwischen Verb und Objekt stehen!

Grammar words

Deutsch	Englisch	Englisches Beispiel	in:
Adverbien der Häufigkeit	adverbs of frequency	always, sometimes, never	G 22
Artikel: *a/an* *the*	article: *a/an* *the* [ðə]/[ði]	a bag, an apple the bag, the apple	G 6 G 7
Fragen mit Fragewörtern	questions with question words	Who …?, What …?, Where …? How …? Why …?	G 11, G 29
Gegenwart: einfache Form, 3. Person Singular, Verlaufsform	simple present 3rd person singular present progressive	We play football. He plays football. Sam is watching the game.	G 21, G 26 – 27, G 40 G 23, G 28 G 33 – 35, G 40
Genitiv: *'s/s', of*	genitive	a girl's house; end of the day	G 12, G 30
Hilfsverben	auxiliaries	can, do, would, must	G 18 – 19, G 27 – 28 G 31, G 41
Imperativ / Befehlsform	imperative	Open the door., Don't write.	G 17
Kurzantworten	short answers	Yes, I am; No, he can't; Yes, he does.	G 5, G 16, G 19, G 27 – 28, G 35
Kurz-/Langformen	short / long forms	I'm; he isn't; they've got; I am; they have; we cannot	G 2 – 4, G 14, G 18, G 31
Mengenangaben	expressions of quantity	a packet of crisps; How much sugar?	G 36 – 37
Negativformen, Verneinung	negatives	isn't; hasn't got; Don't go!; don't like; can't find; doesn't	G 4, G 14, G 17, G 26, G 28, G 33
Personalpronomen (persönl. Fürwörter)	personal pronouns	I, you, he, she, … me, you, him, her, …	G 1 G 25
Plural/Mehrzahl unregelmäßige Formen	plural irregular forms	book – books babies, feet, children	G 8 G 39
Possessivbegleiter	possessive determiners	my, your, his, her, …	G 13
Präpositionen	prepositions	in, on, under, at	G 10, G 32
Satzstellung	word order	I always go swimming on Saturdays.	G 15, G 22, G 43
Singular / Einzahl 3. Person Singular	singular 3rd person singular	a book She walks.	G 8, G 23, G 28
Verben	verbs	to be; have got; to play	G 2, G 14, G 31

one hundred and fifty-nine **159**

Vocabulary

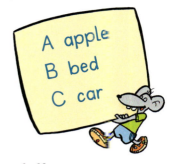

Auf den folgenden Seiten findest du alle neuen englischen Wörter und Ausdrücke. Sie stehen in der Reihenfolge, wie sie im Buch vorkommen. Die Wortliste ist in drei Spalten aufgeteilt:
- Links stehen die englischen Wörter und Sätze.
- In der Mitte werden sie übersetzt.
- Rechts findest du Beispiele, Erklärungen und Tipps, die dir beim Lernen helfen.

Die fett gedruckten Wörter musst du lernen, die normal gedruckten Wörter nicht.
Gleich nach jedem neuen englischen Wort steht die Lautschrift in eckigen Klammern. Sie zeigt dir, wie das neue Wort ausgesprochen wird. Wie du diese Lautzeichen liest, siehst du unten.

Englische Laute

Mitlaute

[b]	**b**ed	[p]	**p**icture
[d]	**d**ay	[r]	**r**ed
[ð]	**th**e	[s]	**s**ix
[f]	**f**amily	[ʃ]	**sh**e
[g]	**g**o	[t]	**t**en
[ŋ]	morni**ng**	[tʃ]	**l**unch
[h]	**h**ouse	[v]	**v**ideo
[j]	**y**ou	[w]	**w**e, **o**ne
[k]	**c**an, mil**k**	[z]	ea**s**y
[l]	**l**etter	[ʒ]	revi**s**ion
[m]	**m**an	[dʒ]	**p**age
[n]	**n**o	[θ]	**th**ank you

Selbstlaute

[ɑː]	c**ar**
[æ]	**a**pple
[e]	p**e**n
[ə]	ag**ai**n
[ɜː]	g**ir**l
[ʌ]	b**u**t
[ɪ]	**i**t
[i]	happ**y**
[iː]	t**ea**cher
[ɒ]	d**o**g
[ɔː]	b**a**ll
[ʊ]	b**oo**k
[u]	Jan**u**ary
[uː]	t**oo**, tw**o**

Doppellaute

[aɪ]	**I**, m**y**
[aʊ]	n**ow**, m**ou**se
[eɪ]	n**a**me, th**ey**
[eə]	th**ere**, p**air**
[ɪə]	h**ere**, id**ea**
[əʊ]	h**ello**
[ɔɪ]	b**oy**
[ʊə]	s**ure**

[ː] der vorangehende Laut ist lang, z. B. *you* [juː]   ['] die folgende Silbe wird betont, z. B. *hello* [heˈləʊ]

Tipps zum Vokabellernen findest du in den Kästen zu Beginn jeder **Unit** sowie auf den **Wordwise**-Seiten.

Am Ende der **Units** kannst du nützliche Ausdrücke für deinen *folder* sammeln, mit denen du dich auf Englisch verständigen kannst.

Außerdem gibt es *word games*. Dies sind kleine Aufgaben, Rätsel und Wortspiele, in denen du die neuen Wörter üben kannst.

Auf den *Vocabulary*-Teil folgt das *Dictionary*, eine alphabetische Wortliste aller englischen Wörter aus dem Buch. Wenn du ein Wort nicht weißt, kannst du es hier nachschlagen.

Abkürzungen und Zeichen

pl	Plural, Mehrzahl	↔	ist das Gegenteil von
p. 12	Auf dieser Seite kommen die Wörter vor.	→	ist verwandt mit
		=	entspricht

Vocabulary V

Unit 1

Unit 1 Thomas Tallis School

VOCABULARY SKILLS

Lies dir das englische Wort, die deutsche Übersetzung und das, was in der rechten Spalte dazu steht, genau durch. Danach deckst du die mittlere und die rechte Spalte ab. Weißt du noch, was das englische Wort auf deutsch heißt?

Du kannst natürlich auch die linke Spalte abdecken und überprüfen, ob du das englische Wort noch weißt.
Auch das Aufschreiben und das laute Vorsagen der englischen Wörter helfen dir beim Lernen.

Check-in

p. 12	**Hi!** [haɪ]	Hi!, Hallo! →	
	I'm (= I am) [aɪm = aɪ ɘm]	ich bin	
	I [aɪ]	ich →	*I* schreibst du immer groß.
	am [əm]	bin	
	eleven [ɪˈlevn]	elf	
	from [frɒm]	aus, von →	Wenn man *from* nicht betont, spricht man es [frəm].
	in [ɪn]	in; hinein, herein	Vor a, e, i, o, u wird *a* zu *an*.
	a [ə], **an** [ən]	ein/-e →	*Pupil* heißt „Schülerin" oder „Schüler".
	pupil [ˈpjuːpl]	Schüler/-in →	Lisa is a pupil *at* Thomas Tallis School.
	at [æt; ət]	an; auf; in; bei; um →	
	hello [helˈəʊ]	hallo	
	My name is … [maɪ ˈneɪm ɪz]	Mein Name ist … ; Ich heiße …	
	my [maɪ]	mein/-e	
	name [neɪm]	Name →	Merk dir bei *name:* Hauptwörter schreibst du immer klein.
	is [ɪz]	ist	
	twelve [twelv]	zwölf	
	too [tuː]	auch →	Satzstellung: I'm from Greenwich, *too*.
	new [njuː]	neu →	
	school [skuːl]	Schule	
	year [jɪə]	Klasse; Jahr	
	seven [ˈsevn]	sieben	
	mouse [maʊs] pl. **mice** [maɪs]	Maus →	
	one [wʌn]	eins; ein/-e	
	and [ænd; ən]	und →	Lisa *and* Terry are new at TTS.
	you [juː]	du, ihr, Sie →	*You* kann im Englischen du/ihr/Sie heißen!
	ten [ten]	zehn	
	five [faɪv]	fünf	
p. 13	**What's your name?** [ˌwɒts jə ˈneɪm]	Wie heißt du/heißen Sie? →	*'s* ist die Abkürzung von *is*.
	what [wɒt]	was	
	your [jɔː]	dein/-e, euer/eure, Ihr/-e	

one hundred and sixty-one **161**

V Vocabulary

Unit 1

p. 13 How old are you? — Wie alt bist du/sind Sie?
[haʊ ˈəʊld ə juː]
how [haʊ] — wie
old [əʊld] — alt →
are [ɑː] — bist, sind, seid →

Where are you from? — Woher kommst du/kommt ihr/kommen Sie? →
[ˌweər ə jə ˈfrɒm]
where [weə] — wo
listening [ˈlɪsnɪŋ] — Hören; *hier:* Hörübung
phone number — Telefonnummer
[ˈfəʊn ˌnʌmbə]
phone (= telephone) — Telefon →
[fəʊn = ˈtelɪfəʊn]
number [ˈnʌmbə] — Zahl, Nummer
to listen [ˈlɪsn] — zuhören; (an)hören →
to write [raɪt] — schreiben →
home [həʊm] — zu Hause; Zuhause; Heim
mobile [ˈməʊbaɪl] — Handy →
German [ˈdʒɜːmən] — Deutsch, deutsch; Deutsche/-r →
or [ɔː] — oder
Your turn. [ˈjɔː tɜːn] — Du bist an der Reihe., Du bist dran.

poster [ˈpəʊstə] — Poster

old ↔ new
Wenn man *are* nicht betont, spricht man es [ə].

Where are you from?   I'm from Greenwich.

Phone ist die Kurzform von *telephone*.

Achtung Aussprache! Das „t" ist stumm.
Das *to* vor dem Verb brauchst du nicht zu lernen.
Handy heißt auf Englisch *mobile*.
Nationalitäten schreibst du immer groß.

Numbers 0–12   C

0	oh [əʊ], zero [ˈzɪərəʊ]				
1	one [wʌn]	5	five [faɪv]	9	nine [naɪn]
2	two [tuː]	6	six [sɪks]	10	ten [ten]
3	three [θriː]	7	seven [ˈsevn]	11	eleven [ɪˈlevn]
4	four [fɔː]	8	eight [eɪt]	12	twelve [twelv]

Language 1

p. 14 friend [frend] — Freund/-in →

but [bʌt] — aber →

big [bɪg] — groß →
here [hɪə] — hier
he [hiː] — er
this [ðɪs] — das; dies; diese/-r/-s

Merk dir bei *friend*: im Englischen gibt es oft nur ein Wort für weibliche und männliche Wortformen.

Wenn man *but* nicht betont, spricht man es [bət].

BIG

162   one hundred and sixty-two

Vocabulary

Unit 1

p. 14
she [ʃiː]	sie →	she ↔ he
that [ðæt]	das	
Mrs [ˈmɪsɪz]	Frau	
tutor [ˈtjuːtə]	Klassenlehrer/-in	
teacher [ˈtiːtʃə]	Lehrer/-in →	Merk dir bei *teacher*: im Englischen gibt es oft nur ein Wort für weibliche und männliche Wortformen.
Hey! [heɪ]	He!	
so [səʊ]	also; so	
tutor group [ˈtjuːtə ˌgruːp]	Klasse (*in einer englischen Schule*)	
cool [kuːl]	cool; klasse →	
football [ˈfʊtbɔːl]	Fußball	
favourite [ˈfeɪvrɪt]	Lieblings- →	Mrs Carter is my *favourite* teacher.
sport [spɔːt]	Sport	
Oh! [əʊ]	Oh!	
no [nəʊ]	nein; kein/-e	
shoe [ʃuː]	Schuh →	Achtung Schreibung!
OK [əʊˈkeɪ]	o.k., okay	
er [ɜː]	äh	
thank you [ˈθæŋk juː]	danke (schön)	
Mr [ˈmɪstə]	Herr	
the [ðə]	der, die (*auch Plural*), das →	Vor a, e, i, o, u sprichst du *the* so: [ði]. Mr Newman
caretaker [ˈkeəˌteɪkə]	Hausmeister/-in →	I'm the *caretaker* at TTS.

p. 15
example [ɪgˈzɑːmpl]	Beispiel	
Go on, please. [gəʊ ˈɒn ˌpliːz]	Mach bitte weiter.	
please [pliːz]	bitte	

Language 2

p. 16
we [wiː]	wir	
right [raɪt]	richtig; rechts; rechte/-r/-s	
classroom [ˈklɑːsruːm]	Klassenzimmer	
yes [jes]	ja →	yes ↔ no
isn't (= is not) [ˈɪznt = ɪz ˈnɒt]	ist nicht	
not [nɒt]	nicht; kein/-e	
who [huː]	wer; wem, wen →	*Who*'s Sam? – He's my friend.
nice [naɪs]	nett; schön →	Mrs Carter is *nice*.
always [ˈɔːlweɪz]	immer	
late [leɪt]	zu spät, spät	
good morning [gʊd ˈmɔːnɪŋ]	guten Morgen	
girl [gɜːl]	Mädchen	
boy [bɔɪ]	Junge →	a *girl* and a *boy*
Sorry! [ˈsɒri]	Entschuldigung!, Verzeihung!	
bag [bæg]	Tasche; Tüte	

V | Vocabulary

Unit 1

p. 16	it [ɪt]	es
	mum [mʌm]	Mutti, Mama
	with [wɪð]	mit; bei
	wrong [rɒŋ]	falsch →
	they [ðeɪ]	sie (Plural)
	grammar ['græmə]	Grammatik
	verb [vɜ:b]	Verb
	to be [bi:]	sein
	short form ['ʃɔ:t fɔ:m]	Kurzform →
	short [ʃɔ:t]	kurz
	form [fɔ:m]	Form
	long form ['lɒŋ fɔ:m]	Langform
	long [lɒŋ]	lang →
	sentence ['sentəns]	Satz →
p. 17	her [hɜ:]	ihr/-e; sie; ihr
	diary ['daɪəri]	Tagebuch
	to put in [pʊt 'ɪn]	einsetzen
	very ['veri]	sehr
	to finish ['fɪnɪʃ]	beenden, fertig machen
	to make [meɪk]	bilden; machen, tun
	question ['kwestʃən]	Frage →
	answer ['ɑ:nsə]	Antwort
	about [ə'baʊt]	über; wegen
	to ask [ɑ:sk]	fragen; hier: (eine Frage) stellen
	partner ['pɑ:tnə]	Partner/-in

right ↔ *wrong*

'They're' is the *short form* of 'they are'.

long ↔ short
This is a *sentence*.

Language 3

p. 18	school bag ['sku:l bæg]	Schultasche, Schulranzen →
	to copy ['kɒpi]	abmalen; abschreiben; kopieren
	grid [grɪd]	Tabelle, Gitter
	exercise book ['eksəsaɪz ˌbʊk]	Heft →
	exercise ['eksəsaɪz]	Übung
	book [bʊk]	Buch →
	to fill in [fɪl 'ɪn]	ausfüllen
	pencil case ['pensl ˌkeɪs]	Federmäppchen
	pen [pen]	Füller
	pencil ['pensl]	Bleistift →
	rubber ['rʌbə]	Radiergummi
	ruler ['ru:lə]	Lineal
	sandwich ['sænwɪdʒ]	belegtes Brot, Sandwich
	apple ['æpl]	Apfel
	picture ['pɪktʃə]	Bild →
	English ['ɪŋglɪʃ]	englisch, Englisch; Engländer/-in →

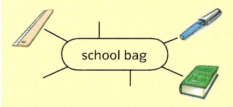

Achtung Schreibung!

pencil → pencil case

I'm English. = „Ich bin Engländer." oder „Ich bin Engländerin."

Vocabulary

Unit 1

p. 18   sound [saʊnd]   Laut; Ton; Geräusch
       word [wɜ:d]   Wort →
       list [lɪst]   Liste
       to say [seɪ]   sagen

'Game' is a *word* with four letters.

Numbers 13–100 A B C

13	thirteen [ˌθɜː'tiːn]	20	twenty ['twenti]	40	forty ['fɔːti]
14	fourteen [ˌfɔː'tiːn]	21	twenty-one [ˌtwenti'wʌn]	50	fifty ['fɪfti]
15	fifteen [ˌfɪf'tiːn]	22	twenty-two [ˌtwenti'tuː]	60	sixty ['sɪksti]
16	sixteen [ˌsɪks'tiːn]	23	twenty-three [ˌtwenti'θriː]	70	seventy ['sevnti]
17	seventeen [ˌsevn'tiːn]	24	twenty-four [ˌtwenti'fɔː]	80	eighty ['eɪti]
18	eighteen [ˌeɪ'tiːn]	…		90	ninety ['naɪnti]
19	nineteen [ˌnaɪn'tiːn]	30	thirty ['θɜːti]	100	one hundred [wʌn 'hʌndrəd]

       to play [pleɪ]   spielen
       order ['ɔːdə]   Reihenfolge
       for [fɔː]   für →
p. 19   song [sɒŋ]   Lied
       alphabet ['ælfəbet]   Alphabet →
       rap [ræp]   Rap
       to clap [klæp]   klatschen
       lesson ['lesn]   Unterrichtsstunde →
       to shout [ʃaʊt]   schreien, rufen
       to do [duː]   machen, tun
       game [geɪm]   Spiel
       to read [riːd]   lesen →
       to spell [spel]   buchstabieren →
       puzzle ['pʌzl]   Rätsel
       letter ['letə]   Buchstabe; Brief →
       tip [tɪp]   Tipp

Gleiche Aussprache: *for* - *four*

the *alphabet*

English *lessons* are OK.

to read
Spell 'Tom'. – T-O-M.
L-E-T-T-E-R-S and a *letter*

The alphabet A B C

a [eɪ]	e [iː]	i [aɪ]	m [em]	q [kjuː]	u [juː]	y [waɪ]
b [biː]	f [ef]	j [dʒeɪ]	n [en]	r [ɑː]	v [viː]	z [zed]
c [siː]	g [dʒiː]	k [keɪ]	o [əʊ]	s [es]	w ['dʌbljuː]	
d [diː]	h [eɪtʃ]	l [el]	p [piː]	t [tiː]	x [eks]	

Language 4

p. 20   window ['wɪndəʊ]   Fenster
       chair [tʃeə]   Stuhl
       board [bɔːd]   Tafel; Brett
       door [dɔː]   Tür

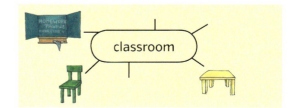

V Vocabulary

Unit 1

p. 20
wall [wɔːl]	Wand; Mauer	
table [ˈteɪbl]	Tisch	
cupboard [ˈkʌbəd]	Schrank →	
desk [desk]	Lehrerpult; Schreibtisch (zu Hause)	Achtung Schreibung!
there's (= there is) [ðeəz = ðeərˌɪz]	es gibt, da ist	
there [ðeə]	da, dort →	here ↔ there
on [ɒn]	auf; am →	Tom is *on* the table.
there are [ðeərˌɑː]	es sind, da sind, es gibt	
crisp [krɪsp]	Kartoffelchip	
behind [bɪˈhaɪnd]	hinter →	Tom is *behind* the book.
chocolate [ˈtʃɒklət]	Schokolade →	Achtung Schreibung!
Wow! [waʊ]	Oh, super!	
party [ˈpɑːti]	Party, Feier	
let's ... [lets]	lass(t) uns ...	
to phone [fəʊn]	anrufen →	to *phone* → a phone
to point [pɔɪnt]	zeigen	
under [ˈʌndə]	unter →	on ↔ under

p. 21
talk [tɔːk]	Unterhaltung, Gespräch	
to match [mætʃ]	zuordnen	
page [peɪdʒ]	Seite →	We're on *page* 19, exercise 6.
homework [ˈhəʊmwɜːk]	Hausaufgabe(n) →	*Homework* hat keine Mehrzahl.
to turn to ... [ˈtɜːn ˌtə]	... aufschlagen	
You're welcome. [jɔːˈwelkəm]	Bitte (schön). →	Thank you. You're welcome.
to practise [ˈpræktɪs]	üben	
phrase [freɪz]	Ausdruck, Redewendung	

Story

p. 22
problem [ˈprɒbləm]	Problem	
cafeteria [ˌkæfəˈtɪəriə]	Cafeteria →	Achtung Aussprache!
joke [dʒəʊk]	Witz	
easy [ˈiːzi]	einfach, leicht	
boring [ˈbɔːrɪŋ]	langweilig	
goodbye [ɡʊdˈbaɪ]	tschüss, auf Wiedersehen; auf Wiederhören →	hello ↔ goodbye
playground [ˈpleɪɡraʊnd]	Schulhof; Spielplatz	
now [naʊ]	jetzt, nun	
Here you are! [ˈhɪə jʊˌɑː]	Bitte schön! →	Where is your homework? – *Here you are!*
to be good at ... [biː ˈɡʊdˌət]	... gut können; gut sein in ...	
Oops! [uːps]	Hoppla!	
ball [bɔːl]	Ball	
tree [triː]	Baum →	

166 one hundred and sixty-six

Vocabulary V

Unit 1

p. 23 **idiot** ['ɪdiət] — Idiot/-in, Dummkopf
to **talk** [tɔːk] — sprechen, reden
to **put** [pʊt] — legen, setzen, stellen, tun
to **sort** [sɔːt] — sortieren
to **look at** ['lʊk æt] — ansehen, anschauen
then [ðen] — dann
to **act** [ækt] — spielen

Wordwise

p. 24 **mind map** ['maɪnd mæp] — Wörternetz (*eine Art Schaubild*) →
vocabulary [vəˈkæbjəlri] — Wortschatz, Vokabular
skill [skɪl] — Fertigkeit, Fähigkeit
folder ['fəʊldə] — Mappe, Hefter, Ordner →
pair [peə] — Paar
to **find** [faɪnd] — finden
adjective ['ædʒɪktɪv] — Adjektiv, Eigenschaftswort

There are *mind maps* for school, classroom and school bag on page 22.

Check-out

p. 25 **to** [tʊ] — an; zu; nach →

of [ɒv] — von →

Love, … [lʌv] — Herzliche Grüße, …, Liebe Grüße, …

different ['dɪfrnt] — anders; andere/-r/-s
can [kæn] — können

Wenn man *to* nicht betont, spricht man es [tə].
Wenn man *of* nicht betont, spricht man es [əv].

For my folder
Hello

Schreibe alle Ausdrücke (*phrases*), die du zum Thema Begrüßung gelernt hast, auf ein Blatt Papier. Lege es in deinen *English folder*. Lass dahinter Platz für weitere *phrases*, damit du deine Sammlung im Laufe des Schuljahres ergänzen kannst.
Rechts siehst du, wie du beginnen könntest. Füge noch mehr Ausdrücke hinzu.

Begrüßung
Hi!
My name is …
…

one hundred and sixty-seven **167**

V Vocabulary

Link-up A

> **Word game**
> Manchmal hörst oder liest du ein englisches Wort, das sich so ähnlich anhört oder schreibt wie ein deutsches Wort. Manche kennst du schon, z. B. *computer*, *skateboard*, *T-shirt*. Diese Wörter haben die gleiche Bedeutung im Englischen und im Deutschen. Schau dir diese neuen englischen Wörter an und ordne sie den deutschen Wörtern zu.

hand	Kostüm
finger	Lampe
paper	Eis
costume	Hand
glass	Papier
hair	Glas
ice	Finger
lamp	Haar

Link-up A Home sweet home

p. 26 **sweet** [swiːt]   süß; niedlich
bedroom [ˈbedrʊm]   Schlafzimmer →
dining room [ˈdaɪnɪŋ rʊm] Esszimmer
bathroom [ˈbɑːθrʊm] Badezimmer →
kitchen [ˈkɪtʃɪn]   Küche
living room [ˈlɪvɪŋ rʊm] Wohnzimmer →
purple [ˈpɜːpl]   lila
grey [ɡreɪ]   grau
green [ɡriːn]   grün
black [blæk]   schwarz
white [waɪt]   weiß
pink [pɪŋk]   rosa, pink
red [red]   rot
blue [bluː]   blau
orange [ˈɒrɪndʒ]   orange(farben)
brown [braʊn]   braun
yellow [ˈjeləʊ]   gelb
room [ruːm]   Zimmer, Raum; Platz →
card [kɑːd]   Karte; Spielkarte →
to **look at** [ˈlʊk æt]   ansehen, anschauen
colour [ˈkʌlə]   Farbe
minute [ˈmɪnɪt]   Minute
then [ðen]   dann
to **close** [kləʊz]   schließen, zumachen
to **answer** [ˈɑːnsə]   beantworten; antworten →

p. 27 **bed** [bed]   Bett
tiny [ˈtaɪni]   winzig
sofa [ˈsəʊfə]   Sofa
funny [ˈfʌni]   lustig; komisch

a *bedroom*

a *bathroom*

Du schreibst *bedroom* und *bathroom* zusammen, *living room* und *dining room* jedoch nicht.

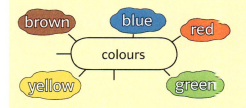

Rooms: bedroom, bathroom, kitchen

 cards

I ask you a question and you *answer* it.

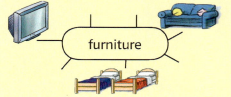

168 one hundred and sixty-eight

Vocabulary V

Link-up A/Unit 2

p. 27	house [haʊs]	Haus →
	TV (= television) [ˌtiː ˈviː = ˈtelɪvɪʒn]	Fernseher; Fernsehen
	computer [kəmˈpjuːtə]	Computer
	furniture [ˈfɜːnɪtʃə]	Möbel →
	dream [driːm]	Traum
	to draw [drɔː]	zeichnen; malen
	to use [juːz]	verwenden; benutzen
	his [hɪz]	sein/-e
	family [ˈfæməli]	Familie →
	brother [ˈbrʌðə]	Bruder
	father [ˈfɑːðə]	Vater
	dad [dæd]	Vati, Papa
	grandfather [ˈɡrænˌfɑːðə]	Großvater →
	grandad [ˈɡrændæd]	Opa →
	sister [ˈsɪstə]	Schwester
	mother [ˈmʌðə]	Mutter
	grandmother [ˈɡrænˌmʌðə]	Großmutter →
	grandma [ˈɡrænmɑː]	Oma
	happy [ˈhæpi]	fröhlich; glücklich →
	more [mɔː]	mehr; weitere
	quiz [kwɪz]	Quiz, Ratespiel

Achtung Schreibung!

Furniture hat keine Mehrzahl.

My father's father is my *grandfather*.

grandad = grandfather

My *grandmother* and grandfather are my mum and dad's mother and father.

Unit 2 Families in Greenwich

VOCABULARY SKILLS

Am besten lernst du die Vokabeln in Ruhe zu Hause. Versuche einen Platz zu finden, an dem du möglichst ungestört arbeiten kannst. Setze dich nach Möglichkeit immer an den gleichen Arbeitsplatz.

Lege dir schon vor dem Lernen alles zurecht, was du dafür brauchst: dein Schreibzeug, deine Hefte und Bücher.

Check-in

p. 28	parents [ˈpeərənts]	Eltern →
	half-sister [ˈhɑːfˌsɪstə]	Halbschwester
	stepfather [ˈstepˌfɑːðə]	Stiefvater
	our [aʊə]	unser/-e
	flat [flæt]	Wohnung
	road [rəʊd]	Straße
	over [ˈəʊvə]	über; vorbei

mum and dad = *parents*

V Vocabulary

Unit 2

p. 28	shop [ʃɒp]	Geschäft, Laden
	its [ɪts]	sein/-e, ihr/-e
	manager [ˈmænɪdʒə]	Geschäftsführer/-in
	small [smɔːl]	klein →
	dog [dɒg]	Hund →
	car [kɑː]	Auto →
p. 29	only child [ˈəʊnli ˌtʃaɪld]	Einzelkind
	only [ˈəʊnli]	einzige/-r/-s; nur; erst; bloß
	child [tʃaɪld] pl. children [ˈtʃɪldrn]	Kind →
	cat [kæt]	Katze →
	interested [ˈɪntrəstɪd]	interessiert
	garden [ˈgɑːdn]	Garten
	drum [drʌm]	Trommel, Plural Schlagzeug →
	shed [ʃed]	Schuppen →
p. 28	text [tekst]	Text
p. 29	to colour [ˈkʌlə]	anmalen, ausmalen; malen
	upstairs [ʌpˈsteəz]	oben (im Gebäude)
	downstairs [ˌdaʊnˈsteəz]	unten (im Gebäude) →
	street [striːt]	Straße

small ↔ big

a *dog*

a *car*

one *child* – two *children*

a *cat*

Can you play the *drums*?

upstairs ↔ downstairs

Language 1

p. 30	family tree [ˌfæməli ˈtriː]	Stammbaum
	married [ˈmærɪd]	verheiratet →
	divorced [dɪˈvɔːst]	geschieden
	uncle [ˈʌŋkl]	Onkel →
	aunt [ɑːnt]	Tante
	cousin [ˈkʌzn]	Cousin/-e →
	son [sʌn]	Sohn
	daughter [ˈdɔːtə]	Tochter
	dinner [ˈdɪnə]	Mittagessen; Abendessen
	next to [ˈnekst tʊ]	neben →
p. 31	European [ˌjʊərəˈpiːən]	europäisch; Europäer/-in
	grandparents [ˈgrænˌpeərnts]	Großeltern
	British [ˈbrɪtɪʃ]	britisch; Brite/Britin →
	Italian [ɪˈtæliən]	italienisch, Italienisch; Italiener/-in →
	because [bɪˈkɒz]	weil, da
	their [ðeə]	ihr/-e →

Als Name schreibst du *uncle* groß, z. B.: *Uncle* David.
My aunt and uncle are my *cousin's* parents.

The blue car is *next to* the grey car.

Nationalitäten schreibst du groß!
Achtung Schreibung!

Gleiche Aussprache: *their* – *they're*

170 one hundred and seventy

Vocabulary

Unit 2

My, your, his, her, our, their A B C

Mit diesen Wörtern kannst du Besitzverhältnisse ausdrücken:

my	mein/meine	**My** brother and **my** parents are in the garden.
your	dein/deine, euer/eure, Ihr/Ihre	**Your** friends are nice. **Your** teacher is OK.
his	sein/seine	**His** drums are in **his** shed.
her	ihr/ihre	**Her** sisters are in **her** grandma's house.
its	sein/seine, ihr/ihre	**Its** rooms are very small. **Its** colour is blue.
our	unser/unsere	**Our** flat is over **our** shop.
their	ihr/ihre	**Their** uncle and **their** cousins are from Greece.

p. 31 **to look** [lʊk] schauen, sehen; aussehen

dead [ded] tot
great [greɪt] großartig; toll
You're lucky. [jɔː ˈlʌki] Du hast Glück.
country [ˈkʌntri] pl. **countries** [ˈkʌntriz] Land →

flag [flæɡ] Flagge, Fahne
Greek [griːk] griechisch, Griechisch; Grieche/Griechin →

Russian [ˈrʌʃn] russisch, Russisch; Russe/Russin →

Turkish [ˈtɜːkɪʃ] türkisch, Türkisch →
French [frentʃ] französisch, Französisch →

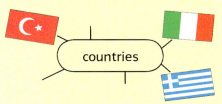

Greek → Greece

Russian → Russia

Turkish → Turkey
French → France

Language 2

p. 32 **trouble** [ˈtrʌbl] Schwierigkeiten
have got/has got [ˈhæv ɡɒt/ˈhæz ɡɒt] haben, besitzen

have/has [hæv/hæz] haben
own [əʊn] eigen →
a lot of [ə ˈlɒt əv] viel/-e, eine Menge
time [taɪm] Zeit; Mal
outside [ˌaʊtˈsaɪd] draußen; nach draußen
hurry [ˈhʌri] Eile
T-shirt [ˈtiːʃɜːt] T-Shirt
wardrobe [ˈwɔːdrəʊb] Kleiderschrank →
magazine [ˌmæɡəˈziːn] Zeitschrift
second [ˈsekənd] Sekunde →
maybe [ˈmeɪbi] vielleicht
dirty [ˈdɜːti] schmutzig, dreckig
mess [mes] Unordnung, Durcheinander →

I have got my *own* bedroom.

There are 60 *seconds* in a minute.

What a *mess!*

one hundred and seventy-one **171**

V Vocabulary

Unit 2

p. 32
later [ˈleɪtə]	später
discman [ˈdɪskmən]	tragbarer CD-Player →
just [dʒʌst]	nur
silly [ˈsɪli]	dumm; albern
well [wel]	na ja, also
to sort out [sɔːt ˈaʊt]	klären, lösen; in Ordnung bringen →

a *discman*

I've got a problem with my sister. We have to *sort* it *out*.

Language 3

p. 34
to clean [kliːn]	aufräumen; putzen, sauber machen →
to call [kɔːl]	anrufen; rufen; nennen
first [fɜːst]	zuerst; als Erste/-r/-s; erste/-r/-s
to take the dog for a walk [teɪk ðə ˈdɒg fɔːr ə ˌwɔːk]	den Hund ausführen →
to take [teɪk]	nehmen; bringen; dauern
walk [wɔːk]	Spaziergang; Wanderung →
rule [ruːl]	Regel
to help [help]	helfen →
to come [kʌm]	kommen
into [ˈɪntə]	in; hinein
call [kɔːl]	Anruf →
polite [pəˈlaɪt]	höflich
the same [seɪm]	derselbe/dieselbe/dasselbe
thing [θɪŋ]	Ding, Sache
music [ˈmjuːzɪk]	Musik →

Clean your room Lisa, it is a mess.

Lisa *takes Barker for a walk*.

Come to the phone. There's a *call* for you Lisa.

Achtung Aussprache!

Language 4

p. 35
which [wɪtʃ]	welche/-r/-s
park [pɑːk]	Park
to open [ˈəʊpn]	öffnen, aufmachen →
up [ʌp]	oben; nach oben
relative [ˈrelətɪv]	Verwandte/-r
me [miː]	mich; mir, *hier:* ich
to think [θɪŋk]	denken
to agree [əˈgriː]	zustimmen
revision [rɪˈvɪʒn]	Wiederholung
place [pleɪs]	Platz, Ort, Stelle →
missing [ˈmɪsɪŋ]	fehlend
e-mail [ˈiːmeɪl]	E-Mail
Bye! [baɪ]	Tschüss!

to open ↔ to close

My favourite *place* is the park.

172 one hundred and seventy-two

Vocabulary

Unit 2

Story

p. 36	fun [fʌn]	Spaß
	project ['prɒdʒekt]	Projekt
	Saturday ['sætədeɪ]	Samstag, Sonnabend →
	afternoon [ˌɑːftə'nuːn]	Nachmittag
	alone [ə'ləʊn]	allein
	too [tuː]	zu →
	loud [laʊd]	laut
	to go [gəʊ]	gehen
	idea [aɪ'dɪə]	Idee, Einfall; Ahnung →
	to come over [ˌkʌm 'əʊvə]	herüberkommen
	clubhouse ['klʌbhaʊs]	Klubhaus
	really ['rɪəli]	wirklich
	thanks [θæŋks]	danke
	Meow! [miːaʊ]	Miau!
	to be a pain [ˌbiː ə 'peɪn]	jdm. auf den Geist gehen (Umgangssprache)
	all [ɔːl]	alle
	thing [θɪŋ]	Ding, Sache
	together [tə'geðə]	zusammen, miteinander →
	to send [send]	schicken, senden
	text message ['tekst ˌmesɪdʒ]	SMS →
p. 37	busy ['bɪzi]	beschäftigt →
	to bring [brɪŋ]	mitbringen; bringen
	clean [kliːn]	sauber
	why [waɪ]	warum →
	to act [ækt]	spielen
	part [pɑːt]	Teil

Saturday schreibt man groß.

My old shoes are *too* small.

I've got an *idea*.

The children walk *together*.

SMS heißt auf Englisch *text message*.

I'm *too* busy to come over.

Why … ? – Because … .

Bringen A B C

Dafür gibt im Englischen zwei Wörter:

*I can **take** you home.*   Ich kann dich nach Hause **bringen**. (= hinbringen)
*Can you **bring** me the ball, please?*   Kannst du mir bitte den Ball **bringen**? (= herbringen)

Wordwise

p. 38	e-mail ['iːmeɪl]	E-Mail →
	missing ['mɪsɪŋ]	fehlend
	CD [ˌsiː'diː]	CD →

Statt *e-mail* heißt es im Englischen oft nur *mail*.

Check-out

| p. 39 | people ['piːpl] | Leute |

one hundred and seventy-three **173**

V Vocabulary

Link-up B

> **For my folder**
> **Hello**
> Ergänze deine *phrases* zum Thema Begrüßung mit *This is my family…, My mum is …, I've got a brother…, Our flat is …*. Du findest bestimmt noch mehr!
>
> **Problems**
> In Unit 2 hast du gelernt, wie man über Probleme spricht und was man sagen kann, wenn man sich streitet. Schreibe die Ausdrücke auf ein Blatt Papier, das du in deinen *folder* legst. Lass auch hier wieder Platz für Ergänzungen.
>
> Probleme/Streit
> *That's a big problem.*
> *It's boring at home.*
> *You're in big trouble!*
> …

> **Word game**
> NAME-ELEVEN-NEW-WHAT-TEACHER … Kannst du die Wortkette fortsetzen? Du kannst allein weiterspielen oder mit anderen. Wenn es nicht mehr weitergeht, fang einfach eine neue Kette an.
>
> NAME-ELEVEN-NEW-WHAT-TEACHER …

Link-up B The hobby gardens

p. 40	**hobby** [ˈhɒbi]	Hobby →	
	to **watch** [wɒtʃ]	(zu)schauen, gucken	
	video [ˈvɪdiəʊ]	Video	
	guitar [gɪˈtɑː]	Gitarre	
	to **go swimming** [gəʊ ˈswɪmɪŋ]	schwimmen gehen	
	to **ride** [raɪd]	fahren; reiten	
	bike [baɪk]	Fahrrad →	
	collector [kəˈlektə]	Sammler/-in	
	corner [ˈkɔːnə]	Ecke	
	to **collect** [kəˈlekt]	sammeln; einsammeln; abholen	
	basketball [ˈbɑːskɪtbɔːl]	Basketball →	
p. 41	**role play** [ˈrəʊl pleɪ]	Rollenspiel	
	role [rəʊl]	Rolle	
	dialogue [ˈdaɪəlɒg]	Dialog; Gespräch	
	Start like this … [ˌstɑːt laɪk ˈðɪs]	Beginne so …	
	day [deɪ]	Tag →	
	week [wiːk]	Woche →	

one *hobby* - two *hobbies*

to ride a *bike*

Basketball is fun!

There are seven days in a *week*.

174 one hundred and seventy-four

Vocabulary

Unit 3

Days of the week
Monday ['mʌndeɪ]	Montag	**Thursday** ['θɜːzdeɪ]	Donnerstag	**Sunday** ['sʌndeɪ]	Sonntag
Tuesday ['tjuːzdeɪ]	Dienstag	**Friday** ['fraɪdeɪ]	Freitag		
Wednesday ['wenzdeɪ]	Mittwoch	**Saturday** ['sætədeɪ]	Samstag, Sonnabend		

Unit 3 Clubs and Hobbies

VOCABULARY SKILLS

Das Lernen geht einfacher mit einer Vokabelkartei. Dazu brauchst du einen Karton mit zwei Fächern und Karteikarten. Schreibe das englische Wort auf die Karte. Du kannst auch ein Bild dazu malen. Auf die Rückseite der Karte schreibst du das deutsche Wort. Die fertigen Karten stellst du in das vordere Fach deines Kartons. Zum Lernen nimmst du eine Karte nach der anderen heraus und prüfst, ob du die Übersetzung auf der Rückseite noch weißt. Wenn du ein Wort gut kannst, stellst du die Karte ins hintere Fach.

Check-in

p. 42			
	club [klʌb]	Klub; Verein →	There are lots of *clubs* at Thomas Tallis School in the afternoon.
	band [bænd]	Band	
	How about … ? ['haʊ ə'baʊt]	Wie steht's mit … ?; Wie wär's mit … ?	
	when [wen]	wann →	*When* is band? – What day and what time?
	Fridays ['fraɪdeɪz]	freitags	
	sports hall ['spɔːts ˌhɔːl]	Sporthalle	
	on Mondays [ˌɒn 'mʌndeɪz]	montags	
	every ['evri]	jede/-r/-s →	We play football *every* Monday.
	to learn [lɜːn]	lernen	
	badminton ['bædmɪntən]	Badminton, Federball	
	volleyball ['vɒlibɔːl]	Volleyball	
	o'clock [ə'klɒk]	Uhr	
	field ['fiːld]	Sportfeld; Wiese	
	Drama Club ['drɑːmə klʌb]	Theaterklub	
	drama ['drɑːmə]	Schauspiel	
	to sing [sɪŋ]	singen →	to *sing* 
	to dance [dɑːns]	tanzen	
	hall [hɔːl]	Aula, Saal; Flur	
	half past (two) ['hɑːf 'pɑːst]	halb (drei) →	In English it is *half past two*. Auf Deutsch sagt man halb drei dazu.

one hundred and seventy-five **175**

V Vocabulary

Unit 3

p. 42	half [hɑːf] pl. **halves** [hɑːvz]	Hälfte	
	past [pɑːst]	nach (*bei Uhrzeiten*)	
p. 43	to tell [tel]	sagen; erzählen	
	time [taɪm]	Uhrzeit	
	What time is it? [ˌwɒt ˈtaɪm ɪz ˌɪt]	Wie viel Uhr ist es?, Wie spät ist es?	
	quarter [ˈkwɔːtə]	Viertel	
	clock [klɒk]	Uhr →	
	to meet [miːt]	sich treffen, treffen →	
	weekend [ˌwiːkˈend]	Wochenende →	

weekend = Saturday and Sunday

Language 1

p. 44	to get up [ˌget ˈʌp]	aufstehen	
	after that [ˈɑːftə ˌðæt]	danach	
	after [ˈɑːftə]	nach →	
	to eat [iːt]	essen	
	breakfast [ˈbrekfəst]	Frühstück	
	to speak [spiːk]	sprechen	
	Bye! [baɪ]	Tschüss! →	
	to see [siː]	sehen; treffen →	
	tonight [təˈnaɪt]	heute Abend; heute Nacht	
	today [təˈdeɪ]	heute	
	to work [wɜːk]	arbeiten; funktionieren →	
	usually [ˈjuːʒəli]	gewöhnlich, normalerweise	
	hour [aʊə]	Stunde →	
	to know [nəʊ]	wissen; kennen	
	What about ... ? [ˌwɒt əˈbaʊt]	Was ist mit ... ?	
	sometimes [ˈsʌmtaɪmz]	manchmal	
	never [ˈnevə]	nie	
	to forget [fəˈget]	vergessen →	
	them [ðem]	sie/ihnen	
p. 45	free [friː]	frei; kostenlos	
	often [ˈɒfn]	oft	
	film [fɪlm]	Film	
	cinema [ˈsɪnəmə]	Kino →	
	How are you? [ˌhaʊ ˈɑː ˌjuː]	Wie geht es dir/euch/Ihnen?	
	fine [faɪn]	gut	
	See you. [ˈsiː ˌjuː]	Bis dann., Bis bald. →	

The children go home *after* school.

Emma's father *works* in a computer shop.

Du sagst: *an hour*.

I never *forget* my homework.

You watch films at the *cinema*.

Bye. Goodbye. *See you*.

176 one hundred and seventy-six

Vocabulary

Unit 3

Language 2

p. 46	to **like** [laɪk]	mögen; gern haben
	to **live** [lɪv]	wohnen, leben
	bus [bʌs] pl. **buses** ['bʌsɪz]	Bus →
	correct [kə'rekt]	richtig
	Dear ... [dɪə]	Liebe/-r ... →
	a lot [ə 'lɒt]	sehr; viel
	practice ['præktɪs]	Übung; Probe; Training
p. 47	to **love** [lʌv]	lieben
	to **chase** [tʃeɪs]	verfolgen; jagen; hinterherrennen →
	by [baɪ]	mit

Dear Sam = Lieber Sam *(im Brief)*

Barker *chases* cats in the garden.

Language 3

p. 48	**these** [ðiːz]	diese (hier)
	those [ðəʊz]	diese (da), die (da); jene →
	over there [ˌəʊvə 'ðeə]	da drüben
	baby ['beɪbi] pl. **babies** ['beɪbiz]	Baby →

These books are new, *those* are old.

one *baby* – two *babies*

Language 4

p. 49	**the same** [seɪm]	derselbe/dieselbe/dasselbe
	genitive ['dʒenɪtɪv]	Genitiv

Story

p. 50	**before** [bɪ'fɔː]	bevor; vor; vorher →
	to **wake up** [ˌweɪk 'ʌp]	aufwachen →
	to **wash** [wɒʃ]	waschen
	face [feɪs]	Gesicht
	again [ə'gen]	noch einmal, wieder
	café ['kæfeɪ]	Café
	also ['ɔːlsəʊ]	auch →
	to **bark** [bɑːk]	bellen
	to **run away** [rʌn ə'weɪ]	wegrennen, weglaufen
	to **throw** [θrəʊ]	werfen →
	to **get lost** [ˌget 'lɒst]	sich verirren, sich verlaufen
	me [miː]	mich; mir
p. 51	**picnic** ['pɪknɪk]	Picknick
	drink [drɪŋk]	Getränk →
	to **fall over** [fɔːl 'əʊvə]	umfallen; *(Person)* hinfallen

after ↔ *before*

I *wake* Lisa *up* every morning.

Barker likes to play, too. = Barker *also* likes to play.

Lisa *throws* balls for Barker.

one hundred and seventy-seven **177**

V Vocabulary

Unit 3/Link-up C

p. 51	evening [ˈiːvnɪŋ]	Abend →
	to sleep [sliːp]	schlafen →
	to fall asleep [ˌfɔːl əˈsliːp]	einschlafen
	quickly [ˈkwɪkli]	schnell
	to happen [ˈhæpn]	geschehen, passieren →

Wordwise

p. 52	to go to bed [ˌgəʊ tə ˈbed]	ins Bett gehen →
	rhyme [raɪm]	Reim
	am [ˌeɪˈem]	vormittags →
	pm [ˌpiːˈem]	nachmittags →

Check-out

| p. 53 | bad [bæd] | schlecht → |

evening ↔ morning

sleep

It's very loud outside. What's *happening*?

am = 0:01–12:00
pm = 12:01–0:00

bad ↔ good

For my folder 📖
Let's …
Schreibe alle Ausdrücke, mit denen du Vorschläge machen und auf Vorschläge reagieren kannst, auf ein Blatt Papier. Lege es in deinen *English folder*.

Vorschläge	Antworter
Let's go to the … club.	OK, that's cool.
Learn to …	That's a bad idea.
…	…

Word game
Eins der Wörter gehört nicht in die Gruppe. Kannst du es finden?
1. *sometimes – often – where – never* 3. *mice – cats – baby – children* 5. *mum – dad – sister – aunt*
2. *chocolate – crisp – apple – eat*   4. *boring – morning – evening – afternoon* 6. *tell – take – talk – table*

Link-up C In town

p. 56	town [taʊn]	Stadt
	map [mæp]	Stadtplan, Landkarte
	museum [mjuːˈziːəm]	Museum
	river [ˈrɪvə]	Fluss →
	bridge [brɪdʒ]	Brücke
	department store [dɪˈpɑːtmənt ˌstɔː]	Kaufhaus, Warenhaus
	supermarket [ˈsuːpəˌmɑːkɪt]	Supermarkt
	newsagent [ˈnjuːzˌeɪdʒnt]	Zeitungsladen
	church [tʃɜːtʃ]	Kirche

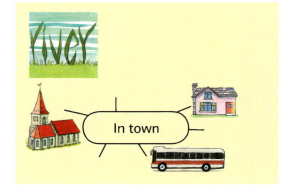

178 one hundred and seventy-eight

Vocabulary

Link-up C/Unit 4

p. 56	**key** [kiː]	Erklärung, Legende; Schlüssel
	bus stop [ˈbʌs ˌstɒp]	Bushaltestelle
	tourist information centre [ˌtʊərɪst ɪnfəˈmeɪʃn sentə]	Touristik-Information
	place [pleɪs]	Platz, Ort, Stelle
	near [nɪə]	in der Nähe von; nahe
	opposite [ˈɒpəzɪt]	gegenüber
	between [bɪˈtwiːn]	zwischen →
p. 57	**on the left** [ˌɒn ðə ˈleft]	links
	left [left]	links; linke/-r/-s →
	on the right [ˌɒn ðə ˈraɪt]	rechts
	to turn [tɜːn]	einbiegen, abbiegen; drehen, wenden
	straight [streɪt]	gerade
	to get to … [ˈget tʊ]	zu/nach … kommen
	Excuse me. [ɪkˈskjuːz miː]	Entschuldigung!, Entschuldige!, Entschuldigen Sie! →
	down [daʊn]	entlang; herunter, hinunter, nach unten
	to cross [krɒs]	überqueren; kreuzen →
	to repeat [rɪˈpiːt]	wiederholen
	to walk [wɔːk]	(zu Fuß) gehen, laufen

The apples are *between* Tom and the bag.

Excuse me, what time is it, please? = Entschuldigung, wie spät ist es bitte?
Sorry, I'm late! = Entschuldige die Verspätung!

Look left, then right, then left, then *cross* the road.

Unit 4 Greenwich project week

VOCABULARY SKILLS

Du behältst neue Wörter besser, wenn du sie dreimal fünf Minuten lang lernst. Zuerst schaust du sie dir fünf Minuten an, nach einer halben Stunde wiederholst du sie, und am Ende deiner Hausaufgaben überprüfst du sie nochmals fünf Minuten. Das bringt mehr als eine viertel oder halbe Stunde am Stück.

Check-in

p. 58	**world** [wɜːld]	Welt →
	time line [ˈtaɪm laɪn]	Zeitleiste
	line [laɪn]	Linie
	to stand [stænd]	stehen
	foot [fʊt] pl. **feet** [fiːt]	Fuß →

one *foot* – two *feet*

one hundred and seventy-nine **179**

V Vocabulary

Unit 4

p. 58	east [iːst]	Osten
	west [west]	Westen
	tunnel [ˈtʌnl]	Tunnel
	north [nɔːθ]	Norden →
	south [saʊθ]	Süden
	on foot [ˌɒn ˈfʊt]	zu Fuß
	spooky [ˈspuːki]	gespenstisch, gruselig →
	ghost [gəʊst]	Geist →

Ghosts are spooky.

VOCABULARY SKILLS
by und on

by bike	mit dem Fahrrad	by bus	mit dem Bus	on foot	zu Fuß
by car	mit dem Auto	by train	mit dem Zug	on skates	mit Inlineskates

p. 59	train [treɪn]	Zug →
	driver [ˈdraɪvə]	Fahrer/-in
	interesting [ˈɪntrəstɪŋ]	interessant
	from all round the world [frəm ɔːl ˌraʊnd ðə ˈwɜːld]	aus der ganzen Welt
	ship [ʃɪp]	Schiff →
	life [laɪf] *pl.* lives [laɪvz]	Leben
	sea [siː]	Meer →
	young [jʌŋ]	jung
	skateboard [ˈskeɪtbɔːd]	Skateboard →
	skates [skeɪts]	Rollschuhe, Inlineskates →
p. 58	without [wɪˈðaʊt]	ohne →
	famous [ˈfeɪməs]	berühmt, bekannt →
	newspaper [ˈnjuːsˌpeɪpə]	Zeitung
	Internet [ˈɪntənet]	Internet
p. 59	sight [saɪt]	Sehenswürdigkeit →
	through [θruː]	durch
	visitor [ˈvɪzɪtə]	Besucher/-in →
	to visit [ˈvɪzɪt]	besuchen →

You can see ships in the *sea* and on *rivers*.

You can't write *without* a pen.
The Cutty Sark is a *famous* ship.

There are a lot of famous *sights* in Greenwich.

I'm not from Greenwich. I'm a *visitor*.
You have to *visit* the Royal Observatory and see the Meridian Line.

Language 1

p. 60	brochure [ˈbrəʊʃə]	Broschüre
	transport [ˈtrænspɔːt]	Verkehrsmittel →
	to show [ʃəʊ]	zeigen
	the Underground [ði ˈʌndəˌgraʊnd]	die Londoner U-Bahn
	us [ʌs]	uns
	fast [fɑːst]	schnell
	scary [ˈskeəri]	unheimlich, gruselig

Achtung Aussprache!

Vocabulary

Unit 4

p. 60	taxi ['tæksi]	Taxi →
	everywhere ['evriweə]	überall
	him [hɪm]	ihn; ihm
	to correct [kəˈrekt]	korrigieren
	to drive [draɪv]	fahren
	kid [kɪd]	Kind →
	of course [ˌəv ˈkɔːs]	selbstverständlich, natürlich
p. 61	way [weɪ]	Weg
	to give [gɪv]	geben
	situation [ˌsɪtjuˈeɪʃn]	Situation
	to leave [liːv]	abfahren; verlassen; lassen

You can say 'child' or 'kid'.

Language 2

p. 62	to sail [seɪl]	segeln →
	to park [pɑːk]	parken
	everything [ˈevriθɪŋ]	alles
	burger [ˈbɜːgə]	Burger →
	Yeah! [jeə]	Ja! (Umgangssprache)
	lunch [lʌntʃ]	Mittagessen
p. 63	the same [seɪm]	derselbe/dieselbe/ dasselbe
	class [klɑːs]	Klasse →

Ships *sail* in the sea.

There are 30 pupils in my *class*.

Language 3

p. 64	to scare [skeə]	erschrecken, Angst einjagen
	head [hed]	Kopf →
	to stop [stɒp]	aufhören; anhalten
	to be scared [ˌbi: ˈskeəd]	Angst haben
	quiet [ˈkwaɪət]	ruhig, still
	person [ˈpɜːsn]	Person →
	programme [ˈprəʊgræm]	Programm
	true [truː]	wahr, richtig
	false [fɔːls]	falsch →
p. 65	to present [prɪˈzent]	präsentieren

one *person* – two people

true ↔ *false*

Language 4

p. 66	to end [end]	zu Ende gehen, enden; beenden
	best [best]	beste/-r/-s
	team [tiːm]	Team, Mannschaft →

There are eleven people in a football *team*.

one hundred and eighty-one **181**

V Vocabulary

Unit 4

p. 66
to **win** [wɪn]	gewinnen	
prize [praɪz]	Preis	
to **mean** [miːn]	bedeuten; meinen →	
end [end]	Ende	

GMT *means* Greenwich Mean Time.

Language 5

p. 67
jolly ['dʒɒli]	fröhlich, vergnügt	
pirate ['paɪrət]	Pirat/-in	
hand [hænd]	Hand	
finger ['fɪŋə]	Finger	
wooden ['wʊdn]	Holz-, hölzern	
leg [leg]	Bein	
parrot ['pærət]	Papagei	
master ['mɑːstə]	Herr, Meister	
ear [ɪə]	Ohr	
full [fʊl]	voll	
ring [rɪŋ]	Ring	
scar [skɑː]	Narbe	
above [ə'bʌv]	über, oberhalb	
lip [lɪp]	Lippe	
cutlass ['kʌtləs]	Entermesser	
hip [hɪp]	Hüfte	
simple present [ˌsɪmpl 'preznt]	Präsens	

Story

p. 68
beautiful ['bjuːtɪfl]	schön, wunderschön, wundervoll →	
captain ['kæptɪn]	Kapitän	
wheel [wiːl]	Steuerrad, Lenkrad; Rad	
tea [tiː]	Tee →	
treasure ['treʒə]	Schatz	
island ['aɪlənd]	Insel →	
suddenly ['sʌdnli]	plötzlich	
bang [bæŋ]	Knall	
to **believe** [bɪ'liːv]	glauben	
eye [aɪ]	Auge →	
help [help]	Hilfe	
awful ['ɔːfl]	schrecklich	
pirate ['paɪrət]	Pirat/-in →	
to **want** [wɒnt]	wollen	
to **give** [gɪv]	geben →	

Achtung Schreibung!

Britain is an *island*.

Achtung Schreibung und Aussprache!

to give

182 one hundred and eighty-two

Vocabulary

Unit 4

p. 68	to **walk the plank** [ˌwɔːk ðə ˈplæŋk]	über eine Schiffsplanke ins Wasser getrieben werden *(alte Strafe für Seeleute)*
	angry [ˈæŋgri]	verärgert, wütend
p. 69	to **fight** [faɪt]	kämpfen; (sich) streiten
	to **run** [rʌn]	rennen, laufen
	fight [faɪt]	Kampf; Streit →
	to **fall** [fɔːl]	fallen
	water [ˈwɔːtə]	Wasser →
	wet [wet]	nass
	something [ˈsʌmθɪŋ]	etwas, irgendetwas
	cake [keɪk]	Kuchen →

to fight → *fight*

There is *water* in the river.

Wordwise

| p. 70 | **last** [lɑːst] | letzte/-r/-s → |

first ↔ *last*

Check-out

| p. 71 | **pronoun** [ˈprəʊnaʊn] | Pronomen, Fürwort |

For my folder
Information
Stell dir vor: du bist in einer fremden Stadt. Welche Gebäude, Sehenswürdigkeiten usw. gibt es dort? Wie kommst du dorthin? Schreibe deine Fragen und möglichen Antworten auf ein Blatt in deinen *English folder*.

Fragen	Antworten
Excuse me, I'm a visitor here. What can I do in … ?	*You can … here.*
Can you tell me the way to … ?	*Go down …*
How do I … ?	*…*
…	

Word game
Schreibe die fehlenden Buchstaben der nebenstehenden Wörter auf einen Zettel. In der richtigen Reihenfolge ergeben sie den Namen einer englischen Stadt.
Du kannst dir selber ähnliche Rätsel für deine Freunde ausdenken. Dazu überlegst du dir zuerst ein englisches Lösungswort und suchst dir dann die passenden englischen Vokabeln.

ti_er	fa_e	h_lp
ga_den	Su_day	bro_n
tra_n	_our	sudd_nly

one hundred and eighty-three **183**

V Vocabulary

Unit 5

Unit 5 Shopping for a birthday

> **VOCABULARY SKILLS**
>
> Hast du schon eine Vokabelkartei angelegt? Dann sind sicher schon ganz viele Karten im hinteren Fach. Schau dir diese Karten alle paar Wochen nochmals an. Wenn du ein Wort nicht mehr weißt, kommt die Karte wieder ins vordere Fach und du lernst sie nochmal.

Check-in

p. 72
shopping	[ˈʃɒpɪŋ]	Einkaufen; Einkäufe
birthday	[ˈbɜːθdeɪ]	Geburtstag →
size	[saɪz]	Größe
extra	[ˈekstrə]	extra, besonders
large	[lɑːdʒ]	groß
medium	[ˈmiːdiəm]	mittel →
photo	[ˈfəʊtəʊ]	Foto
to buy	[baɪ]	kaufen
newspaper	[ˈnjuːsˌpeɪpə]	Zeitung

p. 73
money	[ˈmʌni]	Geld →
penny [ˈpeni] pl. pence (p)	[pens]	Penny (Plural) Pence (britisches Geld) →
pound	[paʊnd]	Pfund →
price	[praɪs]	Preis →
How much is/are ... ?	[haʊ ˈmʌtʃ]	Wie viel kostet/ kosten ... ? →
much	[mʌtʃ]	viel
comic	[ˈkɒmɪk]	Comic(heft)
assistant	[əˈsɪstnt]	Verkäufer/-in
customer	[ˈkʌstəmə]	Kunde/Kundin

s = small   m = *medium*   l = large

English *money*
five *pence* = 5p

one pound = £1
Look at that T-shirt. It's a good *price*.

How much is the pen?   It's two pounds.

Language 1

p. 74
third	[θɜːd]	dritte/-r/-s
March	[mɑːtʃ]	März →
I would like (= I'd like) ...	[aɪ ˈwʊd ˌlaɪk = ˈaɪd laɪk]	ich möchte gern ..., ich hätte gern ...
to invite	[ɪnˈvaɪt]	einladen
pizza	[ˈpiːtsə]	Pizza →
expensive	[ɪkˈspensɪv]	teuer
DVD	[ˌdiː viː ˈdiː]	DVD
lots (of)	[lɒts]	viel
food	[fuːd]	Essen; Lebensmittel →
invitation	[ˌɪnvɪˈteɪʃn]	Einladung →
RSVP	[ˌɑːr es viːˈpiː]	Um Antwort wird gebeten.

p. 75
month	[mʌnθ]	Monat →

Monatsnamen schreibst du groß.

Sandwiches are my favourite *food*.
to invite → *invitation*

day, week, *month*, year

184   one hundred and eighty-four

Vocabulary

Unit 5

Months A B C

January [ˈdʒænjuri]	Januar	**July** [dʒʊˈlaɪ]	Juli
February [ˈfebrʊri]	Februar	**August** [ˈɔːgəst]	August
March [mɑːtʃ]	März	**September** [sepˈtembə]	September
April [ˈeɪprəl]	April	**October** [ɒkˈtəʊbə]	Oktober
May [meɪ]	Mai	**November** [nəʊˈvembə]	November
June [dʒuːn]	Juni	**December** [dɪˈsembə]	Dezember

p. 75 **ordinal number** [ˈɔːdɪnl ˈnʌmbə] — Ordnungszahl

Christmas [ˈkrɪsməs] — Weihnachten

the twenty-first of [ðə ˌtwentɪ ˈfɜːst ˈəv] — der einundzwanzigste →

calendar [ˈkæləndə] — Kalender →

to go shopping [gəʊ ˈʃɒpɪŋ] — einkaufen gehen

My birthday is on *the twenty-first of* May.

Ordinal numbers A B C

first [ˈfɜːst]	erste (-r/-s)	**fourteenth** [fɔːˈtiːnθ]	vierzehnte (-r/-s)
second [ˈseknd]	zweite (-r/-s)	**fifteenth** [fɪfˈtiːnθ]	fünfzehnte (-r/-s)
third [θɜːd]	dritte (-r/-s)	**sixteenth** [sɪksˈtiːnθ]	sechzehnte (-r/-s)
fourth [fɔːθ]	vierte (-r/-s)	**seventeenth** [sevnˈtiːnθ]	siebzehnte (-r/-s)
fifth [fɪfθ]	fünfte (-r/-s)	**eighteenth** [eɪˈtiːnθ]	achzehnte (-r/-s)
sixth [sɪksθ]	sechste (-r/-s)	**nineteenth** [naɪnˈtiːnθ]	neunzehnte (-r/-s)
seventh [ˈsevnθ]	siebte (-r/-s)	**twentieth** [ˈtwentɪɪθ]	zwanzigste (-r/-s)
eighth [eɪtθ]	achte (-r/-s)	**twenty-first** [ˌtwentiˈfɜːst]	einundzwanzigste (-r/-s)
ninth [naɪnθ]	neunte (-r/-s)	**twenty-second** [ˌtwentiˈseknd]	zweiundzwanzigste (-r/-s)
tenth [tenθ]	zehnte (-r/-s)	**twenty-third** [ˌtwentiˈθɜːd]	dreiundzwanzigste (-r/-s)
eleventh [ɪˈlevnθ]	elfte (-r/-s)	…	…
twelfth [twelfθ]	zwölfte (-r/-s)	**thirtieth** [ˈθɜːtiəθ]	dreißigste (-r/-s)
thirteenth [θɜːˈtiːnθ]	dreizehnte (-r/-s)	**thirty-first** [ˌθɜːtiˈfɜːst]	einunddreißigste (-r/-s)

Language 2

p. 76 **present** [ˈpreznt] — Geschenk →

to look for [lʊk fɔː] — suchen

at the moment [æt ðə ˈməʊmənt] — im Augenblick, momentan

still [stɪl] — noch, immer noch

to wait (for) [weɪt] — warten (auf)

sweatshirt [ˈswetʃɜːt] — Sweatshirt

to try on [traɪ ɒn] — anprobieren →

p. 77 **special** [ˈspeʃl] — besondere/-r/-s

the others [ði ˈʌðəz] — die anderen

I want to *try on* this sweatshirt.

one hundred and eighty-five 185

V Vocabulary

Unit 5

p. 77 to guess [ges] — raten, erraten

Language 3

p. 78
- shopping list ['ʃɒpɪŋ ˌlɪst] — Einkaufsliste, Einkaufszettel →
- flour [flaʊə] — Mehl
- box [bɒks] — Schachtel; Karton; Kiste →
- egg [eg] — Ei
- How many … ? [haʊ 'meni] — Wie viele … ?
- many ['meni] — viele →
- to need [niːd] — brauchen
- sugar ['ʃʊgə] — Zucker →
- gram [græm] — Gramm
- packet ['pækɪt] — Päckchen, Packung
- plenty ['plenti] — genug, ausreichend
- a little [ə 'lɪtl] — ein bisschen →
- a few [ə 'fjuː] — ein paar, einige →
- candle ['kændl] — Kerze
- bar [bɑː] — Tafel
- milk [mɪlk] — Milch
- bottle ['bɒtl] — Flasche →
- lemonade [ˌleməˈneɪd] — Limonade
- sweet [swiːt] — Bonbon
- to count [kaʊnt] — zählen →

one *box* – two *boxes*

many friends – *much* money

We only have *a little* sugar and *a little* milk.
We need *a few* eggs.

a *bottle* of milk

How many eggs are there in the box? Let's *count* them.

Wie viel?

How much … ?	Wie viel … ?	**a bag of** apples	eine Tüte Äpfel
How many … ?	Wie viele … ?	**a bottle of** water	eine Flasche Wasser
a lot of money/books	viel Geld/viele Bücher	**a box of** eggs	eine Schachtel Eier
a packet of sugar	ein Päckchen Zucker	**no** chocolate	keine Schokolade

Language 4

p. 79
- recipe ['resɪpi] — Rezept →
- chocolate crispie [ˌtʃɒklət 'krɪspi] — Schokocrossie
- plain chocolate [ˌpleɪn 'tʃɒklət] — Zartbitterschokolade
- tablespoon ['teɪblspuːn] — Esslöffel
- rice crispie [ˌraɪs 'krɪspi] — Rice Krispie, Puffreis
- cornflake ['kɔːnfleɪk] — Cornflake
- raisin ['reɪzn] — Rosine
- to break [breɪk] — brechen

Achtung Aussprache!

Vocabulary

Unit 5

p. 79 piece [piːs] — Stück, Teil
to melt [melt] — schmelzen
bowl [bəʊl] — Schüssel
hot [hɒt] — heiß
to mix [mɪks] — mischen
until [ʌnˈtɪl] — bis
to cover [ˈkʌvə] — bedecken, abdecken
spoonful [ˈspuːnfʊl] — Löffel (voll)
paper case [ˈpeɪpə ˌkeɪs] — Papierförmchen
hard [hɑːd] — hart, fest
ready [ˈredi] — fertig
up [ʌp] — nach oben, hinauf, herauf → *up* ↔ down
voice [vɔɪs] — Stimme

Story

p. 80 **Happy Birthday!** [ˈhæpi ˌbɜːθdeɪ] — Alles Gute zum Geburtstag!
title [ˈtaɪtl] — Überschrift; Titel → The *title* of this book is Red Line 1.
date [deɪt] — Datum
lunchtime [ˈlʌntʃtaɪm] — Mittagszeit
disco [ˈdɪskəʊ] — Disko →

Achtung Schreibung!

sits with his friends [ˌsɪts wɪð hɪz ˈfrendz] — setzt sich zu seinen Freunden
to **sit** [sɪt] — sich setzen; sitzen → to *sit*
to **smile** [smaɪl] — lächeln
back [bæk] — zurück

p. 81 **alarm clock** [əˈlɑːm ˌklɒk] — Wecker →
to **ring** [rɪŋ] — läuten; klingeln
heading [ˈhedɪŋ] — Überschrift
to **understand** [ˌʌndəˈstænd] — verstehen → Can you *understand* me?
better [ˈbetə] — besser
another [əˈnʌðə] — noch ein/eine(-r/-s), ein(e) weitere(-r/-s)

Wordwise

p. 82 **dictionary** [ˈdɪkʃənri] — Wörterbuch →
polite [pəˈlaɪt] — höflich
man [mæn] pl. **men** [men] — Mann →

one *man* – two *men*

Check-out

p. 83 to **sell** [sel] — verkaufen →
right now [ˈraɪt ˌnaʊ] — jetzt gerade
cheese [tʃiːz] — Käse →

sell ↔ buy

V Vocabulary

Unit 6

For my folder
Shopping

Du gehst einkaufen. Was sagst du? Was sagt der Verkäufer/die Verkäuferin? Schreibe alle Ausdrücke, die du beim Einkaufen verwenden kannst, auf ein Blatt Papier für deinen *folder*.

Kunde/Kundin
How much is …?
Excuse me. This T-shirt/… is too small/too ….
Have you got it in …?
Where are …?
…

Verkäufer/Verkäuferin
It's ….

Yes, …/No, …
…

Word game

Schreibe die nebenstehenden Wörter auf Karten. Verteile alle Karten mit der Schrift nach unten auf dem Tisch. Versuche Gegensatzpaare aufzudecken. Wenn du ein Paar gefunden hast, darfst du die beiden Karten behalten. Wenn du mit Freunden/Freundinnen spielst, kannst du das Spiel erweitern: Ihr dürft das Kartenpaar erst dann behalten, wenn ihr mit den beiden Wörtern Sätze gebildet habt, z. B.:
*I've got a **small** dog. – He lives in a **big** house.*

big – right – good – white – short – old – black – new – long – start – small – wrong

Unit 6 At the farm park

> **VOCABULARY SKILLS**
>
> Damit du die Vokabeln gut behältst, kannst du sie mit deinen Freunden/Freundinnen zusammen wiederholen. Nehmt euch in regelmäßigen Abständen Vokabeln aus einer früheren Unit vor. Ihr könnt euch gegenseitig abfragen oder ein Spiel damit machen.

Check-in

p. 86   **farm park** [ˈfɑːm ˌpɑːk]   Farmtierpark
      farm [fɑːm]   Bauernhof →
      both … and [bəʊθ]   sowohl … als auch
      spring [sprɪŋ]   Frühling, Frühjahr

188   one hundred and eighty-eight

Vocabulary

Unit 6

p. 86 summer ['sʌmə] — Sommer
horse [hɔːs] — Pferd →
sheep [ʃiːp] pl. sheep [ʃiːp] — Schaf →
goose [guːs] pl. geese [giːs] — Gans
pig [pɪɡ] — Schwein
to stay [steɪ] — übernachten; bleiben
hostel ['hɒstl] — Herberge
night [naɪt] — Nacht
animal ['ænɪml] — Tier →
pets corner [,pets 'kɔːnə] — Streichelzoo
pet [pet] — Haustier
to feed [fiːd] — füttern →
kid [kɪd] — Zicklein
animal snacks ['ænɪml ,snæks] — Tierfutter
snack [snæk] — Snack, Imbiss
gift shop ['ɡɪft ʃɒp] — Geschenkladen, Souvenirshop →

> You can ride a bike or you can ride a *horse*.
> one *sheep* – a lot of *sheep*
>
> animals
>
> feed
>
> You can buy presents in a *gift shop*.

Besondere Pluralformen

family	famil**ies**	sheep	**sheep**	child	**children**
baby	bab**ies**			mouse	**mice**
country	countr**ies**			foot	**feet**
hobby	hobb**ies**			goose	**geese**
sandwich	sandwich**es**				

Be careful! [,biː 'keəfl] — Sei vorsichtig! →
goat [ɡəʊt] — Ziege
hungry ['hʌŋɡri] — hungrig →
lamb [læm] — Lamm
born [bɔːn] — geboren
everybody ['evri,bɒdi] — jede/-r/-s
tractor ['træktə] — Traktor →
mini ['mɪni] — Mini-
opening time ['əʊpnɪŋ taɪm] — Öffnungszeit
ticket ['tɪkɪt] — Eintrittskarte; Fahrkarte
adult ['ædʌlt] — Erwachsene/-r
postcard ['pəʊstkɑːd] — Postkarte →
super ['suːpə] — super, toll
pullover ['pʊləʊvə] — Pullover
milking barn ['mɪlkɪŋ bɑːn] — Melkstall
to milk [mɪlk] — melken

> *Be careful* the table is wet!
>
> I'm *hungry*. Have you got a sandwich?

V Vocabulary

Unit 6

p. 86
- **barn** [bɑ:n] — Stall; Scheune →
- **farmer** ['fɑ:mə] — Bauer/Bäuerin, Landwirt/-in →
- **cow** [kaʊ] — Kuh
- to **try** [traɪ] — versuchen, probieren
- **real** [rɪəl] — echt
- **safari ride** [sə'fɑ:ri ˌraɪd] — Safarifahrt

p. 87
- **plural** ['plʊərl] — Plural, Mehrzahl →
- **woman** ['wʊmən] pl. **women** ['wɪmɪn] — Frau →
- **chicken** ['tʃɪkɪn] — Huhn, Hähnchen
- **season** ['si:zn] — Jahreszeit →
- **jumbled** ['dʒʌmbld] — durcheinander geworfen
- **trip** [trɪp] — Ausflug

Language 1

p. 88
- to **pack** [pæk] — packen
- **uniform** ['ju:nɪfɔ:m] — Uniform →
- **clothes** pl. [kləʊðz] — Kleidung, Kleider
- to **wear** [weə] — tragen →
- **sunglasses** pl. ['sʌnˌglɑ:sɪz] — Sonnenbrille
- **trainer** ['treɪnə] — Turnschuh →
- **quick** [kwɪk] — schnell
- **cold** [kəʊld] — kalt
- **sunny** ['sʌni] — sonnig
- to **rain** [reɪn] — regnen →
- **welly** ['weli] — Gummistiefel
- **jeans** pl. [dʒi:nz] — Jeans
- **cap** [kæp] — Kappe, Schirmmütze
- **trousers** pl. ['traʊzəz] — Hose →
- **skirt** [skɜ:t] — Rock

p. 89
- **weather** ['weðə] — Wetter
- **both** [bəʊθ] — beide
- **warm** [wɔ:m] — warm
- **windy** ['wɪndi] — windig →
- **poem** ['pəʊɪm] — Gedicht
- **wind** [wɪnd] — Wind
- **nose** [nəʊz] — Nase
- **sun** [sʌn] — Sonne
- to **swim** [swɪm] — schwimmen →

The cows live in the *barn*.
farm → *farmer*

The *plural* of 'child' is 'children'.
one *woman* – two *women*

English pupils *wear* a school uniform.

It's *raining*.

One pair of *trousers* → three pairs of *trousers*

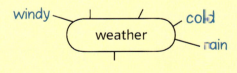

190 one hundred and ninety

Vocabulary

Unit 6

Schreibweisen der -ing-Form

to read	reading	to come	coming	to get	getting
to pack	packing	to take	taking	to put	putting
to see	seeing	to have	having	to run	running
to be	being	to make	making	to swim	swimming

Language 2

p. 90 to **carry** [ˈkæri] — tragen
across [əˈkrɒs] — auf der anderen Seite von; über

to **cut** [kʌt] — schneiden
piece [piːs] — Stück; Teil →

That cake looks nice. Can I have a *piece*, please?

dessert [dɪˈzɜːt] — Nachtisch →
surprise [səˈpraɪz] — Überraschung

First we eat pizza, then *dessert* – my favourite.

p. 91 **simple present** [ˌsɪmpl ˈpreznt] — Präsens

present progressive [ˌpreznt prəˈgresɪv] — Verlaufsform der Gegenwart

to **drink** [drɪŋk] — trinken →
radio [ˈreɪdiəʊ] — Radio →

After a race I *drink* lots of juice.

Language 3

p. 92 **must** [mʌst] — müssen →
needn't [ˈniːdnt] — nicht müssen, nicht brauchen →

We *must* wear uniform to school.
We *needn't* wear uniform to the farm park.

some [sʌm] — einige, ein Paar; etwas →
scone [skɒn] — brötchenartiges Gebäck

some – something – somewhere

Story

p. 94 to **hear** [hɪə] — hören
Oink! [ɔɪŋk] — Grunz!
little [ˈlɪtl] — klein →
to **laugh** [lɑːf] — lachen →
to **think** [θɪŋk] — denken; glauben
next [nekst] — als nächste/-r/-s
cute [kjuːt] — süß, niedlich
around … [əˈraʊnd] — um … herum
to **pat** [pæt] — tätscheln
Go away! [ˌgəʊ əˈweɪ] — Geh weg!

p. 95 **grass** [grɑːs] — Gras →
ham [hæm] — Schinken

big ↔ little
Achtung Schreibung!

one hundred and ninety-one 191

V Vocabulary

Unit 6/Unit 7

Wordwise
p. 96 **other** [ˈʌðə] andere/-r/-s

Check-out
p. 97 **regular** [ˈregjələ] regelmäßig
irregular [ɪˈregjələ] unregelmäßig →

regular ↔ *irregular*

For my folder
Phone calls

Du kannst inzwischen auf Englisch telefonieren. Schreibe ein Telefongespräch, in dem du dich mit jemandem für eine bestimmte Uhrzeit verabredest, für deinen *English folder* auf.

Das sagst du:

Hi!/Hello.
What are you doing?
…

Das sagt dein Gesprächspartner:

Hi, it's …
I'm …. And you?
…

Word game

Benutze das *dictionary* am Ende des Buchs und schlage die vier nebenstehenden Fragen nach. Die richtigen Lösungen ergeben eine neue Frage. Lies sie laut vor und antworte darauf.
Du kannst auch mit deinen Freunden/Freundinnen um die Wette nach Wörtern suchen. Ihr müsst mindestens zu dritt sein. Einer fragt die anderen nach einem Wort im *dictionary*, z. B.: *What comes after/before … ?*
Wer zuerst antwortet, bekommt einen Punkt und darf die nächste Frage stellen.

Welches Wort steht
1. vor *dog*?
2. nach *yes*?
3. nach *season*?
4. nach *end*?

Unit 7 The school year

VOCABULARY SKILLS

Schreibe die englischen Wörter, die du lernen möchtest, auf kleine Zettel. Die deutsche Bedeutung kommt in einer anderen Farbe auf die Rückseite. Lege die Zettel mit den deutschen Wörtern nach oben vor dich hin.

Jedesmal wenn du das englische Wort weißt, darfst du die Karte wegnehmen. Kannst du das Wort noch nicht, legst du die Karte wieder zu den anderen.

Check-in
p. 98 **full** [fʊl] voll
event [ɪˈvent] Veranstaltung →
planner [ˈplænə] Jahresplaner

A school disco is an *event*.

192 one hundred and ninety-two

Vocabulary

Unit 7

p. 98	festival	['festɪvl]	Festival; Fest
	lantern	['læntən]	Laterne →
	procession	[prə'seʃn]	Umzug
	to organize	['ɔ:gənaɪz]	organisieren
	kind	[kaɪnd]	Art
	even	['i:vn]	sogar
	to remember	[rɪ'membə]	denken an, nicht vergessen; sich erinnern an →
	sports day	['spɔ:ts deɪ]	Sportfest
	next	[nekst]	nächste/-r/-s
	fair	[feə]	Fest; Markt, Jahrmarkt
	charity	['tʃærɪti]	Wohltätigkeitsverein →
	stall	[stɔ:l]	Stand →
	play	[pleɪ]	Theaterstück
	to turn	[tɜ:n]	sich umdrehen
p. 99	to compare	[kəm'peə]	vergleichen

I *remember* the lantern procession in 2005.

We collect money for *charities*.

Language 1

p. 100	long jump	['lɒŋ ˌdʒʌmp]	Weitsprung →
	race	[reɪs]	Rennen, Lauf
	cricket	['krɪkɪt]	Kricket
	ice-cream	[ˌaɪs'kri:m]	Eis →
	juice	[dʒu:s]	Saft
	exciting	[ɪk'saɪtɪŋ]	aufregend
p. 101	conjunction	[kən'dʒʌŋkʃn]	Konjunktion, Bindewort
	preposition	[ˌprepə'zɪʃn]	Präposition
	style	[staɪl]	Stil
	to connect	[kə'nekt]	verbinden →

Conjunctions *connect* sentences.

Machen

to **do** homework	Hausaufgaben **machen**	to **do** the long jump	Weitsprung **machen**
to **do** sports	Sport **machen**	to **do** an excercise	eine Übung **machen**

Language 3

p. 104	scene	[si:n]	Kulisse
	opening night	['əʊpnɪŋ ˌnaɪt]	Premiere →
	hard	[hɑ:d]	hart, fest; schwierig, schwer
	actor	['æktə]	Schauspieler →
	actress	['æktrəs]	Schauspielerin →
	younger	[jʌŋgə]	jüngere/-r/-s
	may	[meɪ]	dürfen
	to paint	[peɪnt]	streichen; malen →

The *opening night* is the first night of a play or a film.

to act → *actor*
to act → *actress*

to *paint*

one hundred and ninety-three **193**

Vocabulary

Unit 7

p. 104
	scenery [ˈsiːnəri]	Bühnenbild
	to **build** [bɪld]	bauen, aufbauen
	work [wɜːk]	Arbeit
	tired [taɪəd]	müde
	Lord Mayor [ˌlɔːd ˈmeə]	Oberbürgermeister

Kein, keine A B C

Lisa **can't** speak German.	Lisa kann **kein** Deutsch.
No idea.	**Keine** Ahnung.
It's a flat, **not** a house.	Es ist eine Wohnung, **kein** Haus.
Mark **hasn't got** a bike.	Mark hat **kein** Fahrrad.

Story

p. 106
	part [pɔːt]	Rolle
	ill [ɪl]	krank
	library [ˈlaɪbrəri]	Bibliothek, Bücherei →
	stage [steɪdʒ]	Bühne
	excited [ɪkˈsaɪtɪd]	aufgeregt
	ear [ɪə]	Ohr →

p. 107
	Guess what! [ɡes ˈwɒt]	Rate mal!
	to **guess** [ɡes]	raten, erraten
	secret [ˈsiːkrət]	Geheimnis
	finally [ˈfaɪnəli]	endlich, schließlich
	audience [ˈɔːdiəns]	Publikum →
	curtain [ˈkɜːtn]	Vorhang
	to **whisper** [ˈwɪspə]	flüstern
	tail [teɪl]	Schwanz, *hier:* Schweif
	to **wave** [weɪv]	winken →

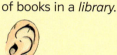

There are lots and lots of books in a *library*.

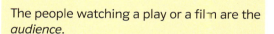

The people watching a play or a film are the *audience*.

to *wave*

Wordwise

p. 108
	meaning [ˈmiːnɪŋ]	Bedeutung
	underlined [ˌʌndəˈlaɪnd]	unterstrichen
	above [əˈbʌv]	über, oberhalb; oben

For my folder 📖
I like ...

Schreibe alle Ausdrücke auf, mit denen du sagen kannst, was du über eine Sache denkst, was du magst/nicht magst und warum du es magst/nicht magst. Die Liste rechts hilft dir. Schau dir auch deine bisher gesammelten Ausdrücke in deinem *English folder* nochmal an. Kannst du sie ergänzen?

Was ich mag/nicht mag:
I think ... is ...	nice
... is ... because ...	boring
I like ... because it's ...	I have fun there
I don't like ... because I must ...	I'm good at ...
	...

Dictionary

English – German

In dieser alphabetischen Liste ist das Vokabular von *Red Line 1* enthalten. Namen werden in einer gesonderten Liste am Ende des Vokabulars aufgelistet.
Wendungen, die aus mehreren Wörtern bestehen, werden meist unter mehreren Stichwörtern aufgeführt. So ist z. B. *a little* sowohl unter *a* als auch unter *little* zu finden.
Die Fundstellen verweisen auf das erstmalige Vorkommen der Wörter, z. B.
about [əˈbaʊt] über **I U1,** 17 kommt zum ersten Mal in Band I, Unit 1, Seite 17, vor.
colour [ˈkʌlə] Farbe **I LUA,** 26 kommt zum ersten Mal in Band I, Link-up A, Seite 26, vor.
bad [bæd] böse ⟨**I ER,** 120⟩ kommt zum ersten Mal in Band I, Extras, Seite 120, vor.
Ist die Fundstelle mit Spitzklammern versehen, weist das darauf hin, dass das Wort zum fakultativen Wortschatz zählt.

A

a [ə], **an** [ən] ein/-e **I U1,** 12
　a few [ə ˈfjuː] ein paar, einige **I U5,** 78
　a little [ə ˈlɪtl] ein bisschen **I U5,** 78
　a lot [ə ˈlɒt] sehr; viel **I U3,** 46
　a lot of [ə ˈlɒt əv] viel/-e, eine Menge **I U2,** 32
about [əˈbaʊt] über; wegen **I U1,** 17
above [əˈbʌv] über, oberhalb ⟨**I U4,** 67⟩; über, oberhalb; oben **I U7,** 108
across [əˈkrɒs] auf der anderen Seite von; über **I U6,** 90
to **act** [ækt] spielen ⟨**I U1,** 23⟩; **I U2,** 37
action [ˈækʃn] Bewegung ⟨**I ER,** 115⟩
actor [ˈæktə] Schauspieler **I U7,** 104
actress [ˈæktrəs] Schauspielerin **I U7,** 104
adjective [ˈædʒɪktɪv] Adjektiv, Eigenschaftswort **I U1,** 24
adult [ˈædʌlt] Erwachsene/-r **I U6,** 86
after [ˈɑːftə] nach **I U3,** 44
　after that [ˈɑːftə ˌðæt] danach **I U3,** 44
afternoon [ˌɑːftəˈnuːn] Nachmittag **I U2,** 36
again [əˈgen] noch einmal, wieder **I U3,** 50
… **ago** [əˈgəʊ] vor … ⟨**I ER,** 120⟩
to **agree** [əˈgriː] zustimmen ⟨**I U2,** 35⟩
alarm clock [əˈlɑːm ˌklɒk] Wecker **I U5,** 81
all [ɔːl] alle **I U2,** 36
alone [əˈləʊn] allein **I U2,** 36
alphabet [ˈælfəbet] Alphabet **I U1,** 19
already [ɔːlˈredi] schon ⟨**I ER,** 121⟩
also [ˈɔːlsəʊ] auch **I U3,** 50
always [ˈɔːlweɪz] immer **I U1,** 16
am [ˌeɪˈem] vormittags **I U3,** 52
am [əm] bin **I U1,** 12
at **anchor** [ət ˈæŋkə] vor Anker ⟨**I ER,** 118⟩
and [ænd; ən] und **I U1,** 12

angry [ˈæŋgri] verärgert, wütend **I U4,** 68
animal [ˈænɪml] Tier **I U6,** 86
　animal snacks [ˈænɪml ˌsnæks] Tierfutter **I U6,** 86
another [əˈnʌðə] noch ein/eine(-r/-s), ein(e) weitere(-r/-s) **I U5,** 81; ein/-e andere/-r ⟨**I ER,** 123⟩
answer [ˈɑːnsə] Antwort **I U1,** 17
to **answer** [ˈɑːnsə] beantworten; antworten **I LUA,** 26
anywhere [ˈeniweə] irgendwohin ⟨**I ER,** 119⟩
apple [ˈæpl] Apfel **I U1,** 18
April [ˈeɪprəl] April **I U5,** 75
are [ɑː] bist, sind, seid **I U1,** 13
　aren't (= are not) [ɑːnt = ɑː ˈnɒt] bist/sind/seid nicht **I U1,** 17
around … [əˈraʊnd] um … herum **I U6,** 94
　around [əˈraʊnd] rund um ⟨**I ER,** 128⟩
to **arrive** [əˈraɪv] ankommen ⟨**I ER,** 125⟩
to **ask** [ɑːsk] fragen; (eine Frage) stellen **I U1,** 17
assistant [əˈsɪstnt] Verkäufer/-in **I U5,** 73
at [æt; ət] an; auf; in; bei; um **I U1,** 12
　at the moment [æt ðə ˈməʊmənt] im Augenblick, momentan **I U5,** 76
audience [ˈɔːdiəns] Publikum **I U7,** 107
August [ˈɔːgəst] August **I U5,** 75
aunt [ɑːnt] Tante **I U2,** 30
autumn [ˈɔːtəm] Herbst **I U6,** 87
awful [ˈɔːfl] schrecklich **I U4,** 68

B

baby [ˈbeɪbi] pl. **babies** [ˈbeɪbiz] Baby **I U3,** 48
back [bæk] zurück **I U5,** 80
bad [bæd] böse ⟨**I ER,** 120⟩; schlecht **I U3,** 53

badminton [ˈbædmɪntən] Badminton, Federball **I U3,** 42
bag [bæg] Tasche; Tüte **I U1,** 16
ball [bɔːl] Ball **I U1,** 22
band [bænd] Band **I U3,** 42
bang [bæŋ] Knall **I U4,** 68
bar [bɑː] Tafel **I U5,** 78
to **bark** [bɑːk] bellen **I U3,** 50
barn [bɑːn] Stall; Scheune **I U6,** 86
basketball [ˈbɑːskɪtbɔːl] Basketball **I LUB,** 40
bathroom [ˈbɑːθrʊm] Badezimmer **I LUA,** 26
to **be** [biː] sein **I U1,** 16
　Be careful! [ˌbiː ˈkeəfl] Sei vorsichtig! **I U6,** 86
　to be a pain [ˌbiː ə ˈpeɪn] jdm. auf den Geist gehen (*Umgangssprache*) **I U2,** 36
　to be good at … [ˌbiː ˈgʊd ət] … gut können; gut sein in … **I U1,** 22
　to be scared [ˌbiː ˈskeəd] Angst haben **I U4,** 64
beard [bɪəd] Bart ⟨**I ER,** 118⟩
beautiful [ˈbjuːtɪfl] schön, wunderschön, wundervoll **I U4,** 68
because [bɪˈkɒz] weil, da **I U2,** 31
to **become** [bɪˈkʌm] werden ⟨**I ER,** 127⟩
bed [bed] Bett **I LUA,** 27
　to go to bed [ˌgəʊ tə ˈbed] ins Bett gehen **I U3,** 52
bedroom [ˈbedrʊm] Schlafzimmer **I LUA,** 26
before [bɪˈfɔː] bevor; vor; vorher **I U3,** 50
behind [bɪˈhaɪnd] hinter **I U1,** 20
to **believe** [bɪˈliːv] glauben **I U4,** 68
bell [bel] Glocke ⟨**I ER,** 124⟩
best [best] beste/-r/-s **I U4,** 66
better [ˈbetə] besser **I U5,** 81
between [bɪˈtwiːn] zwischen **I LUC,** 56
big [bɪg] groß **I U1,** 14
bike [baɪk] Fahrrad **I LUB,** 40
birthday [ˈbɜːθdeɪ] Geburtstag **I U5,** 72

Dictionary

English – German

black [blæk] schwarz I LUA, 26
to **blow up** [bləʊ 'ʌp] in die Luft jagen ⟨I ER, 128⟩
blue [bluː] blau I LUA, 26
board [bɔːd] Tafel; Brett I U1, 20
on **board** [ˈɒn bɔːd] an Bord ⟨I ER, 118⟩
boat [bəʊt] Boot ⟨I ER, 122⟩
book [bʊk] Buch I U1, 18
boring [ˈbɔːrɪŋ] langweilig I U1, 22
born [bɔːn] geboren I U6, 86
to **borrow** [ˈbɒrəʊ] ausleihen ⟨I ER, 126⟩
both [bəʊθ] beide I U5, 89
both ... and [bəʊθ] sowohl ... als auch I U6, 86
bottle [ˈbɒtl] Flasche I U5, 78
bowl [bəʊl] Schüssel ⟨I U5, 79⟩
box [bɒks] Schachtel; Karton; Kiste I U5, 78
boy [bɔɪ] Junge I U1, 16
to **break** [breɪk] brechen ⟨I U5, 79⟩
breakfast [ˈbrekfəst] Frühstück I U3, 44
bridge [brɪdʒ] Brücke I LUC, 56
to **bring** [brɪŋ] mitbringen; bringen I U2, 37
British [ˈbrɪtɪʃ] britisch; Brite/Britin I U2, 31
brochure [ˈbrəʊʃə] Broschüre I U4, 60
brother [ˈbrʌðə] Bruder I LUA, 27
brought [brɔːt] brachte ⟨I ER, 118⟩
brown [braʊn] braun I LUA, 26
to **build** [bɪld] bauen, aufbauen I U7, 104
burger [ˈbɜːgə] Burger I U4, 62
bus [bʌs] pl. **buses** [ˈbʌsɪz] Bus I U3, 46
bus stop [ˈbʌs ˌstɒp] Bushaltestelle I LUC, 56
busy [ˈbɪzi] beschäftigt I U2, 37
but [bʌt] aber I U1, 14
to **buy** [baɪ] kaufen I U5, 72
by [baɪ] mit I U3, 47
Bye! [baɪ] Tschüss! ⟨I U2, 35⟩; I U3, 44

C

cabin [ˈkæbɪn] Kajüte ⟨I ER, 118⟩
cabin boy [ˈkæbɪn ˌbɔɪ] Schiffsjunge ⟨I ER, 118⟩
café [ˈkæfeɪ] Café I U3, 50
cafeteria [ˌkæfəˈtɪəriə] Cafeteria I U1, 22
cake [keɪk] Kuchen I U4, 69
calendar [ˈkæləndə] Kalender I U5, 75
call [kɔːl] Anruf I U2, 34
to **call** [kɔːl] anrufen; rufen; nennen I U2, 34
came down ... [ˌkeɪm 'daʊn] fuhr ... herunter ⟨I ER, 127⟩

camera [ˈkæmrə] Kamera ⟨I ER, 122⟩
can [kæn] können I U1, 25
candle [ˈkændl] Kerze I U5, 78
cap [kæp] Kappe, Schirmmütze I U6, 88
captain [ˈkæptɪn] Kapitän I U4, 68
car [kɑː] Auto I U2, 28
card [kɑːd] Karte; Spielkarte I LUA, 26
caretaker [ˈkeəˌteɪkə] Hausmeister/-in I U1, 14
carol-singing [ˈkærəl ˌsɪŋɪŋ] Weihnachtslieder singen ⟨I ER, 129⟩
carrot [ˈkærət] Karotte ⟨I ER, 129⟩
to **carry** [ˈkæri] tragen I U6, 90
cat [kæt] Katze I U2, 29
to **catch** [kætʃ] fangen ⟨I ER, 119⟩; ⟨I ER, 126⟩
caught [kɔːt] fing ⟨I ER, 127⟩
CD [ˌsiːˈdiː] CD I U2, 38
centre [ˈsentə] Zentrum; Mitte I LUC, 56
tourist information centre [ˌtʊərɪst ɪnfəˈmeɪʃn sentə] Touristik-Information I LUC, 56
chair [tʃeə] Stuhl I U1, 20
chant [tʃɑːnt] Sprechgesang ⟨I ER, 114⟩
charity [ˈtʃærɪti] Wohltätigkeitsverein I U7, 98
to **chase** [tʃeɪs] verfolgen; jagen; hinterherrennen I U3, 47
to **check-in** [ˈtʃekɪn] einchecken I U1, 12
to **check-out** [ˈtʃekaʊt] auschecken I U1, 12
cheese [tʃiːz] Käse I U5, 83
chicken [ˈtʃɪkɪn] Huhn, Hähnchen I U6, 87
child [tʃaɪld] pl. **children** [ˈtʃɪldrən] Kind I U2, 29
to **chime** [tʃaɪm] schlagen ⟨I ER, 120⟩
chimney [ˈtʃɪmni] Kamin ⟨I ER, 129⟩
chocolate [ˈtʃɒklət] Schokolade I U1, 20
chocolate crispie [ˌtʃɒklət 'krɪspi] Schokocrossie I U5, 79
plain **chocolate** [ˌpleɪn 'tʃɒklət] Zartbitterschokolade ⟨I U5, 79⟩
chorus [ˈkɔːrəs] Refrain ⟨I ER, 129⟩
Christmas [ˈkrɪsməs] Weihnachten I U5, 75; ⟨I ER, 128⟩
Christmas Day [ˌkrɪsməs 'deɪ] 1. Weihnachtstag ⟨I ER, 129⟩
Christmas Eve [ˌkrɪsməs 'iːv] Heiliger Abend ⟨I ER, 129⟩
Christmas pudding [ˌkrɪsməs 'pʊdɪŋ] Plumpudding ⟨I ER, 129⟩
church [tʃɜːtʃ] Kirche I LUC, 56
cinema [ˈsɪnəmə] Kino I U3, 45
to **clap** [klæp] klatschen I U1, 19
class [klɑːs] Klasse I U4, 63

classroom [ˈklɑːsruːm] Klassenzimmer I U1, 16
clean [kliːn] sauber I U2, 37
to **clean** [kliːn] aufräumen; putzen, sauber machen I U2, 34
clever [ˈklevə] klug ⟨I ER, 125⟩
clock [klɒk] Uhr I U3, 43
alarm clock [əˈlɑːm ˌklɒk] Wecker I U5, 81
to **close** [kləʊz] schließen, zumachen I LUA, 26
closed [kləʊzd] geschlossen ⟨I ER, 122⟩
clothes pl. [kləʊðz] Kleidung, Kleider I U6, 88
club [klʌb] Klub; Verein I U3, 42
clubhouse [ˈklʌbhaʊs] Klubhaus I U2, 36
coach [kəʊtʃ] Kutsche ⟨I ER, 126⟩
coin [kɔɪn] Münze ⟨I ER, 126⟩
cold [kəʊld] kalt I U6, 85
to **collect** [kəˈlekt] sammeln; einsammeln; abholen I LUB, 40
collector [kəˈlektə] Sammler/-in I LUB, 40
colour [ˈkʌlə] Farbe I LUA, 26
to **colour** [ˈkʌlə] anmalen, ausmalen; malen I U2, 29
to **come** [kʌm] kommen I U2, 34
to come over [ˌkʌm 'əʊvə] herüberkommen I U2, 36
comic [ˈkɒmɪk] Comic(heft) I U5, 73
communication [kəˌmjuːnɪˈkeɪʃn] Verständigung, Kommunikation, Vermittlung I U6, 89
communication skills [kəˌmjuːnɪˈkeɪʃn 'skɪlz] Gesprächstechniken I U6, 89
to **compare** [kəmˈpeə] vergleichen I U7, 99
computer [kəmˈpjuːtə] Computer I LUA, 27
conjunction [kənˈdʒʌŋkʃn] Konjunktion, Bindewort I U7, 101
to **connect** [kəˈnekt] verbinden I U7, 101
cook [kʊk] Koch/Köchin ⟨I ER, 125⟩
to **cook** [kʊk] kochen ⟨I ER, 125⟩
cool [kuːl] cool; klasse I U1, 14
to **copy** [ˈkɒpi] abmalen; abschreiben; kopieren I U1, 18
corner [ˈkɔːnə] Ecke I LUB, 40
cornflake [ˈkɔːnfleɪk] Cornflake ⟨I U5, 79⟩
correct [kəˈrekt] richtig I U3, 46
to **correct** [kəˈrekt] korrigieren I U4, 60
to **count** [kaʊnt] zählen I U5, 78
country [ˈkʌntri] pl. **countries** [ˈkʌntriz] Land I U2, 31
in the country [ˌɪn ðə ˈkʌntri] auf dem Land ⟨I ER, 124⟩

Dictionary D

English – German

cousin ['kʌzn] Cousin/-e I U2, 30
to cover ['kʌvə] bedecken, abdecken ⟨I U5, 79⟩
cow [kaʊ] Kuh I U6, 86
cracker ['krækə] Knallbonbon ⟨I ER, 127⟩
crew [kru:] Besatzung ⟨I ER, 118⟩
cricket ['krɪkɪt] Kricket I U7, 100
crisp [krɪsp] Kartoffelchip I U1, 20
to cross [krɒs] überqueren; kreuzen I LUC, 57
to crouch [kraʊtʃ] kauern ⟨I ER, 115⟩
cupboard ['kʌbəd] Schrank I U1, 20
curtain ['kɜ:tn] Vorhang I U7, 107
customer ['kʌstəmə] Kunde/Kundin I U5, 73
to cut [kʌt] schneiden I U6, 90
cute [kju:t] süß, niedlich I U6, 94
cutlass ['kʌtləs] Entermesser ⟨I U4, 67⟩

D

dad [dæd] Vati, Papa I LUA, 27
to dance [dɑ:ns] tanzen I U3, 42
date [deɪt] Datum I U5, 80
daughter ['dɔ:tə] Tochter I U2, 30
day [deɪ] Tag I LUB, 41
dead [ded] tot I U2, 31
dear [dɪə] Schatz ⟨I ER, 127⟩
Dear … [dɪə] Liebe/-r … I U3, 46
December [dɪ'sembə] Dezember I U5, 75
department store [dɪ'pɑ:tmənt ˌstɔ:] Kaufhaus, Warenhaus I LUC, 56
desk [desk] Lehrerpult; Schreibtisch (zu Hause) I U1, 20
dessert [dɪ'zɜ:t] Nachtisch I U6, 90
dialogue ['daɪəlɒg] Dialog; Gespräch I LUB, 41
diamond ['daɪəmənd] Rhombus ⟨I ER, 114⟩
diary ['daɪəri] Tagebuch I U1, 17
dictionary ['dɪkʃənri] Wörterbuch I U5, 82
Did … get in? [dɪd … ˌget ɪn] Ist … reingekommen? ⟨I ER, 119⟩
did happen [dɪd 'hæpn] ist geschehen ⟨I ER, 119⟩
did lose [dɪd lu:z] hat verloren ⟨I ER, 120⟩
Did you know …? [dɪd jɔ: 'nəʊ] Habt ihr gewusst …? ⟨I ER, 123⟩
didn't see … ['dɪdənt ˌsi:] sah … nicht ⟨I ER, 127⟩
different ['dɪfrənt] anders; andere/-r/-s I U1, 25
ding [dɪŋ] bim ⟨I ER, 120⟩

dining room ['daɪnɪŋ rʊm] Esszimmer I LUA, 26
dinner ['dɪnə] Mittagessen; Abendessen I U2, 30
dirty ['dɜ:ti] schmutzig, dreckig I U2, 32
discman ['dɪskmən] tragbarer CD-Player I U2, 32
disco ['dɪskəʊ] Disko I U5, 80
divorced [dɪ'vɔ:st] geschieden I U2, 30
to do [du:] machen, tun I U1, 19
dog [dɒg] Hund I U2, 28
 to take the dog for a walk [teɪk ðə 'dɒg fɔ:r ə ˌwɔ:k] den Hund ausführen I U2, 34
door [dɔ:] Tür I U1, 20
down [daʊn] entlang; herunter, hinunter, nach unten I LUC, 57
downstairs [ˌdaʊn'steəz] unten (im Gebäude) I U2, 29
drama ['drɑ:mə] Schauspiel I U3, 42
 Drama Club ['drɑ:mə ˌklʌb] Theaterklub I U3, 42
to draw [drɔ:] zeichnen; malen I LUA, 27
dream [dri:m] Traum I LUA, 27
drink [drɪŋk] Getränk I U3, 51
to drink [drɪŋk] trinken I U6, 91
to drive [draɪv] fahren I U4, 60
driver ['draɪvə] Fahrer/-in I U4, 59
drum [drʌm] Trommel, Plural Schlagzeug I U2, 29
DVD [ˌdi: vi: 'di:] DVD I U5, 74

E

each other [ˌi:tʃ 'ʌðə] einander ⟨I ER, 121⟩
ear [ɪə] Ohr ⟨I U4, 67⟩; I U7, 106
east [i:st] Osten I U4, 58
Easter ['i:stə] Ostern ⟨I ER, 128⟩
easy ['i:zi] einfach, leicht I U1, 22
to eat [i:t] essen I U3, 44
egg [eg] Ei I U5, 78
e-mail ['i:meɪl] E-Mail ⟨I U2, 35⟩; I U2, 38
end [end] Ende I U4, 66
to end [end] zu Ende gehen, enden; beenden I U4, 66
English ['ɪŋglɪʃ] englisch, Englisch; Engländer/-in I U1, 18
er [ɜ:] äh I U1, 14
European [ˌjʊərə'pi:ən] europäisch; Europäer/-in I U2, 31
even ['i:vn] sogar I U7, 98
evening ['i:vnɪŋ] Abend I U3, 51
event [ɪ'vent] Veranstaltung I U7, 98
every ['evri] jede/-r/-s I U3, 42

everybody ['evriˌbɒdi] jede/-r/-s I U6, 86
everything ['evriθɪŋ] alles I U4, 62
everywhere ['evriweə] überall I U4, 60
example [ɪg'zɑ:mpl] Beispiel I U1, 15
excited [ɪk'saɪtɪd] aufgeregt I U7, 106
exciting [ɪk'saɪtɪŋ] aufregend I U7, 100
Excuse me. [ɪk'skju:z mi] Entschuldigung!, Entschuldige!, Entschuldigen Sie! I LUC, 57
exercise ['eksəsaɪz] Übung I U1, 18
 exercise book ['eksəsaɪz ˌbʊk] Heft I U1, 18
expensive [ɪk'spensɪv] teuer I U5, 74
to explain [ɪk'spleɪn] erklären ⟨I ER, 122⟩
extra ['ekstrə] extra, besonders I U5, 72
eye [aɪ] Auge I U4, 68

F

face [feɪs] Gesicht I U3, 50
fair [feə] Fest; Markt, Jahrmarkt I U7, 98
to fall [fɔ:l] fallen I U4, 69
 to fall asleep [ˌfɔ:l ə'sli:p] einschlafen I U3, 51
 to fall over [fɔ:l 'əʊvə] umfallen; (Person) hinfallen I U3, 51
false [fɔ:ls] falsch I U4, 64
family ['fæməli] Familie I LUA, 27
family tree [ˌfæməli 'tri:] Stammbaum I U2, 30
famous ['feɪməs] berühmt, bekannt I U4, 58
far [fɑ:] weit ⟨I ER, 121⟩
farm [fɑ:m] Bauernhof I U6, 86
 farm park ['fɑ:m ˌpɑ:k] Farmtierpark I U6, 86
farmer ['fɑ:mə] Bauer/Bäuerin, Landwirt/-in I U6, 86
fast [fɑ:st] schnell I U4, 60
 faster ['fɑ:stə] schneller ⟨I ER, 121⟩
 fastest ['fɑ:stɪst] schnellste/-r/-s ⟨I ER, 118⟩
father ['fɑ:ðə] Vater I LUA, 27
favourite ['feɪvrɪt] Lieblings- I U1, 14
February ['febrʊri] Februar I U5, 75
to feed [fi:d] füttern I U6, 86
to feel [fi:l] fühlen ⟨I ER, 121⟩
festival ['festɪvl] Festival; Fest I U7, 98
a few [ə 'fju:] ein paar, einige I U5, 78
field [fi:ld] Sportfeld; Wiese I U3, 42
fight [faɪt] Kampf; Streit I U4, 69
to fight [faɪt] kämpfen; (sich) streiten I U4, 69
to fill in [fɪl 'ɪn] ausfüllen I U1, 18
film [fɪlm] Film I U3, 45

one hundred and ninety-seven 197

D Dictionary

English – German

finally ['faɪnəli] endlich, schließlich I U7, 107
to find [faɪnd] finden I U1, 24
fine [faɪn] gut I U3, 45
finger ['fɪŋə] Finger ⟨I U4, 67⟩
to finish ['fɪnɪʃ] beenden, fertig machen I U1, 17
fire ['faɪə] Feuer ⟨I ER, 128⟩
fireworks ['faɪəwɜːks] Feuerwerk ⟨I ER, 128⟩
first [fɜːst] zuerst; als Erste/-r/-s; erste/-r/-s I U2, 34
flag [flæg] Flagge, Fahne I U2, 31
flat [flæt] Wohnung I U2, 28
flour [flaʊə] Mehl I U5, 78
flower [flaʊə] Blume ⟨I ER, 128⟩
folder ['fəʊldə] Mappe, Hefter, Ordner I U1, 24
to follow ['fɒləʊ] folgen ⟨I ER, 119⟩
food [fuːd] Essen; Lebensmittel I U5, 74
foot [fʊt] pl. **feet** [fiːt] Fuß I U4, 58
football ['fʊtbɔːl] Fußball I U1, 14
for [fɔː] für I U1, 18
to forget [fə'get] vergessen I U3, 44
form [fɔːm] Form I U1, 16
free [friː] frei; kostenlos I U3, 45
French [frentʃ] französisch, Französisch I U2, 31
Friday ['fraɪdeɪ] Freitag I LUB, 41
Fridays ['fraɪdeɪz] freitags I U3, 42
friend [frend] Freund/-in I U1, 14
from [frɒm] aus, von I U1, 12
 from all round the world [frɒm ɔːl ˌraʊnd ðə 'wɜːld] aus der ganzen Welt I U4, 59
fruit [fruːt] Obst ⟨I ER, 129⟩
full [fʊl] voll ⟨I U4, 67⟩; I U7, 98
fun [fʌn] Spaß I U2, 36
funny ['fʌni] lustig; komisch I LUA, 27
furniture ['fɜːnɪtʃə] Möbel I LUA, 27

G

game [geɪm] Spiel I U1, 19
garden ['gɑːdn] Garten I U2, 29
genitive ['dʒenɪtɪv] Genitiv ⟨I U3, 49⟩
German ['dʒɜːmən] Deutsch, deutsch; Deutsche/-r I U1, 13
to get lost [ˌget 'lɒst] sich verirren, sich verlaufen I U3, 50
to get to … ['get tʊ] zu/nach … kommen I LUC, 57
to get up [ˌget 'ʌp] aufstehen I U3, 44
ghost [gəʊst] Geist I U4, 58

gift shop ['gɪft ˌʃɒp] Geschenkladen, Souvenirshop I U6, 86
girl [gɜːl] Mädchen I U1, 16
to give [gɪv] geben ⟨I U4, 61⟩; I U4, 68
glass [glɑːs] Glas ⟨I ER, 129⟩
to go [gəʊ] gehen I U2, 36
 Go away! [ˌgəʊ ə'weɪ] Geh weg! I U6, 94
 to go on [gəʊ 'ɒn] weitermachen I U1, 15
 to go shopping [gəʊ 'ʃɒpɪŋ] einkaufen gehen I U5, 75
 to go swimming [gəʊ 'swɪmɪŋ] schwimmen gehen I LUB, 40
 to go to bed [gəʊ tə 'bed] ins Bett gehen I U3, 52
goat [gəʊt] Ziege I U6, 86
gold [gəʊld] Gold ⟨I ER, 124⟩
good [gʊd] gut I U1, 16
 good morning [gʊd 'mɔːnɪŋ] guten Morgen I U1, 16
 good tidings [ˌgʊd 'taɪdɪŋz] gute Botschaft ⟨I ER, 129⟩
goodbye [gʊd'baɪ] tschüss, auf Wiedersehen; auf Wiederhören I U1, 22
goose [guːs] pl. **geese** [giːs] Gans I U6, 86
gram [græm] Gramm I U5, 78
grammar ['græmə] Grammatik I U1, 16
grandad ['grændæd] Opa I LUA, 27
grandfather ['grænˌfɑːðə] Großvater I LUA, 27
grandma ['grænmɑː] Oma I LUA, 27
grandmother ['grænˌmʌðə] Großmutter I LUA, 27
grandparents ['grænˌpeərnts] Großeltern I U2, 31
grass [grɑːs] Gras I U6, 95
great [greɪt] großartig; toll I U2, 31
Greek [griːk] griechisch, Griechisch; Grieche/Griechin I U2, 31
green [griːn] grün I LUA, 26
grey [greɪ] grau I LUA, 26
grid [grɪd] Tabelle, Gitter I U1, 18
group [gruːp] Klasse; Gruppe I U1, 14
to guess [ges] raten, erraten ⟨I U5, 77⟩; I U7, 107
 Guess what! [ges 'wɒt] Rate mal! I U7, 107
guide [gaɪd] Führer/-in ⟨I ER, 118⟩
guitar [gɪ'tɑː] Gitarre I LUB, 40
guy [gaɪ] Guy-Fawkes-Puppe ⟨I ER, 128⟩
guys [gaɪz] Leute ⟨I ER, 119⟩

H

had [hæd] hatte ⟨I ER, 119⟩
half [hɑːf] pl. **halves** [hɑːvz] Hälfte I U3, 42
 half past (two) [ˌhɑːf 'pɑːst] halb (drei) I U3, 42
half-sister ['hɑːfˌsɪstə] Halbschwester I U2, 28
hall [hɔːl] Aula, Saal; Flur I U3, 42
ham [hæm] Schinken I U6, 95
hand [hænd] Hand ⟨I U4, 67⟩; ⟨I ER, 125⟩
to happen ['hæpn] geschehen, passieren I U3, 51
 happened ['hæpnd] geschah ⟨I ER, 123⟩
happy ['hæpi] fröhlich; glücklich I LUA, 27
 Happy Birthday! ['hæpi ˌbɜːθdeɪ] Alles Gute zum Geburtstag I U5, 80
 Happy New Year ['hæpi ˌnjuː jɪə] gutes neues Jahr ⟨I ER, 129⟩
hard [hɑːd] hart, fest ⟨I U5, 79⟩; hart, fest; schwierig, schwer I U7, 104
hat [hæt] Hut ⟨I ER, 124⟩
to have [hæv] haben I U2, 32
 to have got ['hæv gɒt] haben, besitzen I U2, 32
he [hiː] er I U1, 14
 he's (= he is) [hiːz = hiː ɪz] er ist I U1, 14
head [hed] Kopf I U4, 64
heading ['hedɪŋ] Überschrift I U5, 81
headteacher [ˌhed'tiːtʃə] Schulleiter/-in ⟨I ER, 121⟩
to hear [hɪə] hören I U6, 94
hello ['heləʊ] hallo I U1, 12
help [help] Hilfe I U4, 68
to help [help] helfen I U2, 34
her [hɜː] ihr/-e; sie; ihr I U1, 17
here [hɪə] hier I U1, 14
 here's (= here is) [hɪəz = 'hɪər ɪz] hier ist I U1, 14
 Here you are! ['hɪə juː ɑː] Bitte schön! I U1, 22
Hey! [heɪ] He! I U1, 14
Hi! [haɪ] Hi!, Hallo! I U1, 12
him [hɪm] ihn; ihm I U4, 60
hip [hɪp] Hüfte ⟨I U4, 67⟩
his [hɪz] sein/-e I LUA, 27
hobby ['hɒbi] Hobby I LUB, 40
hold [həʊld] Laderaum ⟨I ER, 118⟩
home [həʊm] zu Hause, Zuhause; Heim I U1, 13
homework ['həʊmwɜːk] Hausaufgaben I U1, 21

Dictionary

English – German

horse [hɔːs] Pferd **I U6**, 86
hostel [ˈhɒstl] Herberge **I U6**, 86
hot [hɒt] heiß ⟨**I U5**, 79⟩; ⟨**I ER**, 113⟩
hour [aʊə] Stunde **I U3**, 44
house [haʊs] Haus **I LUA**, 27
how [haʊ] wie **I U1**, 13
  How about ...? [ˈhaʊ əˌbaʊt] Wie steht's mit ...?, Wie wär's mit ...? **I U3**, 42
  How are you? [haʊ ˈɑː juː] Wie geht es dir/euch/Ihnen? **I U3**, 45
  How many ...? [haʊ ˈmeni] Wie viele ...? **I U5**, 78
  How much is/are ...? [haʊ ˈmʌtʃ] Wie viel kostet/kosten ...? **I U5**, 73
  How old are you? [haʊ ˈəʊld ə juː] Wie alt bist du/sind Sie? **I U1**, 13
hungry [ˈhʌŋɡri] hungrig **I U6**, 86
hurry [ˈhʌri] Eile **I U2**, 32

I

I [aɪ] ich **I U1**, 12
  I'm (= I am) [aɪm = aɪ əm] ich bin **I U1**, 12
  I would like (= I'd like) ... [aɪ wʊd laɪk = aɪd laɪk] Ich möchte gern ..., Ich hätte gern **I U5**, 74
ice-cream [ˌaɪsˈkriːm] Eis **I U7**, 100
idea [aɪˈdɪə] Idee, Einfall; Ahnung **I U2**, 36
idiot [ˈɪdiət] Idiot/-in, Dummkopf **I U1**, 23
ill [ɪl] krank **I U7**, 106
in [ɪn] in; hinein, herein **I U1**, 12
to **include** [ɪnˈkluːd] enthalten ⟨**I ER**, 113⟩
information [ˌɪnfəˈmeɪʃn] Information(en); Auskunft **I LUC**, 56
  tourist information centre [ˌtʊərɪst ɪnfəˈmeɪʃn sentə] Touristik-Information **I LUC**, 56
interested [ˈɪntrəstɪd] interessiert **I U2**, 29
interesting [ˈɪntrəstɪŋ] interessant **I U4**, 59
Internet [ˈɪntənet] Internet ⟨**I U4**, 58⟩; ⟨**I ER**, 129⟩
into [ˈɪntə] in; hinein **I U2**, 34
invitation [ˌɪnvɪˈteɪʃn] Einladung **I U5**, 74
to **invite** [ɪnˈvaɪt] einladen **I U5**, 74
irregular [ɪˈreɡjələ] unregelmäßig **I U6**, 97
is [ɪz] ist **I U1**, 12

isn't (= is not) [ˈɪznt = ɪz ˈnɒt] ist nicht **I U1**, 16
  ... is high [ɪz ˈhaɪ] ... steht hoch ⟨**I ER**, 120⟩
island [ˈaɪlənd] Insel **I U4**, 68
it [ɪt] es **I U1**, 16
  it's (= it is) [ɪts = ɪt ɪz] es ist **I U1**, 16
Italian [ɪˈtæliən] italienisch, Italienisch; Italiener/-in **I U2**, 31
its [ɪts] sein/-e, ihr/-e **I U2**, 28

J

January [ˈdʒænjuri] Januar **I U5**, 75
jeans pl. [dʒiːnz] Jeans **I U6**, 88
joke [dʒəʊk] Witz **I U1**, 22
jolly [ˈdʒɒli] fröhlich, vergnügt ⟨**I U4**, 67⟩
juice [dʒuːs] Saft **I U7**, 100
July [dʒʊˈlaɪ] Juli **I U5**, 75
jumbled [ˈdʒʌmbld] durcheinander geworfen **I U6**, 87
to **jump** [dʒʌmp] springen ⟨**I ER**, 115⟩
June [dʒuːn] Juni **I U5**, 75
just [dʒʌst] nur **I U2**, 32

K

key [kiː] Erklärung, Legende; Schlüssel **I LUC**, 56
kid [kɪd] Kind **I U4**, 60; Zicklein **I U6**, 86
to **kill** [kɪl] töten ⟨**I ER**, 128⟩
kin [kɪn] Verwandte/-r ⟨**I ER**, 129⟩
kind [kaɪnd] Art **I U7**, 98
kitchen [ˈkɪtʃɪn] Küche **I LUA**, 26
to **know** [nəʊ] wissen; kennen **I U3**, 44

L

lads [lædz] Jungs ⟨**I ER**, 120⟩
lamb [læm] Lamm **I U6**, 86
land [lænd] Festland ⟨**I ER**, 119⟩
language [ˈlæŋɡwɪdʒ] Sprache **I U1**, 12
lantern [ˈlæntən] Laterne **I U7**, 98
large [lɑːdʒ] groß **I U5**, 72
last [lɑːst] letzte/-r/-s **I U4**, 70
  last, as usual [ˈlɑːst əz ˈjuːʒl] wie üblich Letzte/-r ⟨**I ER**, 118⟩
late [leɪt] zu spät, spät **I U1**, 16
later [ˈleɪtə] später **I U2**, 32
to **laugh** [lɑːf] lachen **I U6**, 94
to **learn** [lɜːn] lernen **I U3**, 42
to **leave** [liːv] abfahren; verlassen; lassen **I U4**, 61

left [left] links; linke/-r/-s **I LUC**, 57
  on the left [ˌɒn ðə ˈleft] links **I LUC**, 57
leg [leɡ] Bein ⟨**I U4**, 67⟩
lemonade [ˌleməˈneɪd] Limonade **I U5**, 78
lesson [ˈlesn] Unterrichtsstunde **I U1**, 19
let's ... [lets] lass(t) uns ... **I U1**, 20
letter [ˈletə] Buchstabe; Brief **I U1**, 19
library [ˈlaɪbrəri] Bibliothek, Bücherei **I U7**, 106
life [laɪf] pl. **lives** [laɪvz] Leben **I U4**, 59
to **lift anchor** [ˌlɪft ˈæŋkə] den Anker lichten ⟨**I ER**, 118⟩
  lifted the anchor [lɪftɪd ði ˈæŋkə] lichtete den Anker ⟨**I ER**, 122⟩
like [laɪk] wie, ähnlich **I LUB**, 41
to **like** [laɪk] mögen; gern haben **I U3**, 46
line [laɪn] Linie **I U4**, 58
lip [lɪp] Lippe ⟨**I U4**, 67⟩
list [lɪst] Liste **I U1**, 18
to **listen** [ˈlɪsn] zuhören; (an)hören **I U1**, 13
listening [ˈlɪsnɪŋ] Hören; Hörübung **I U1**, 13
  listening skills [ˌlɪsnɪŋ ˈskɪlz] Hörtechniken **I U4**, 67
little [ˈlɪtl] klein **I U6**, 94
  a little [ə ˈlɪtl] ein bisschen **I U5**, 78
to **live** [lɪv] wohnen, leben **I U3**, 46
lived [lɪvd] lebte ⟨**I ER**, 120⟩
living room [ˈlɪvɪŋ ruːm] Wohnzimmer **I LUA**, 26
long [lɒŋ] lang **I U1**, 16
  long form [ˈlɒŋ fɔːm] Langform **I U1**, 16
  long jump [ˈlɒŋ ˌdʒʌmp] Weitsprung **I U7**, 100
to **look** [lʊk] schauen, sehen; aussehen **I U2**, 31
  to **look at** [ˈlʊk æt] ansehen, anschauen ⟨**I U1**, 123⟩; **I LUA**, 26
  to **look for** [ˈlʊk fɔː] suchen **I U5**, 76
lost [lɒst] verlor ⟨**I ER**, 123⟩
a lot [ə ˈlɒt] sehr; viel **I U3**, 46
  a lot of [ə ˈlɒt əv] viel/-e, eine Menge **I U2**, 32
lots (of) [lɒts] viel **I U5**, 74
loud [laʊd] laut **I U2**, 36
Love, ... [lʌv] Herzliche Grüße, ..., Liebe Grüße, ... **I U1**, 25
to **love** [lʌv] lieben **I U3**, 47
You're lucky. [jɔː ˈlʌki] Du hast Glück. **I U2**, 31
lunch [lʌntʃ] Mittagessen **I U4**, 62
lunchtime [ˈlʌntʃtaɪm] Mittagszeit **I U5**, 80

Dictionary

English – German

M

magazine [ˌmægəˈziːn] Zeitschrift **I U2**, 32
to make [meɪk] bilden; machen, tun **I U1**, 17
  make people laugh [ˌmeɪk piːpl ˈlɑːf] Leute zum Lachen bringen ⟨**I ER**, 128⟩
man [mæn] pl. **men** [men] Mann **I U5**, 82
manager [ˈmænɪdʒə] Geschäftsführer/-in **I U2**, 28
many [ˈmeni] viele **I U5**, 78
map [mæp] Stadtplan, Landkarte **I LUC**, 56
March [mɑːtʃ] März **I U5**, 74
market [ˈmɑːkɪt] Markt ⟨**I ER**, 126⟩
married [ˈmærɪd] verheiratet **I U2**, 30
master [ˈmɑːstə] Herr, Meister ⟨**I U4**, 67⟩
to match [mætʃ] zuordnen **I U1**, 21
May [meɪ] Mai **I U5**, 75
may [meɪ] dürfen **I U7**, 104
maybe [ˈmeɪbi] vielleicht **I U2**, 32
me [miː] mich; mir, ich ⟨**I U2**, 35⟩; mich; mir **I U3**, 50
to mean [miːn] bedeuten; meinen **I U4**, 66
meaning [ˈmiːnɪŋ] Bedeutung **I U7**, 108
medium [ˈmiːdiəm] mittel **I U5**, 72
to meet [miːt] sich treffen, treffen **I U3**, 43
megaphone [ˈmegəfəʊn] Megafon ⟨**I ER**, 122⟩
to melt [melt] schmelzen ⟨**I U5**, 79⟩
menu [ˈmenjuː] Speisekarte ⟨**I ER**, 113⟩
Meow! [miːˈaʊ] Miau! **I U2**, 36
mess [mes] Unordnung, Durcheinander **I U2**, 32
text **message** [ˈtekst ˌmesɪdʒ] SMS **I U2**, 36
milk [mɪlk] Milch **I U5**, 78
to milk [mɪlk] melken **I U6**, 86
  milking barn [ˈmɪlkɪŋ ˌbɑːn] Melkstall **I U6**, 86
mind map [ˈmaɪnd mæp] Wörternetz (eine Art Schaubild) **I U1**, 24
mini [ˈmɪni] Mini- **I U6**, 86
minute [ˈmɪnɪt] Minute **I LUA**, 26
missing [ˈmɪsɪŋ] fehlend ⟨**I U2**, 35⟩; **I U2**, 38
to mix [mɪks] mischen ⟨**I U5**, 79⟩
mobile [ˈməʊbaɪl] Handy **I U1**, 13
at the **moment** [ˌæt ðə ˈməʊmənt] im Augenblick, momentan **I U5**, 76
Monday [ˈmʌndeɪ] Montag **I LUB**, 41
on Mondays [ˌɒn ˈmʌndeɪz] montags **I U3**, 42
money [ˈmʌni] Geld **I U5**, 73
month [mʌnθ] Monat **I U5**, 75
more [mɔː] mehr; weitere **I LUA**, 27
morning [ˈmɔːnɪŋ] Morgen; Vormittag **I U1**, 16
mother [ˈmʌðə] Mutter **I LUA**, 27
mouse [maʊs] pl. **mice** [maɪs] Maus **I U1**, 12
mouth [maʊθ] Maul ⟨**I ER**, 125⟩
Mr [ˈmɪstə] Herr **I U1**, 14
Mrs [ˈmɪsɪz] Frau **I U1**, 14
much [mʌtʃ] viel **I U5**, 73
mum [mʌm] Mutti, Mama **I U1**, 16
museum [mjuːˈziːəm] Museum **I LUC**, 56
music [ˈmjuːzɪk] Musik **I U2**, 34
must [mʌst] müssen **I U6**, 92
my [maɪ] mein/-e **I U1**, 12
  My name is … [maɪ ˈneɪm ɪz] Mein Name ist …; Ich heiße … **I U1**, 12

N

name [neɪm] Name **I U1**, 12
near [nɪə] in der Nähe von; nahe **I LUC**, 56
to need [niːd] brauchen **I U5**, 78
needn't [ˈniːdnt] nicht müssen, nicht brauchen **I U6**, 92
neighbour [ˈneɪbə] Nachbar/-in ⟨**I ER**, 129⟩
never [ˈnevə] nie **I U3**, 44
new [njuː] neu **I U1**, 12
newsagent [ˈnjuːzˌeɪdʒnt] Zeitungsladen **I LUC**, 56
newspaper [ˈnjuːsˌpeɪpə] Zeitung ⟨**I U4**, 58⟩; **I U5**, 72
next [nekst] als nächste/-r/-s **I U6**, 94; nächste/-r/-s **I U7**, 98
  next to [ˈnekst tʊ] neben **I U2**, 30
nice [naɪs] nett; schön **I U1**, 16
night [naɪt] Nacht **I U6**, 86
no [nəʊ] nein; kein/-e **I U1**, 14
nobody [ˈnəʊbədi] niemand ⟨**I ER**, 123⟩
noise [nɔɪz] Geräusch ⟨**I ER**, 125⟩
north [nɔːθ] Norden **I U4**, 58
nose [nəʊz] Nase **I U6**, 89
not [nɒt] nicht; kein/-e **I U1**, 16
November [nəʊˈvembə] November **I U5**, 75
now [naʊ] jetzt, nun **I U1**, 22
number [ˈnʌmbə] Zahl, Nummer **I U1**, 13

O

o'clock [əˈklɒk] Uhr **I U3**, 42
October [ɒkˈtəʊbə] Oktober **I U5**, 75
of [ɒv] von **I U1**, 25
  of course [ˌɒv ˈkɔːs] selbstverständlich, natürlich **I U4**, 60
often [ˈɒfn] oft **I U3**, 45
Oh! [əʊ] Oh! **I U1**, 14
Oink! [ɔɪnk] Grunz! **I U6**, 94
OK [əʊˈkeɪ] o.k., okay **I U1**, 14
old [əʊld] alt **I U1**, 13
on [ɒn] auf; am **I U1**, 20
  on foot [ˌɒn ˈfʊt] zu Fuß **I U4**, 58
  on Mondays [ˌɒn ˈmʌndeɪz] montags **I U3**, 42
  on the left [ˌɒn ðə ˈleft] links **I LUC**, 57
  on the right [ˌɒn ðə ˈraɪt] rechts **I LUC**, 57
only [ˈəʊnli] einzige/-r/-s; nur; erst; bloß **I U2**, 29
  only child [ˈəʊnli ˌtʃaɪld] Einzelkind **I U2**, 29
Oops! [uːps] Hoppla! **I U1**, 22
to open [ˈəʊpn] öffnen, aufmachen **I U2**, 35
opening night [ˈəʊpnɪŋ ˌnaɪt] Premiere **I U7**, 104
opening time [ˈəʊpnɪŋ ˌtaɪm] Öffnungszeit **I U6**, 86
opposite [ˈɒpəzɪt] gegenüber **I LUC**, 56
or [ɔː] oder **I U1**, 13
orange [ˈɒrɪndʒ] orange(farben) **I LUA**, 26
order [ˈɔːdə] Reihenfolge **I U1**, 18
ordinal number [ˈɔːdɪnl ˌnʌmbə] Ordnungszahl **I U5**, 75
to organize [ˈɔːɡənaɪz] organisieren **I U7**, 98
other [ˈʌðə] andere/-r/-s **I U6**, 96
the **others** [ði ˈʌðəz] die anderen ⟨**I U5**, 77⟩
our [aʊə] unser/-e **I U2**, 28
outside [ˌaʊtˈsaɪd] draußen; nach draußen **I U2**, 32
over [ˈəʊvə] über; vorbei **I U2**, 28
  over there [ˌəʊvə ˈðeə] da drüben **I U3**, 48
own [əʊn] eigen **I U2**, 32

P

to pack [pæk] packen **I U6**, 88
packet [ˈpækɪt] Päckchen, Packung **I U5**, 78

Dictionary

English – German

page [peɪdʒ] Seite I U1, 21
to be a pain [ˌbiː ə ˈpeɪn] jdm. auf den Geist gehen (*Umgangssprache*) I U2, 36
to paint [peɪnt] streichen; malen I U7, 104
pair [peə] Paar I U1, 24
paper case [ˈpeɪpə ˌkeɪs] Papierförmchen ⟨I U5, 79⟩
paper hat [ˌpeɪpə ˈhæt] Papierhut ⟨I ER, 129⟩
papers [ˈpeɪpəz] Papiere ⟨I ER, 119⟩
parents [ˈpeərənts] Eltern I U2, 28
park [pɑːk] Park I U2, 35
to park [pɑːk] parken I U4, 62
Parliament [ˈpɑːləmənt] Parlament ⟨I ER, 128⟩
parrot [ˈpærət] Papagei ⟨I U4, 67⟩
part [pɑːt] Teil I U2, 37; Rolle I U7, 106
partner [ˈpɑːtnə] Partner/-in I U1, 17
party [ˈpɑːti] Party, Feier I U1, 20
past [pɑːst] nach (*bei Uhrzeiten*) I U3, 42
to pat [pæt] tätscheln I U6, 94
patch [pætʃ] Augenklappe ⟨I ER, 118⟩
pen [pen] Füller I U1, 18
pencil [ˈpensl] Bleistift I U1, 18
pencil case [ˈpensl ˌkeɪs] Federmäppchen I U1, 18
penny [ˈpeni] pl. pence (p) [pens] Penny, *Plural* Pence (*britisches Geld*) I U5, 73
people [ˈpiːpl] Leute I U2, 39
to perform [pəˈfɔːm] ausführen ⟨I ER, 115⟩
person [ˈpɜːsn] Person I U4, 64
pet [pet] Haustier I U6, 86
pets corner [ˈpets ˌkɔːnə] Streichelzoo I U6, 86
Phew! [fjuː] Mensch! ⟨I ER, 122⟩
phone (= telephone) [fəʊn = ˈtelɪfəʊn] Telefon I U1, 13
phone number [ˈfəʊn ˌnʌmbə] Telefonnummer I U1, 13
to phone [fəʊn] anrufen I U1, 20
photo [ˈfəʊtəʊ] Foto I U5, 72
phrase [freɪz] Ausdruck; Redewendung I U1, 21
pickpocket [ˈpɪkˌpɒkɪt] Taschendieb/-in ⟨I ER, 124⟩
picnic [ˈpɪknɪk] Picknick I U3, 51
picture [ˈpɪktʃə] Bild I U1, 18
piece [piːs] Stück, Teil ⟨I U5, 79⟩; I U6, 90
pig [pɪɡ] Schwein I U6, 86
pink [pɪŋk] rosa, pink I LUA, 26
pirate [ˈpaɪrət] Pirat/-in ⟨I U4, 67⟩; I U4, 68

pizza [ˈpiːtsə] Pizza I U5, 74
place [pleɪs] Platz, Ort, Stelle ⟨I U2, 35⟩; I LUC, 56
plain chocolate [ˌpleɪn ˈtʃɒklət] Zartbitterschokolade ⟨I U5, 79⟩
plan [plæn] Plan I U5, 75
plank [plæŋk] Planke; Brett I U4, 68
planner [ˈplænə] Jahresplaner I U7, 98
play [pleɪ] Theaterstück I U7, 98
to play [pleɪ] spielen I U1, 18
playground [ˈpleɪɡraʊnd] Schulhof; Spielplatz I U1, 22
please [pliːz] bitte I U1, 15
plenty [ˈplenti] genug, ausreichend I U5, 78
plural [ˈplʊərl] Plural, Mehrzahl I U6, 87
pm [ˌpiːˈem] nachmittags I U3, 52
pocket [ˈpɒkɪt] (Hosen-)Tasche ⟨I ER, 125⟩
poem [ˈpəʊɪm] Gedicht I U6, 89
to point [pɔɪnt] zeigen I U1, 20
police [pəˈliːs] Polizei ⟨I ER, 122⟩
policeman [pəˈliːsmən] Polizist ⟨I ER, 122⟩
polite [pəˈlaɪt] höflich ⟨I U2, 34⟩; I U5, 82
pony [ˈpəʊni] Pony ⟨I ER, 113⟩
poor [pɔː] arm ⟨I ER, 119⟩; ⟨I ER, 125⟩; ⟨I ER, 128⟩
popcorn [ˈpɒpkɔːn] Popcorn ⟨I ER, 113⟩
postcard [ˈpəʊstkɑːd] Postkarte I U6, 86
poster [ˈpəʊstə] Poster I U1, 13
pound [paʊnd] Pfund I U5, 73
practice [ˈpræktɪs] Übung; Probe; Training I U3, 46
to practise [ˈpræktɪs] üben I U1, 21
to prepare [prɪˈpeə] vorbereiten ⟨I ER, 114⟩
preposition [ˌprepəˈzɪʃn] Präposition I U7, 101
present [ˈpreznt] Geschenk I U5, 76; Gegenwart I U6, 91
to present [prɪˈzent] präsentieren ⟨I U4, 65⟩; ⟨I ER, 114⟩
present progressive [ˌpreznt prəˈɡresɪv] Verlaufsform der Gegenwart I U6, 91
presentation [ˌpreznˈteɪʃn] Präsentation ⟨I ER, 115⟩
price [praɪs] Preis I U5, 73
prize [praɪz] Preis I U4, 66
problem [ˈprɒbləm] Problem I U1, 22
procession [prəˈseʃn] Umzug I U7, 98
programme [ˈprəʊɡræm] Programm I U4, 64
present progressive [ˌpreznt prəˈɡresɪv] Verlaufsform der Gegenwart I U6, 91
project [ˈprɒdʒekt] Projekt I U2, 36

pronoun [ˈprəʊnaʊn] Pronomen, Fürwort I U4, 71
to pull [pʊl] ziehen ⟨I ER, 129⟩
pullover [ˈpʊləʊvə] Pullover I U6, 86
pupil [ˈpjuːpl] Schüler/-in I U1, 12
purple [ˈpɜːpl] lila I LUA, 26
Purr! [pɜː] Schnurr! ⟨I ER, 125⟩
to push [pʊʃ] stoßen ⟨I ER, 127⟩
to put [pʊt] legen, setzen, stellen, tun I U1, 23
to put in [pʊt ˌɪn] einsetzen I U1, 17
puzzle [ˈpʌzl] Rätsel I U1, 19

Q

quarter [ˈkwɔːtə] Viertel I U3, 43
question [ˈkwestʃən] Frage I U1, 17
quick [kwɪk] schnell I U6, 88
quickly [ˈkwɪkli] schnell I U3, 51
quiet [ˈkwaɪət] ruhig, still I U4, 64
quiz [kwɪz] Quiz, Ratespiel I LUA, 27

R

rabbit [ˈræbɪt] Kaninchen ⟨I ER, 113⟩
race [reɪs] Rennen, Lauf I U7, 100
race ring [ˈreɪs ˌrɪŋ] Rennbahn ⟨I ER, 113⟩
radio [ˈreɪdiəʊ] Radio I U6, 91
to rain [reɪn] regnen I U6, 88
raisin [ˈreɪzn] Rosine ⟨I U5, 79⟩
rap [ræp] Rap I U1, 19
rat [ræt] Ratte ⟨I ER, 119⟩
to read [riːd] lesen I U1, 19
reading skills [ˌriːdɪŋ ˈskɪlz] Lesetechniken I U3, 50
ready [ˈredi] fertig ⟨I U5, 79⟩
real [rɪəl] echt I U6, 86
real talk [ˌrɪəl ˈtɔːk] echtes Alltagsenglisch I U1, 12
really [ˈrɪəli] wirklich I U2, 36
recipe [ˈresɪpi] Rezept I U5, 79
red [red] rot I LUA, 26
regular [ˈreɡjələ] regelmäßig I U6, 97
reindeer [ˈreɪndɪə] Rentier ⟨I ER, 129⟩
relative [ˈrelətɪv] Verwandte/-r ⟨I U2, 35⟩
to remember [rɪˈmembə] denken an, nicht vergessen; sich erinnern an I U7, 98
to repeat [rɪˈpiːt] wiederholen I LUC, 57
reporter [rɪˈpɔːtə] Reporter/-in ⟨I ER, 122⟩
revision [rɪˈvɪʒn] Wiederholung I U2, 35
rhyme [raɪm] Reim I U3, 52

two hundred and one **201**

D Dictionary

English – German

rice crispie [ˌraɪs ˈkrɪspi] Rice Krispie, Puffreis ⟨I U5, 79⟩
rich [rɪtʃ] reich ⟨I ER, 125⟩
ride [raɪd] Ritt I U6, 86
to **ride** [raɪd] fahren; reiten I LUB, 40
right [raɪt] richtig; rechts; rechte/-r/-s I U1, 16
  on the **right** [ˌɒn ðə ˈraɪt] rechts I LUC, 57
right now [ˈraɪt ˌnaʊ] jetzt gerade I U5, 83
ring [rɪŋ] Ring ⟨I U4, 67⟩
to **ring** [rɪŋ] läuten; klingeln I U5, 81
river [ˈrɪvə] Fluss I LUC, 56
road [rəʊd] Straße I U2, 28
role [rəʊl] Rolle I LUB, 41
  role play [ˈrəʊl ˌpleɪ] Rollenspiel I LUB, 41
room [ruːm] Zimmer, Raum; Platz I LUA, 26
round … [raʊnd] um … herum I U4, 59
RSVP [ˌɑːr ˌes viːˈpiː] Um Antwort wird gebeten. I U5, 74
rubber [ˈrʌbə] Radiergummi I U1, 18
rubbish [ˈrʌbɪʃ] Abfall ⟨I ER, 124⟩
rule [ruːl] Regel I U2, 34
ruler [ˈruːlə] Lineal I U1, 18
to **run** [rʌn] rennen, laufen I U4, 69
  to **run away** [ˌrʌn əˈweɪ] wegrennen, weglaufen I U3, 50
Russian [ˈrʌʃn] russisch, Russisch; Russe/Russin I U2, 31

S

safari [səˈfɑːri] Safari I U6, 86
  safari ride [səˈfɑːri ˌraɪd] Safarifahrt I U6, 86
to **sail** [seɪl] segeln I U4, 62
  sailed [seɪld] segelte ⟨I ER, 118⟩
the **same** [seɪm] derselbe/dieselbe/dasselbe ⟨I U2, 34⟩; ⟨I U3, 49⟩; I U4, 63
sandwich [ˈsænwɪdʒ] belegtes Brot, Sandwich I U1, 18
Saturday [ˈsætədeɪ] Samstag, Sonnabend I U2, 36
saved my life [ˌseɪvd maɪ ˈlaɪf] hast mir das Leben gerettet ⟨I ER, 127⟩
saw [sɔː] sah ⟨I ER, 121⟩
to **say** [seɪ] sagen I U1, 18
scar [skɑː] Narbe ⟨I U4, 67⟩
to **scare** [skeə] erschrecken, Angst einjagen I U4, 64
scared [skeəd] ängstlich ⟨I ER, 118⟩

scary [ˈskeəri] unheimlich, gruselig I U4, 60
scene [siːn] Kulisse I U7, 104; Szene ⟨I ER, 124⟩
scenery [ˈsiːnəri] Bühnenbild I U7, 104
school [skuːl] Schule I U1, 12
  school bag [ˈskuːl ˌbæg] Schultasche, Schulranzen I U1, 18
scone [skɒn] brötchenartiges Gebäck I U6, 92
to **scream** [skriːm] schreien ⟨I ER, 126⟩
sea [siː] Meer I U4, 59
seasick [ˈsiːsɪk] seekrank ⟨I ER, 121⟩
season [ˈsiːzn] Jahreszeit I U6, 87
second [ˈsekənd] Sekunde I U2, 32; zweite/-r/-s I U5, 75
secret [ˈsiːkrət] Geheimnis I U7, 107
to **see** [siː] sehen; treffen I U3, 44
  See you. [ˈsiː ˌjuː] Bis dann., Bis bald. I U3, 45
to **sell** [sel] verkaufen I U5, 83
to **send** [send] schicken, senden I U2, 36
sentence [ˈsentəns] Satz I U1, 16
September [sepˈtembə] September I U5, 75
she [ʃiː] sie I U1, 14
  she's (= she is) [ʃiːz = ʃi: ɪz] sie ist I U1, 14
shed [ʃed] Schuppen I U2, 29
sheep [ʃiːp] pl. **sheep** [ʃiːp] Schaf I U6, 86
ship [ʃɪp] Schiff I U4, 59
shoe [ʃuː] Schuh I U1, 14
shop [ʃɒp] Geschäft, Laden I U2, 28
shopping [ˈʃɒpɪŋ] Einkaufen; Einkäufe I U5, 72
  shopping list [ˈʃɒpɪŋ ˌlɪst] Einkaufsliste, Einkaufszettel I U5, 78
  to **go shopping** [ˌgəʊ ˈʃɒpɪŋ] einkaufen gehen I U5, 75
short [ʃɔːt] kurz I U1, 16
  short form [ˈʃɔːt ˌfɔːm] Kurzform I U1, 16
to **shout** [ʃaʊt] schreien, rufen I U1, 19
show [ʃəʊ] Aufführung ⟨I ER, 113⟩
to **show** [ʃəʊ] zeigen I U4, 60
sight [saɪt] Sehenswürdigkeit I U4, 59
silk [sɪlk] Seide ⟨I ER, 126⟩
silly [ˈsɪli] Dummerchen ⟨I ER, 119⟩; dumm; albern I U2, 32
simple present [ˌsɪmpl ˈpreznt] Präsens ⟨I U4, 67⟩; I U6, 91
to **sing** [sɪŋ] singen I U3, 42
sister [ˈsɪstə] Schwester I LUA, 27
to **sit** [sɪt] sich setzen; sitzen I U5, 80
sits with his friends [ˌsɪts wɪð hɪz ˈfrendz] setzt sich zu seinen Freunden I U5, 80

situation [ˌsɪtjuˈeɪʃn] Situation I U4, 61
size [saɪz] Größe I U5, 72
skates [skeɪts] Rollschuhe, Inlineskates I U4, 59
skateboard [ˈskeɪtbɔːd] Skateboard I U4, 59
skill [skɪl] Fertigkeit, Fähigkeit I U1, 24
skirt [skɜːt] Rock I U6, 88
to **sleep** [sliːp] schlafen I U3, 51
small [smɔːl] klein I U2, 28
  smaller [ˈsmɔːlə] kleiner ⟨I ER, 121⟩
to **smile** [smaɪl] lächeln I U5, 80
snack [snæk] Snack, Imbiss I U6, 86
so [səʊ] also; so I U1, 15
sofa [ˈsəʊfə] Sofa I LUA, 27
some [sʌm] einige, ein paar, etwas I U6, 92
something [ˈsʌmθɪŋ] etwas, irgendetwas I U4, 69
sometimes [ˈsʌmtaɪmz] manchmal I U3, 44
son [sʌn] Sohn I U2, 30
song [sɒŋ] Lied I U1, 15
soon [suːn] bald ⟨I ER, 124⟩
Sorry! [ˈsɒri] Entschuldigung!, Verzeihung! I U1, 16
to **sort** [sɔːt] sortieren I U1, 23
  to **sort out** [ˌsɔːt ˈaʊt] klären, lösen; in Ordnung bringen I U2, 32
sound [saʊnd] Laut; Ton; Geräusch I U1, 18
south [saʊθ] Süden I U4, 58
to **speak** [spiːk] sprechen I U3, 44
special [ˈspeʃl] besondere/-r/-s I U5, 77
to **spell** [spel] buchstabieren I U1, 19
spooky [ˈspuːki] gespenstisch, gruselig I U4, 58
spoonful [ˈspuːnfʊl] Löffel (voll) ⟨I U5, 79⟩
sport [spɔːt] Sport I U1, 14
sports day [ˈspɔːts ˌdeɪ] Sportfest I U7, 98
sports hall [ˈspɔːts ˌhɔːl] Sporthalle I U3, 42
spring [sprɪŋ] Frühling, Frühjahr I U6, 86
stage [steɪdʒ] Bühne I U7, 106
stall [stɔːl] Stand I U7, 98
to **stand** [stænd] stehen I U4, 58
to **stand up** [ˈstænd ˌʌp] aufstehen ⟨I ER, 115⟩
to **stare** [steə] starren ⟨I ER, 119⟩
to **start** [stɑːt] anfangen, beginnen I LUB, 41
  Start like this [ˌstɑːt laɪk ˈðɪs] Beginne so I LUB, 41
to **stay** [steɪ] übernachten; bleiben I U6, 86

Dictionary D

English – German

to **steal** [stiːl] stehlen ⟨IER, 122⟩
stepfather [ˈstepˌfɑːðə] Stiefvater IU2, 28
still [stɪl] noch, immer noch IU5, 76
stocking [ˈstɒkɪŋ] Strumpf ⟨IER, 129⟩
to **stop** [stɒp] aufhören; anhalten IU4, 64
stored [stɔːd] gelagert ⟨IER, 118⟩
story [ˈstɔːri] Geschichte IU1, 12
storyteller [ˈstɔːriˌtelə] Erzähler/-in ⟨IER, 124⟩
straight [streɪt] gerade ILUC, 57
  straight into ... [ˈstreɪt ˌɪntə] geradewegs in ... hinein ⟨IER, 122⟩
strange [streɪndʒ] merkwürdig ⟨IER, 123⟩
street [striːt] Straße IU2, 29
style [staɪl] Stil IU7, 101
suddenly [ˈsʌdnli] plötzlich IU4, 68
sugar [ˈʃʊɡə] Zucker IU5, 78
summer [ˈsʌmə] Sommer IU6, 86
sun [sʌn] Sonne IU6, 89
Sunday [ˈsʌndeɪ] Sonntag ILUB, 41
sunglasses pl. [ˈsʌnˌɡlɑːsɪz] Sonnenbrille IU6, 88
sunny [ˈsʌni] sonnig IU6, 88
super [ˈsuːpə] super, toll IU6, 86
supermarket [ˈsuːpəˌmɑːkɪt] Supermarkt ILUC, 56
surprise [səˈpraɪz] Überraschung IU6, 90
sweatshirt [ˈswetʃɜːt] Sweatshirt IU5, 76
sweet [swiːt] Bonbon IU5, 78; süß; niedlich ILUA, 26
to **swim** [swɪm] schwimmen IU6, 89
to go **swimming** [ɡəʊ ˈswɪmɪŋ] schwimmen gehen ILUB, 40

T

table [ˈteɪbl] Tisch IU1, 20
tablespoon [ˈteɪblspuːn] Esslöffel ⟨IU5, 79⟩
tail [teɪl] Schwanz, Schweif IU7, 107
to **take** [teɪk] nehmen; bringen; dauern IU2, 34
  to take pictures [teɪk ˈpɪktʃəz] Fotos schießen ⟨IER, 122⟩
  to take the dog for a walk [teɪk ðə ˈdɒɡ fɔːr ə ˌwɔːk] den Hund ausführen IU2, 34
talk [tɔːk] Unterhaltung, Gespräch IU1, 21
to **talk** [tɔːk] sprechen, reden IU1, 23

taxi [ˈtæksi] Taxi IU4, 60
tea [tiː] Tee IU4, 68
teacher [ˈtiːtʃə] Lehrer/-in IU1, 14
team [tiːm] Team, Mannschaft IU4, 66
telescope [ˈtelɪskəʊp] Fernrohr ⟨IER, 119⟩
to **tell** [tel] sagen; erzählen IU3, 43
text [tekst] Text IU2, 28
  text message [ˈtekst ˌmesɪdʒ] SMS IU2, 36
thank you [ˈθæŋk juː] danke (schön) IU1, 14
Thank you very much. [ˈθæŋk juː ˌveri ˈmʌtʃ] Vielen Dank. ⟨IER, 125⟩
thanks [θæŋks] danke IU2, 36
  thanks a lot [ˈθæŋks ə ˌlɒt] vielen Dank ⟨IER, 120⟩
that [ðæt] das IU1, 14
  that's (= that is) [ðæts = ðæt ɪz] das ist IU1, 14
the [ðə] der, die (auch Plural), das IU1, 14
  the twenty-first of [ðə ˌtwenti ˈfɜːst ˌɒv] der einundzwanzigste IU5, 75
theatre [ˈθɪətə] Theater ⟨IER, 113⟩
their [ðeə] ihr/-e IU2, 31
them [ðem] sie/ihnen IU3, 44
then [ðen] dann ⟨IU1, 23⟩; ILUA, 26
there [ðeə] da, dort IU1, 20
  there are [ðeərˈɑː] es sind, da sind, es gibt IU1, 20
  there's (= there is) [ðeəz = ðeərˈɪz] es gibt; da ist IU1, 20
these [ðiːz] diese (hier) IU3, 48
they [ðeɪ] sie (Plural) IU1, 16
thing [θɪŋ] Ding, Sache ⟨IU2, 34⟩; IU2, 36
to **think** [θɪŋk] denken ⟨IU2, 35⟩; denken; glauben IU6, 94
third [θɜːd] dritte/-r/-s IU5, 74
this [ðɪs] das; dies; diese/-r/-s IU1, 14
those [ðəʊz] diese (da), die (da); jene IU3, 48
through [θruː] durch IU4, 59
to **throw** [θrəʊ] werfen IU3, 50
Thursday [ˈθɜːzdeɪ] Donnerstag ILUB, 41
ticket [ˈtɪkɪt] Eintrittskarte; Fahrkarte IU6, 86
  ticket collector [ˈtɪkɪt kəˌlektə] Eintrittskartenkontrolleur/-in ⟨IER, 119⟩
time [taɪm] Zeit; Mal IU2, 32; Uhrzeit IU3, 43

time line [ˈtaɪm laɪn] Zeitleiste IU4, 58
tiny [ˈtaɪni] winzig ILUA, 27
tip [tɪp] Tipp IU1, 19
tired [taɪəd] müde IU7, 104
title [ˈtaɪtl] Überschrift; Titel IU5, 80
to [tʊ] an; zu; nach IU1, 25
today [təˈdeɪ] heute IU3, 44
together [təˈɡeðə] zusammen, miteinander IU2, 36
tonight [təˈnaɪt] heute Abend; heute Nacht IU3, 44
too [tuː] auch IU1, 12; zu IU2, 36
tourist [ˈtʊərɪst] Tourist/-in ILUC, 56
  tourist information centre [ˌtʊərɪst ɪnfəˈmeɪʃn sentə] Touristik-Information ILUC, 56
town [taʊn] Stadt ILUC, 56
toy [tɔɪ] Spielzeug ⟨IER, 129⟩
tractor [ˈtræktə] Traktor IU6, 86
tradition [trəˈdɪʃn] Tradition ⟨IER, 129⟩
train [treɪn] Zug IU4, 59
trainer [ˈtreɪnə] Turnschuh IU6, 88
transport [ˈtrænspɔːt] Verkehrsmittel IU4, 60
treasure [ˈtreʒə] Schatz IU4, 68
tree [triː] Baum IU1, 22
trip [trɪp] Ausflug IU6, 87
trouble [ˈtrʌbl] Schwierigkeiten IU2, 32
trousers pl. [ˈtraʊzəz] Hose IU6, 88
true [truː] wahr, richtig IU4, 64
to **try** [traɪ] versuchen, probieren IU6, 86
  to try on [traɪ ˈɒn] anprobieren IU5, 76
T-shirt [ˈtiːʃɜːt] T-Shirt IU2, 32
tuck shop [ˈtʌkʃɒp] Süßwarengeschäft (in einer Schule) ⟨IER, 113⟩
Tuesday [ˈtjuːzdeɪ] Dienstag ILUB, 41
tunnel [ˈtʌnl] Tunnel IU4, 58
turkey [ˈtɜːki] Truthahn ⟨IER, 129⟩
Turkish [ˈtɜːkɪʃ] türkisch, Türkisch IU2, 31
turn [tɜːn] an der Reihe IU1, 13
to **turn** [tɜːn] einbiegen, abbiegen; drehen, wenden ILUC, 57; sich umdrehen ⟨IU7, 98⟩; ⟨IER, 124⟩
  to turn to ... [ˈtɜːn tə] ... aufschlagen IU1, 21
tutor [ˈtjuːtə] Klassenlehrer/-in IU1, 14
  tutor group [ˈtjuːtə ɡruːp] Klasse (in einer englischen Schule) IU1, 14
TV (= television) [ˌtiːˈviː = ˈtelɪvɪʒn] Fernseher; Fernsehen ILUA, 27

two hundred and three **203**

Dictionary

English – German

U

uncle ['ʌŋkl] Onkel I U2, 30
under ['ʌndə] unter I U1, 20
underlined [ˌʌndə'laɪnd] unterstrichen I U7, 108
to understand [ˌʌndə'stænd] verstehen I U5, 81
unhappy [ʌn'hæpi] unglücklich ⟨I ER, 126⟩
uniform ['juːnɪfɔːm] Uniform I U6, 88
unit ['juːnɪt] Kapitel; Lektion I U1, 12
until [ʌn'tɪl] bis ⟨I U5, 79⟩
up [ʌp] oben; nach oben ⟨I U2, 35⟩; nach oben, hinauf, herauf I U5, 79
upstairs [ʌp'steəz] oben (im Gebäude) I U2, 29
us [ʌs] uns I U4, 60
to use [juːz] verwenden; benutzen I LUA, 27
used to sleep [juːs tə 'sliːp] immer schlief ⟨I ER, 118⟩
useful ['juːsfl] nützlich I U1, 12
  useful phrase ['juːsfl ˌfreɪz] nützlicher Ausdruck I U1, 12
usually ['juːʒəli] gewöhnlich, normalerweise I U3, 44

V

Valentine's Day ['væləntaɪnz ˌdeɪ] Valentinstag ⟨I ER, 128⟩
verb [vɜːb] Verb I U1, 16
very ['veri] sehr I U1, 17
video ['vɪdiəʊ] Video I LUB, 40
to visit ['vɪzɪt] besuchen I U4, 59
visitor ['vɪzɪtə] Besucher/-in I U4, 59
vocabulary [və'kæbjəlri] Wortschatz, Vokabular I U1, 24
  vocabulary skills [və'kæbjəlri 'skɪlz] Wortschatztechniken I U1, 24
voice [vɔɪs] Stimme I U5, 79
volleyball ['vɒlibɔːl] Volleyball I U3, 42

W

to wait [weɪt] warten I U5, 76
  to wait for ['weɪt fɔː] warten auf I U5, 76
to wake up [ˌweɪk 'ʌp] aufwachen I U3, 50
walk [wɔːk] Spaziergang; Wanderung I U2, 34
  to take the dog for a walk [teɪk ðə 'dɒg fɔːr ə ˌwɔːk] den Hund ausführen I U2, 34

to walk [wɔːk] (zu Fuß) gehen, laufen I LUC, 57
  to walk the plank [ˌwɔːk ðə 'plæŋk] über eine Schiffsplanke ins Wasser getrieben werden (alte Strafe für Seeleute) I U4, 68
wall [wɔːl] Wand; Mauer I U1, 20
to want [wɒnt] wollen I U4, 68
  wanted ['wɒntɪd] wollte ⟨I ER, 122⟩
wardrobe ['wɔːdrəʊb] Kleiderschrank I U2, 32
warm [wɔːm] warm I U6, 89
was [wɒz] war ⟨I ER, 118⟩
to wash [wɒʃ] waschen I U3, 50
to watch [wɒtʃ] (zu)schauen, gucken I LUB, 40
  Watch out! [ˌwɒtʃ 'aʊt] Vorsicht! ⟨I ER, 125⟩
water ['wɔːtə] Wasser I U4, 69
to wave [weɪv] winken I U7, 107
way [weɪ] Weg I U4, 61
we [wiː] wir I U1, 16
to wear [weə] tragen I U6, 88
weather ['weðə] Wetter I U6, 89
Wednesday ['wenzdeɪ] Mittwoch I LUB, 41
week [wiːk] Woche I LUB, 41
weekend [ˌwiːk'end] Wochenende I U3, 43
Welcome ... ['welkəm] Willkommen ... ⟨I ER, 110⟩; ⟨I ER, 118⟩
well [wel] na ja, also I U2, 32
welly ['weli] Gummistiefel I U6, 88
went [went] ging ⟨I ER, 118⟩
were [wɜː] waren ⟨I ER, 118⟩
west [west] Westen I U4, 58
wet [wet] nass I U4, 69
what [wɒt] was I U1, 13
  what's (= what is) [wɒts = wɒt 'ɪz] was ist I U1, 13
  What's your name? [ˌwɒts jə 'neɪm] Wie heißt du/heißen Sie? I U1, 13
  What about ... ? [ˌwɒt ə'baʊt] Was ist mit ... ? I U3, 44
  what it was like [ˌwɒt ɪt wɒz 'laɪk] wie es war ⟨I ER, 119⟩
  What time is it? [ˌwɒt 'taɪm ɪz ɪt] Wie viel Uhr ist es?, Wie spät ist es? I U3, 43
wheel [wiːl] Steuerrad, Lenkrad; Rad I U4, 68
when [wen] wann I U3, 42
where [weə] wo; wohin I U1, 13
  Where are you from? [ˌweər ə jə 'frɒm] Woher kommst du/kommt ihr/kommen Sie? I U1, 13

which [wɪtʃ] welche/-r/-s I U2, 35
to whisper ['wɪspə] flüstern I U7, 107
whistling ['wɪslɪŋ] pfeifen ⟨I ER, 124⟩
white [waɪt] weiß I LUA, 26
who [huː] wer; wem, wen I U1, 16
  who else [huː 'els] wer sonst ⟨I ER, 123⟩
  who's (= who is) [huːz = huː 'ɪz] wer ist I U1, 16
whose luck is down [huːz ˌlʌk ɪz 'daʊn] der kein Glück hat ⟨I ER, 127⟩
why [waɪ] warum I U2, 37
to win [wɪn] gewinnen I U4, 66
wind [wɪnd] Wind I U6, 39
window ['wɪndəʊ] Fenster I U1, 20
windy ['wɪndi] windig I U6, 89
to wink [wɪŋk] zwinkern ⟨I ER, 118⟩
winter ['wɪntə] Winter I U6, 87
to wish [wɪʃ] wünschen ⟨I ER, 129⟩
with [wɪð] mit; bei I U1, 16
without [wɪ'ðaʊt] ohne I U4, 58
woman ['wʊmən] pl. women ['wɪmɪn] Frau I U6, 87
wooden ['wʊdn] hölzern ⟨I U4, 67⟩
Woof! [wʊf] Wuf! ⟨I ER, 115⟩
word [wɜːd] Wort I U1, 18
work [wɜːk] Arbeit I U7, 104
to work [wɜːk] arbeiten; funktionieren I U3, 44
worked [wɜːkt] arbeiteten ⟨I ER, 118⟩
worker ['wɜːkə] Arbeiter/-in ⟨I ER, 113⟩
world [wɜːld] Welt I U4, 58
  from all round the world [frɒm ɔːl ˌraʊnd ðə 'wɜːld] aus der ganzen Welt I U4, 59
Wow! [waʊ] Oh, super! I U1, 20
to write [raɪt] schreiben I U1, 13
wrong [rɒŋ] falsch I U1, 16

Y

Yeah! [jeə] Ja! (Umgangssprache) I U4, 62
year [jɪə] Klasse; Jahr I U1, 12
  Year 7 [jɪə 'sevn] 7. Klasse I U1, 12
yellow ['jeləʊ] gelb I LUA, 26
yes [jes] ja I U1, 16
you [juː] du, ihr, Sie I U1, 12
  you're (= you are) [jɔː = juː 'ɑː] du bist; ihr seid; Sie sind I U1, 14
  You're lucky. [jɔː 'lʌki] Du hast Glück. I U2, 31
  You're welcome. [jɔː 'welkəm] Bitte (schön). I U1, 21

Dictionary D

English – German

young [jʌŋ] jung ⟩U4, 59
younger [ˈjʌŋɡə] jüngere/-r/-s ⟩U7, 104
your [jɔː] dein/-e, euer/eure, Ihr/-e
⟩U1, 13
Your turn. [ˈjɔː tɜːn] Du bist an der Reihe., Du bist dran. ⟩U1, 13
yourselves [jɔːˈselvz] selbst ⟨IER, 122⟩

Z

zero [ˈzɪərəʊ] Null ⟩U1, 13

Boys' names

Ben [ben] ⟩U2, 28
David [ˈdeɪvɪd] ⟩U2, 30
Fred [fred] ⟨U2, 55⟩
James [dʒeɪmz] ⟩U2, 30
Jason [ˈdʒeɪsn] ⟨IER, 118⟩
Kadar [ˈkədaː] ⟩U1, 15
Marco [ˈmɑːkəʊ] ⟩U1, 15
Mehmet [ˈmemet] ⟩U1, 15
Paul [pɔːl] ⟨IER, 118⟩
Peter [ˈpiːtə] ⟩U1, 13
Phil [fɪl] ⟩U2, 30
Richard [ˈrɪtʃəd] ⟩U2, 28
Rob [rɒb] ⟩U2, 28
Rudolph [ˈruːdɒlf] ⟨IER, 127⟩
Sam [sæm] ⟩U1, 15
Ted [ted] ⟩U2, 29
Terry [ˈteri] ⟩U1, 12
Thomas [ˈtɒməs] ⟩U1, 19
Tim [tɪm] ⟩LUA, 27
Tom [tɒm] ⟩U1, 12
Tony [ˈtəʊni] ⟩LUA, 27

Girls' names

Alexandra [ˌælɪɡˈzaːndrə] ⟩U1, 15
Alice [ˈælɪs] ⟨IER, 124⟩
Alison [ˈælɪsən] ⟩U3, 46
Cassie [ˈkæsi] ⟨IER, 113⟩
Dorothy [ˈdɒrəθi] ⟨IER, 113⟩
Elena [ˈelɪnə] ⟩U2, 30
Emma [ˈemə] ⟩U1, 14
Farah [ˈfɑːrə] ⟩U2, 28
Fiona [fiˈəʊnə] ⟩U2, 39
Grace [ɡreɪs] ⟩U2, 29
Jade [dʒeɪd] ⟩U2, 28
Lisa [ˈliːsə] ⟩U1, 12
Lucy [ˈluːsi] ⟩U3, 49
Nasreen [nʌsˈriːn] ⟩U2, 28
Nicola [ˈnɪklə] ⟨U2, 35⟩

Nina [ˈniːnə] ⟩U1, 15
Peg [peɡ] ⟨U4, 67⟩
Polly [ˈpɒli] ⟩U6, 94
Rachel [ˈreɪtʃl] ⟩U2, 30
Sarah [ˈseərə] ⟩U2, 30
Sue [suː] ⟩U2, 28
Susan [ˈsuːzn] ⟩U2, 30
Suzanne [suːˈzæn] ⟩U1, 13
Tamara [təˈmɑːrə] ⟩LUA, 27
Tess [tes] ⟩LUA, 27
Tilly [ˈtɪli] ⟩LUA, 27
Tracy [ˈtreɪsi] ⟩U2, 30

Surnames

Adams [ˈædəmz] ⟨IER, 110⟩
Brook [brʊk] ⟩U1, 14
Brown [braʊn] ⟩U4, 60
Carter [ˈkɑːtə] ⟩U1, 14
Cole [kəʊl] ⟨IER, 110⟩
Dudley [ˈdʌdli] ⟨IER, 122⟩
Fisher [ˈfɪʃə] ⟨IER, 112⟩
Green [ɡriːn] ⟩U2, 39
Jackson [ˈdʒæksn] ⟩U1, 12
Martin [ˈmɑːtɪn] ⟨IER, 110⟩
Monte [ˈmɒnteɪ] ⟩U2, 30
Moodie [ˈmuːdi] ⟨IER, 119⟩
Newman [ˈnjuːmən] ⟩U1, 14
Sanderson [ˈsɑːndəsn] ⟨IER, 118⟩
Smith [smɪθ] ⟩U6, 93
Spencer [ˈspensə] ⟩U1, 16
Taylor [ˈteɪlə] ⟩U1, 12
Tiny [ˈtaɪni] ⟩U1, 12
Wood [wʊd] ⟨IER, 110⟩

Place names

Apple Tree Road [ˈæpl triː ˌrəʊd] ⟩LUC, 56
Athens [ˈæθənz] ⟩U1, 15
Blackheath [ˌblækˈhiːθ] ⟩U4, 61
Blackheath Park [ˈblækhiːθ ˌpɑːk] ⟩U3, 47
Bristol [ˈbrɪstl] ⟩U1, 14
Britain [ˈbrɪtn] ⟩U2, 31
Brook Street [ˈbrʊk ˌstriːt] ⟩LUC, 56
Cardiff [ˈkɑːdɪf] ⟩U1, 16
Cat Street [ˈkæt ˌstriːt] ⟩LUC, 56
China [ˈtʃaɪnə] ⟨IER, 118⟩
Chocolate Island [ˌtʃɒklət ˈaɪlənd] ⟩U4, 68
Church Street [ˈtʃɜːtʃ ˌstriːt] ⟩U4, 59
Cotswold [ˈkɒtswəʊld] ⟩U6, 86
Dog Street [dɒɡ ˌstriːt] ⟩LUC, 56

England [ˈɪŋɡlənd] ⟩U1, 13
France [frɑːns] ⟩U2, 31
Germany [ˈdʒɜːməni] ⟩U2, 31
Greece [ɡriːs] ⟩U2, 31
Greenwich [ˈɡrenɪdʒ] ⟩U1, 12
Hither Farm Road [ˈhɪðə fɑːm ˌrəʊd] ⟩U2, 29
Holbourne Road [ˈhəʊbɔːn ˌrəʊd] ⟩U2, 28
Istanbul [ˌɪstænˈbʊl] ⟩U1, 15
Italy [ˈɪtəli] ⟩U2, 31
Leicester [ˈlestə] ⟩U2, 33
London [ˈlʌndən] ⟩U1, 12
Mouse Road [ˈmaʊs ˌrəʊd] ⟩LUC, 56
North Sea [ˌnɔːθ ˈsiː] ⟨IER, 119⟩
Old Road [ˈəʊld ˌrəʊd] ⟩LUC, 56
Paris [ˈpærɪs] ⟩U1, 15
Park Road [ˈpɑːk ˌrəʊd] ⟩LUC, 56
Pond Road [ˈpɒnd ˌrəʊd] ⟩U2, 28
River Road [ˈrɪvə ˌrəʊd] ⟩LUC, 56
Rome [rəʊm] ⟩U1, 15
Russia [ˈrʌʃə] ⟩U2, 31
Shanghai [ˌʃæŋˈhaɪ] ⟩U4, 68
Shoe Street [ˈʃuː ˌstriːt] ⟩LUC, 56
Thames [temz] ⟩U4, 58
Turkey [ˈtɜːki] ⟩U2, 31
Wendover Road [ˈwendəʊvə ˌrəʊd] ⟩U2, 29

Other names

Angelo's Pizza Place [ˈændʒələʊz ˌpiːtsə pleɪs] ⟩U5, 74
Arsenal [ˈɑːsnl] ⟨IER, 114⟩
Barker [ˈbɑːkə] ⟩U2, 28
Barny Forge [ˌbɑːrni ˈfɔːdʒ] ⟨IER, 124⟩
Baywood School [ˈbeɪwʊd ˌskuːl] ⟨IER, 110⟩
Blackjack [ˈblækdʒæk] ⟨IER, 120⟩
Blacky [ˈblæki] ⟨IER, 124⟩
Bluewater [ˈbluːˌwɔːtə] ⟨IER, 111⟩
Bow Church [ˈbəʊ ˌtʃɜːtʃ] ⟨IER, 124⟩
Buzz [bʌz] ⟩U1, 18
Cutty Sark [ˌkʌti ˈsɑːk] ⟩U4, 59
Dick Whittington [ˌdɪk ˈwɪtɪŋtən] ⟩U7, 98
Docklands Light Railway (= DLR) [ˈd = kləndz ˌlaɪt ˈreɪlweɪ] ⟩U4, 59
From Here to Chelsea [frɒm hɪə tə ˈtʃelsi] ⟩U3, 45
George Buckingham [ˌdʒɔːdʒ ˈbʌkɪŋəm] ⟨IER, 124⟩
Greenwich Mean Time (= GMT) [ˌɡrenɪdʒ ˈmiːn taɪm] ⟩U4, 58
The Greenwich Foot Tunnel [ðə ˈɡrenɪdʒ fʊt ˌtʌnl] ⟩U4, 58

D Dictionary

English – German

Grumpy Greg [ˈgrʌmpi ˌgreg] ⟨I U4, 67⟩
Guy Fawkes [ˌgaɪ ˈfɔːks] ⟨I ER, 127⟩
Jazz Café [ˈdʒæz ˌkæfeɪ] I U3, 50
King James I [kɪŋ ˈdʒeɪmz ðə ˌfɜːst] ⟨I ER, 127⟩
Lady Anne Fitwarren [ˌleɪdi ˌæn fɪtsˈwɒrn] ⟨I ER, 124⟩
Lord Mayor [ˌlɔːd ˈmeə] ⟨I U7, 104⟩; ⟨I ER, 124⟩

Meridian Line [məˈrɪdiən ˌlaɪn] I U4, 58
Power Ball [ˈpaʊə ˌbɔːl] I U3, 48
Royal Observatory [ˌrɔɪəl əbˈzɜːvətri] I U4, 58
Samba Band [ˈsæmbə ˌbænd] I U7, 106
Sissy Forge [ˌsɪsi ˈfɔːdʒ] ⟨I ER, 124⟩
Stouty Burke [ˌstaʊti ˈbɜːk] ⟨I ER, 124⟩
Thames Barrier [ˌtemz ˈbæriə] ⟨I ER, 121⟩

Thames Festival Lantern Procession [ˌtemz ˈfestɪvl ˈlæntən prəˈseʃn] I U7, 98
Thomas Tallis School [ˌtɒməs ˈtælɪs ˌskuːl] I U1, 12
Tiger [ˈtaɪgə] I U2, 29
Turn again, Whittington [ˌtɜːn əgen ˈwɪtɪŋtən] I U7, 98
the Underground [ði ˈʌndəˌgraʊnd] I U4, 60
Velvet [ˈvelvɪt] ⟨I ER, 113⟩

Dictionary D

German – English

A

abbiegen to turn [tɜ:n]
abdecken to cover [ˈkʌvə]
Abend evening [ˈi:vnɪŋ]
Abendessen dinner [ˈdɪnə]
aber but [bʌt]
abfahren to leave [li:v]
Abfall rubbish [ˈrʌbɪʃ]
abholen to collect [kəˈlekt]
abmalen to copy [ˈkɒpi]
abschreiben to copy [ˈkɒpi]
achte/-r/-s eighth [eɪtθ]
Adjektiv adjective [ˈædʒɪktɪv]
ähnlich like [laɪk]
Ahnung idea [aɪˈdɪə]
albern silly [ˈsɪli]
alle all [ɔ:l]
allein alone [əˈləʊn]
alles everything [ˈevrɪθɪŋ]
Alles Gute zum Geburtstag! Happy Birthday! [ˈhæpi ˌbɜ:θdeɪ]
Alphabet alphabet [ˈælfəbet]
also well [wel]; so [səʊ]
alt old [əʊld]
am on [ɒn]
an to [tʊ]; at [æt; ət]
andere/-r/-s different [ˈdɪfrnt]; other [ˈʌðə]
  ein/-e andere/-r another [əˈnʌθə]
anders different [ˈdɪfrnt]
anfangen to start [sta:t]
Angst einjagen to scare [skeə]
Angst haben to be scared [ˌbi: ˈskeəd]
ängstlich scared [skeəd]
anhalten to stop [stɒp]
anhören to listen [ˈlɪsn]
den Anker lichten to lift anchor [ˌlɪft ˈæŋkə]
vor Anker at anchor [ˌət ˈæŋkə]
ankommen to arrive [əˈraɪv]
anmalen to colour [ˈkʌlə]
anprobieren to try on [traɪ ˈɒn]
Anruf call [kɔ:l]
anrufen to phone [fəʊn]; to call [kɔ:l]
ansehen to look at [ˈlʊk æt]
Antwort answer [ˈɑ:nsə]
antworten to answer [ˈɑ:nsə]
Apfel apple [ˈæpl]
April April [ˈeɪprəl]
Arbeit work [wɜ:k]
arbeiten to work [wɜ:k]
Arbeiter/-in worker [ˈwɜ:kə]
arbeiteten worked [wɜ:kt]
arm poor [pɔ:]
Art kind [kaɪnd]

auch too [tu:]; also [ˈɔ:lsəʊ]
auf on [ɒn]; at [æt; ət]
  auf Wiederhören goodbye [gʊdˈbaɪ]
  auf Wiedersehen goodbye [gʊdˈbaɪ]
aufbauen to build [bɪld]
Aufführung show [ʃəʊ]
aufgeregt excited [ɪkˈsaɪtɪd]
aufhören to stop [stɒp]
aufmachen to open [ˈəʊpn]
aufräumen to clean [kli:n]
aufregend exciting [ɪkˈsaɪtɪŋ]
… aufschlagen to turn to … [ˈtɜ:n ˌtə]
aufstehen to get up [getˈʌp]; to stand up [ˈstænd ʌp]
aufwachen to wake up [ˌweɪk ˈʌp]
Auge eye [aɪ]
im Augenblick at the moment [ˌæt ðə ˈməʊmənt]
Augenklappe patch [pætʃ]
August August [ˈɔ:gəst]
Aula hall [hɔ:l]
aus from [frɒm]
  aus der ganzen Welt from all round the world [frɒm ɔ:l ˌraʊnd ðə ˈwɜ:ld]
auschecken to check-out [ˈtʃekaʊt]
Ausdruck phrase [freɪz]
Ausflug trip [trɪp]
ausführen to perform [pəˈfɔ:m]
ausfüllen to fill in [fɪl ˈɪn]
Auskunft information [ˌɪnfəˈmeɪʃn]
ausleihen to borrow [ˈbɒrəʊ]
ausmalen to colour [ˈkʌlə]
ausreichend plenty [ˈplenti]
aussehen to look [lʊk]
Auto car [kɑ:]

B

Baby baby [ˈbeɪbi]
Badminton badminton [ˈbædmɪntən]
bald soon [su:n]
Ball ball [bɔ:l]
Bart beard [bɪəd]
Basketball basketball [ˈbɑ:skɪtbɔ:l]
bauen to build [bɪld]
Bauer/Bäuerin farmer [ˈfɑ:mə]
Bauernhof farm [fɑ:m]
Baum tree [tri:]
beantworten to answer [ˈɑ:nsə]
bedecken to cover [ˈkʌvə]
bedeuten to mean [mi:n]
Bedeutung meaning [ˈmi:nɪŋ]
beenden to finish [ˈfɪnɪʃ]; to end [end]
beginnen to start [stɑ:t]
bei with [wɪð]; at [æt; ət]

beide both [bəʊθ]
Bein leg [leg]
bekannt famous [ˈfeɪməs]
bellen to bark [bɑ:k]
benutzen to use [ju:z]
berühmt famous [ˈfeɪməs]
Besatzung crew [kru:]
beschäftigt busy [ˈbɪzi]
besitzen have got [ˈhæv gɒt]
besondere/-r/-s special [ˈspeʃl]
besonders extra [ˈekstrə]
besser better [ˈbetə]
beste/-r/-s best [best]
besuchen to visit [ˈvɪzɪt]
Besucher/-in visitor [ˈvɪzɪtə]
Bett bed [bed]
bevor before [bɪˈfɔ:]
Bewegung action [ˈækʃn]
Bibliothek library [ˈlaɪbrəri]
Bild picture [ˈpɪktʃə]
bilden to make [meɪk]
bin am [əm]
Bindewort conjunction [kənˈdʒʌŋkʃn]
bis until [ʌnˈtɪl]
  Bis bald. See you. [ˈsi: ˌju:]
  Bis dann. See you. [ˈsi: ˌju:]
ein bisschen a little [əˈlɪtl]
bist are [ɑ:]
bitte please [pli:z]
Bitte (schön). You're welcome. [jɔ: ˈwelkəm]; Here you are! [ˈhɪə jʊˌɑ:]
bleiben to stay [steɪ]
Bleistift pencil [ˈpensl]
bloß only [ˈəʊnli]
Blume flower [flaʊə]
Bonbon sweet [swi:t]
Boot boat [bəʊt]
an Bord on board [ˈɒn bɔ:d]
böse bad [bæd]
brachte brought [brɔ:t]
brauchen to need [ni:d]
braun brown [braʊn]
brechen to break [breɪk]
Brett board [bɔ:d]; plank [plæŋk]
Brief letter [ˈletə]
bringen to take [teɪk]; to bring [brɪŋ]
britisch British [ˈbrɪtɪʃ]
Broschüre brochure [ˈbrəʊʃə]
Brücke bridge [brɪdʒ]
Bruder brother [ˈbrʌðə]
Buch book [bʊk]
Bücherei library [ˈlaɪbrəri]
Buchstabe letter [ˈletə]
buchstabieren to spell [spel]
Bühne stage [steɪdʒ]
Bühnenbild scenery [ˈsi:nəri]

two hundred and seven **207**

D Dictionary

German – English

Burger burger [ˈbɜːgə]
Bus bus [bʌs] pl. buses [ˈbʌsɪz]
Bushaltestelle bus stop [ˈbʌs ˌstɒp]

C

Café café [ˈkæfeɪ]
Cafeteria cafeteria [ˌkæfəˈtɪərɪə]
CD CD [ˌsiːˈdiː]
Comic(heft) comic [ˈkɒmɪk]
Computer computer [kəmˈpjuːtə]
cool cool [kuːl]
Cornflake cornflake [ˈkɔːnfleɪk]
Cousin/-e cousin [ˈkʌzn]

D

da there [ðeə]; because [bɪˈkɒz]
　da drüben over there [ˌəʊvə ˈðeə]
　da ist there's (= there is) [ðeəz = ðeərˈɪz]
　da sind there are [ðeərˈɑː]
danach after that [ˈɑːftə ˌðæt]
danke (schön) thank you [ˈθæŋk juː]
dann then [ðen]
das the [ðə]; this [ðɪs]; that [ðæt]
Datum date [deɪt]
dauern to take [teɪk]
dein/-e your [jɔː]
denken to think [θɪŋk]
denken an to remember [rɪˈmembə]
der the [ðə]
derselbe/dieselbe/dasselbe the same [seɪm]
deutsch German [ˈdʒɜːmən]
Deutsche/-r German [ˈdʒɜːmən]
Dezember December [dɪˈsembə]
Dialog dialogue [ˈdaɪəlɒg]
die the [ðə]
die (da) those [ðəʊz]
die anderen the others [ði ˈʌðəz]
Dienstag Tuesday [ˈtjuːzdeɪ]
dies this [ðɪs]
diese/-r/-s this [ðɪs]
　diese (da) those [ðəʊz]
　diese (hier) these [ðiːz]
Ding thing [θɪŋ]
Disko disco [ˈdɪskəʊ]
Donnerstag Thursday [ˈθɜːzdeɪ]
dort there [ðeə]
draußen outside [ˌaʊtˈsaɪd]
dreckig dirty [ˈdɜːti]
drehen to turn [tɜːn]
dritte/-r/-s third [θɜːd]

du you [juː]
dumm silly [ˈsɪli]
Dummerchen silly [ˈsɪli]
Dummkopf idiot [ˈɪdɪət]
durch through [θruː]
Durcheinander mess [mes]
durcheinander geworfen jumbled [ˈdʒʌmbld]
dürfen may [meɪ]
DVD DVD [ˌdiː viː ˈdiː]

E

echt real [rɪəl]
Ei egg [eg]
Eigenschaftswort adjective [ˈædʒɪktɪv]
einander each other [ˌiːtʃ ˈʌðə]
ein/-e a [ə], an [ən]; one [wʌn]
einbiegen to turn [tɜːn]
einchecken to check-in [ˈtʃekɪn]
einfach easy [ˈiːzi]
Einfall idea [aɪˈdɪə]
einige some [sʌm]; a few [ə ˈfjuː]
Einkäufe shopping [ˈʃɒpɪŋ]
Einkaufen shopping [ˈʃɒpɪŋ]
einkaufen gehen to go shopping [gəʊ ˈʃɒpɪŋ]
Einkaufsliste shopping list [ˈʃɒpɪŋ ˌlɪst]
Einkaufszettel shopping list [ˈʃɒpɪŋ ˌlɪst]
einladen to invite [ɪnˈvaɪt]
Einladung invitation [ˌɪnvɪˈteɪʃn]
einsammeln to collect [kəˈlekt]
einschlafen to fall asleep [ˌfɔːl əˈsliːp]
einsetzen to put in [pʊtˈɪn]
Eintrittskarte ticket [ˈtɪkɪt]
Eintrittskartenkontrolleur/-in ticket collector [ˈtɪkɪt kəˌlektə]
Einzelkind only child [ˈəʊnli ˌtʃaɪld]
einzige/-r/-s only [ˈəʊnli]
Eis ice-cream [ˌaɪsˈkriːm]
Eltern parents [ˈpeərənts]
E-Mail e-mail [ˈiːmeɪl]
Ende end [end]
enden to end [end]
endlich finally [ˈfaɪnəli]
Engländer/-in English [ˈɪŋglɪʃ]
englisch, Englisch English [ˈɪŋglɪʃ]
Entermesser cutlass [ˈkʌtləs]
enthalten to include [ɪnˈkluːd]
entlang down [daʊn]
Entschuldige! Excuse me. [ɪkˈskjuːz mi]
Entschuldigen Sie! Excuse me. [ɪkˈskjuːz mi]
Entschuldigung! Excuse me. [ɪkˈskjuːz mi]

Entschuldigung! Sorry! [ˈsɒri]
er he [hiː]
sich erinnern an to remember [rɪˈmembə]
erklären to explain [ɪkˈspleɪn]
Erklärung key [kiː]
erraten to guess [ges]
erschrecken to scare [skeə]
erst only [ˈəʊnli]
erste/-r/-s first [fɜːst]
Erwachsene/-r adult [ˈædʌlt]
erzählen to tell [tel]
Erzähler/-in storyteller [ˈstɔːrɪˌtelə]
es it [ɪt]
　es gibt there's (= there is) [ðeəz = ðeərˈɪz]; there are [ðeərˈɑː]
　es ist it's (= it is) [ɪts = ɪt ɪz]
　es sind there are [ðeərˈɑː]
essen to eat [iːt]
Essen food [fuːd]
Esslöffel tablespoon [ˈteɪblspuːn]
Esszimmer dining room [ˈdaɪnɪŋ rʊm]
etwas some [sʌm]; something [ˈsʌmθɪŋ]
euer/eure your [jɔː]
Europäer/-in European [ˌjʊərəˈpiːən]
europäisch European [ˌjʊərəˈpiːən]
extra extra [ˈekstrə]

F

Fähigkeit skill [skɪl]
Fahne flag [flæg]
fahren to ride [raɪd]; to drive [draɪv]
Fahrer/-in driver [ˈdraɪvə]
Fahrkarte ticket [ˈtɪkɪt]
Fahrrad bike [baɪk]
fallen to fall [fɔːl]
falsch false [fɔːls]; wrong [rɒŋ]
Familie family [ˈfæməli]
fangen to catch [kætʃ]
Farbe colour [ˈkʌlə]
Farmtierpark farm park [ˈfɑːm ˌpɑːk]
Februar February [ˈfebruri]
Federball badminton [ˈbædmɪntən]
Federmäppchen pencil case [ˈpensl ˌkeɪs]
fehlend missing [ˈmɪsɪŋ]
Feier party [ˈpɑːti]
Fenster window [ˈwɪndəʊ]
Fernrohr telescope [ˈteliskəʊp]
Fernsehen TV (= television) [ˌtiː viː = ˈtelɪvɪʒn]
Fernseher TV (= television) [ˌtiː viː = ˈtelɪvɪʒn]

208 two hundred and eight

Dictionary D

German – English

fertig ready ['redi]
fertig machen to finish ['fɪnɪʃ]
Fertigkeit skill [skɪl]
fest hard [hɑːd]
Fest festival ['festɪvl]; fair [feə]
Festival festival ['festɪvl]
Festland land [lænd]
Feuer fire ['faɪə]
Feuerwerk fireworks ['faɪəwɜːks]
Film film [fɪlm]
finden to find [faɪnd]
fing caught [kɔːt]
Finger finger ['fɪŋgə]
Flagge flag [flæg]
Flasche bottle ['bɒtl]
Flur hall [hɔːl]
Fluss river ['rɪvə]
flüstern to whisper ['wɪspə]
folgen to follow ['fɒləʊ]
Form form [fɔːm]
Foto photo ['fəʊtəʊ]
   Fotos schießen to take pictures [teɪk 'pɪktʃəz]
Frage question ['kwestʃən]
fragen to ask [ɑːsk]
französisch, Französisch French [frentʃ]
Frau woman ['wʊmən]; Mrs ['mɪsɪz]
frei free [friː]
Freitag Friday ['fraɪdeɪ]
freitags Fridays ['fraɪdeɪz]
Freund/-in friend [frend]
fröhlich happy ['hæpi]; jolly ['dʒɒli]
Frühjahr spring [sprɪŋ]
Frühling spring [sprɪŋ]
Frühstück breakfast ['brekfəst]
fühlen to feel [fiːl]
fuhr ... herunter came down ... [keɪm 'daʊn]
Führer/-in guide [gaɪd]
Füller pen [pen]
fünfte/-r/-s fifth [fɪfθ]
funktionieren to work [wɜːk]
für for [fɔː]
Fürwort pronoun ['prəʊnaʊn]
Fuß foot [fʊt] pl. feet [fiːt]
Fußball football ['fʊtbɔːl]
füttern to feed [fiːd]

G

Gans goose [guːs]
geben to give [gɪv]
geboren born [bɔːn]
Geburtstag birthday ['bɜːθdeɪ]
Gedicht poem ['pəʊɪm]
gegenüber opposite ['ɒpəzɪt]
Geh weg! Go away! [ˌgəʊ ə'weɪ]
Geheimnis secret ['siːkrət]
gehen to go [gəʊ]; to walk [wɔːk]
Geist ghost [gəʊst]
gelagert stored [stɔːd]
Geld money ['mʌni]
Genitiv genitive ['dʒenɪtɪv]
genug plenty ['plenti]
gerade straight [streɪt]
geradewegs in ... hinein straight into ... ['streɪt ˌɪntə]
Geräusch sound [saʊnd]; noise [nɔɪz]
gern haben to like [laɪk]
geschah happened ['hæpnd]
Geschäft shop [ʃɒp]
Geschäftsführer/-in manager ['mænɪdʒə]
geschehen to happen ['hæpn]
Geschenk present ['preznt]
Geschenkladen gift shop ['gɪft ˌʃɒp]
Geschichte story ['stɔːri]
geschieden divorced [dɪ'vɔːst]
geschlossen closed [kləʊzd]
Gesicht face [feɪs]
gespenstisch spooky ['spuːki]
Gespräch talk [tɔːk]; dialogue ['daɪəlɒg]
Getränk drink [drɪŋk]
gewinnen to win [wɪn]
gewöhnlich usually ['juːʒəli]
ging went [went]
Gitarre guitar [gɪ'tɑː]
Gitter grid [grɪd]
Glas glass [glɑːs]
glauben to think [θɪŋk]; to believe [bɪ'liːv]
Glocke bell [bel]
glücklich happy ['hæpi]
Gold gold [gəʊld]
Gramm gram [græm]
Grammatik grammar ['græmə]
Gras grass [grɑːs]
grau grey [greɪ]
Grieche/Griechin Greek [griːk]
griechisch, Griechisch Greek [griːk]
groß large [lɑːdʒ]; big [bɪg]
großartig great [greɪt]
Größe size [saɪz]
Großeltern grandparents ['grænˌpeərnts]
Großmutter grandmother ['grænˌmʌðə]
Großvater grandfather ['grænˌfɑːðə]
grün green [griːn]
Gruppe group [gruːp]
gruselig spooky ['spuːki]; scary ['skeəri]
gucken to watch [wɒtʃ]

Gummistiefel welly ['weli]
gut good [gʊd]; fine [faɪn]
gut können to be good at ... [ˌbiː 'gʊd ˌət]
   ... gut können; gut sein in ... to be good at ... [ˌbiː 'gʊd ˌət]
gute Botschaft good tidings [ˌgʊd 'taɪdɪŋz]
guten Morgen good morning [gʊd 'mɔːnɪŋ]
gutes neues Jahr Happy New Year ['hæpi ˌnjuː jɪə]

H

haben have got ['hæv gɒt]; have [hæv]
Hähnchen chicken ['tʃɪkɪn]
halb half [hɑːf]
halb (drei) half past (two) [ˌhɑːf 'pɑːst]
hallo hello [he'ləʊ]; hi [haɪ]
Hand hand [hænd]
hart hard [hɑːd]
hatte had [hæd]
Hausaufgaben homework ['həʊmwɜːk]
Hausmeister/-in caretaker ['keəˌteɪkə]
Haustier pet [pet]
Heft exercise book ['eksəsaɪz ˌbʊk]
Hefter folder ['fəʊldə]
Heiliger Abend Christmas Eve [ˌkrɪsməs 'iːv]
Heim home [həʊm]
heiß hot [hɒt]
helfen to help [help]
herauf up [ʌp]
Herberge hostel ['hɒstl]
Herbst autumn ['ɔːtəm]
herein in [ɪn]
Herr Mr ['mɪstə]; master ['mɑːstə]
herüberkommen to come over [ˌkʌm 'əʊvə]
herunter down [daʊn]
heute today [tə'deɪ]
   heute Abend tonight [tə'naɪt]
   heute Nacht tonight [tə'naɪt]
Hi! Hi! [haɪ]
hier here [hɪə]
Hilfe help [help]
hinauf up [ʌp]
hinein into ['ɪntə]; in [ɪn]
hinfallen to fall over [fɔːl 'əʊvə]
hinter behind [bɪ'haɪnd]
hinterherrennen to chase [tʃeɪs]
hinunter down [daʊn]
Hobby hobby ['hɒbi]
höflich polite [pə'laɪt]

two hundred and nine **209**

Dictionary

German – English

Holz- wooden ['wʊdn]
hölzern wooden ['wʊdn]
Hoppla! Oops! [u:ps]
hören to listen ['lɪsn]; to hear [hɪə]
Hören listening ['lɪsnɪŋ]
Hose trousers ['traʊzəz]
(Hosen-)Tasche pocket ['pɒkɪt]
Hüfte hip [hɪp]
Huhn chicken ['tʃɪkɪn]
Hund dog [dɒg]
hungrig hungry ['hʌŋgri]
Hut hat [hæt]

I

ich I [aɪ]; me [mi:]
Idee idea [aɪ'dɪə]
Idiot/-in idiot ['ɪdɪət]
ihm him [hɪm]
ihn him [hɪm]
ihnen them [ðem]
ihr you [ju:]; her [hɜ:]; your [jɔ:]
ihr/-e their [ðeə]; its [ɪts]; her [hɜ:]
Imbiss snack [snæk]
immer always ['ɔ:lweɪz]
immer noch still [stɪl]
in into ['ɪntə]; in [ɪn]; at [æt; ət]
   in der Nähe von near [nɪə]
   in Ordnung bringen to sort out [sɔ:t 'aʊt]
Information(en) information [ˌɪnfə'meɪʃn]
Inlineskates skates [skeɪts]
Insel island ['aɪlənd]
interessant interesting ['ɪntrəstɪŋ]
interessiert interested ['ɪntrəstɪd]
Internet Internet ['ɪntənet];
irgendetwas something ['sʌmθɪŋ]
irgendwohin anywhere ['enɪweə]
ist is [ɪz]
Italiener/-in Italian [ɪ'tælɪən]
italienisch, Italienisch Italian [ɪ'tælɪən]

J

ja yes [jes]
jagen to chase [tʃeɪs]
Jahr year [jɪə]
Jahresplaner planner ['plænə]
Jahreszeit season ['si:zn]
Jahrmarkt fair [feə]
Januar January ['dʒænjuri]
Jeans jeans [dʒi:nz]
jede/-r/-s everybody ['evrɪˌbɒdi]; every

['evri]
jene those [ðəʊz]
jetzt now [naʊ]
jetzt gerade right now ['raɪt ˌnaʊ]
Juli July [dʒʊ'laɪ]
jung young [jʌŋ]
Junge boy [bɔɪ]
jüngere/-r/-s younger ['jʌŋgə]
Jungs lads [lædz]
Juni June [dʒu:n]

K

Kajüte cabin ['kæbɪn]
Kalender calendar ['kæləndə]
kalt cold [kəʊld]
Kamera camera ['kæmrə]
Kamin chimney ['tʃɪmni]
Kampf fight [faɪt]
kämpfen to fight [faɪt]
Kaninchen rabbit ['ræbɪt]
Kapitän captain ['kæptɪn]
Kapitel unit ['ju:nɪt]
Kappe cap [kæp]
Karotte carrot ['kærət]
Karte card [kɑ:d]
Kartoffelchip crisp [krɪsp]
Karton box [bɒks]
Katze cat [kæt]
kauern to crouch [kraʊtʃ]
kaufen to buy [baɪ]
Kaufhaus department store [dɪ'pɑ:tmənt ˌstɔ:]
kein/-e not [nɒt]; no [nəʊ]
kennen to know [nəʊ]
Kerze candle ['kændl]
Kind kid [kɪd]; child [tʃaɪld]
Kino cinema ['sɪnəmə]
Kirche church [tʃɜ:tʃ]
Kiste box [bɒks]
klären to sort out [sɔ:t 'aʊt]
klasse cool [ku:l]
Klasse tutor group ['tju:tə ˌgru:p]; year [jɪə]; group [gru:p]; class [klɑ:s]
Klassenlehrer/-in tutor ['tju:tə]
Klassenzimmer classroom ['klɑ:sru:m]
klatschen to clap [klæp]
Kleider clothes pl. [kləʊðz]
Kleiderschrank wardrobe ['wɔ:drəʊb]
Kleidung clothes pl. [kləʊðz]
klein small [smɔ:l]; little [lɪtl]
   kleiner smaller [smɔ:lə]
Klub club [klʌb]
Klubhaus clubhouse ['klʌbhaʊs]
klug clever ['klevə]

Knall bang [bæŋ]
Knallbonbon cracker ['krækə]
Koch/Köchin cook [kʊk]
kochen to cook [kʊk]
komisch funny ['fʌni]
kommen to come [kʌm]
Kommunikation communication [kəˌmju:nɪ'keɪʃn]
Konjunktion conjunction [kən'dʒʌŋkʃn]
können can [kæn]
Kopf head [hed]
kopieren to copy ['kɒpi]
korrigieren to correct [kə'rekt]
kostenlos free [fri:]
krank ill [ɪl]
kreuzen to cross [krɒs]
Kricket cricket ['krɪkɪt]
Küche kitchen ['kɪtʃɪn]
Kuchen cake [keɪk]
Kuh cow [kaʊ]
Kulisse scene [si:n]
Kunde/Kundin customer ['kʌstəmə]
kurz short [ʃɔ:t]
Kurzform short form [ʃɔ:t fɔ:m]
Kutsche coach [kəʊtʃ]

L

lächeln to smile [smaɪl]
lachen to laugh [lɑ:f]
Laden shop [ʃɒp]
Laderaum hold [həʊld]
Lamm lamb [læm]
Land country ['kʌntri]
   auf dem Land in the country [ˌɪn ðə 'kʌntri]
Landkarte map [mæp]
Landwirt/-in farmer ['fɑ:mə]
lang long [lɒŋ]
Langform long form ['lɒŋ fɔ:m]
langweilig boring ['bɔ:rɪŋ]
lassen to leave [li:v]
lass(t) uns ... let's ... [lets]
Laterne lantern ['læntən]
Lauf race [reɪs]
laufen to walk [wɔ:k]; to run [rʌn]
laut loud [laʊd]
Laut sound [saʊnd]
läuten to ring [rɪŋ]
leben to live [lɪv]
Leben life [laɪf]
   hast mir das Leben gerettet saved my life [ˌseɪvd maɪ 'laɪf]
Lebensmittel food [fu:d]
lebte lived [lɪvd]

Dictionary D

German – English

legen to put [pʊt]
Legende key [kiː]
Lehrer/-in teacher ['tiːtʃə]
Lehrerpult desk [desk]
leicht easy ['iːzi]
Lektion unit ['juːnɪt]
Lenkrad wheel [wiːl]
lernen to learn [lɜːn]
lesen to read [riːd]
letzte/-r/-s last [lɑːst]
Leute people ['piːpl]; guys [gaɪz]
   Leute zum Lachen bringen make people laugh [meɪk piːpl 'lɑːf]
Liebe/-r ... Dear ... [dɪə]
   Liebe Grüße, ... Love, ... [lʌv]
lieben to love [lʌv]
Lieblings- favourite ['feɪvrɪt]
Lied song [sɒŋ]
lila purple ['pɜːpl]
Limonade lemonade [ˌleməˈneɪd]
Lineal ruler ['ruːlə]
Linie line [laɪn]
linke/-r/-s left [left]
links on the left [ɒn ðə 'left]; left [left]
Lippe lip [lɪp]
Liste list [lɪst]
Löffel (voll) spoonful ['spuːnfʊl]
lösen to sort out [sɔːt 'aʊt]
in die **Luft jagen** to blow up [bləʊ 'ʌp]
lustig funny ['fʌni]

M

machen to make [meɪk]; to do [duː]
Mädchen girl [gɜːl]
Mai May [meɪ]
Mal time [taɪm]
malen to paint [peɪnt]; to draw [drɔː]; to colour ['kʌlə]
Mama mum [mʌm]
manchmal sometimes ['sʌmtaɪmz]
Mann man [mæn]
Mannschaft team [tiːm]
Mappe folder ['fəʊldə]
Markt fair [feə]; market ['mɑːkɪt]
März March [mɑːtʃ]
Mauer wall [wɔːl]
Maul mouth [maʊθ]
Maus mouse [maʊs] pl mice [maɪs]
Meer sea [siː]
Megafon megaphone ['megəfəʊn]
Mehl flour [flaʊə]
mehr more [mɔː]
Mehrzahl plural ['plʊərəl]
mein/-e my [maɪ]

meinen to mean [miːn]
Meister master ['mɑːstə]
melken to milk [mɪlk]
Melkstall milking barn ['mɪlkɪŋ ˌbɑːn]
eine **Menge** a lot of [əˈlɒt ˌɒv]
Mensch! Phew! [fjuː]
merkwürdig strange [streɪndʒ]
mich me [miː]
Milch milk [mɪlk]
Mini- mini ['mɪni]
Minute minute ['mɪnɪt]
mir me [miː]
mischen to mix [mɪks]
mit by [baɪ]; with [wɪð]
mitbringen to bring [brɪŋ]
miteinander together [təˈgeðə]
Mittagessen lunch [lʌntʃ]; dinner ['dɪnə]
Mittagszeit lunchtime ['lʌntʃtaɪm]
Mitte centre ['sentə]
mittel medium ['miːdiəm]
Mittwoch Wednesday ['wenzdeɪ]
Möbel furniture ['fɜːnɪtʃə]
mögen to like [laɪk]
momentan at the moment [ət ðə 'məʊmənt]
Monat month [mʌnθ]
Montag Monday ['mʌndeɪ]
montags on Mondays [ˌɒn 'mʌndeɪz]
Morgen morning ['mɔːnɪŋ]
müde tired [taɪəd]
Münze coin [kɔɪn]
Museum museum [mjuːˈziːəm]
Musik music ['mjuːzɪk]
müssen must [mʌst]
Mutti mum [mʌm]

N

na ja well [wel]
nach to [tʊ]; after ['ɑːftə]
   nach (bei Uhrzeiten) past [pɑːst]
   nach draußen outside [ˌaʊt'saɪd]
   nach oben up [ʌp]
   nach unten down [daʊn]
Nachbar/-in neighbour ['neɪbə]
Nachmittag afternoon [ˌɑːftəˈnuːn]
nachmittags pm [ˌpiːˈem]
nächste/-r/-s next [nekst]
Nacht night [naɪt]
Nachtisch dessert [dɪˈzɜːt]
nahe near [nɪə]
Name name [neɪm]
Narbe scar [skɑː]
Nase nose [nəʊz]

nass wet [wet]
natürlich of course [ˌɒv 'kɔːs]
neben next to ['nekst tʊ]
nehmen to take [teɪk]
nein no [nəʊ]
nennen to call [kɔːl]
nett nice [naɪs]
neu new [njuː]
neunte/-r/-s ninth [naɪnθ]
nicht not [nɒt]
nie never ['nevə]
niedlich sweet [swiːt]; cute [kjuːt]
niemand nobody ['nəʊbədi]
noch still [stɪl]
   noch ein/eine(-r/-s) another [əˈnʌðə]
   noch einmal again [əˈgen]
Norden north [nɔːθ]
normalerweise usually ['juːʒəli]
November November [nəʊˈvembə]
Null zero ['zɪərəʊ]
Nummer number ['nʌmbə]
nun now [naʊ]
nur only ['əʊnli]; just [dʒʌst]
nützlich useful ['juːsfl]
nützlicher Ausdruck useful phrase ['juːsfl ˌfreɪz]

O

oben above [əˈbʌv]; up [ʌp]
oben (im Gebäude) upstairs [ʌpˈsteəz]
oberhalb above [əˈbʌv]
Obst fruit [fruːt]
oder or [ɔː]
öffnen to open ['əʊpn]
Öffnungszeit opening time ['əʊpnɪŋ ˌtaɪm]
oft often ['ɒfn]
ohne without [wɪˈðaʊt]
Ohr ear [ɪə]
o.k. OK [əʊˈkeɪ]
okay OK [əʊˈkeɪ]
Oktober October [ɒkˈtəʊbə]
Opa grandad ['grændæd]
orange(farben) orange ['ɒrɪndʒ]
Ordner folder ['fəʊldə]
Ordnungszahl ordinal number ['ɔːdɪnl ˌnʌmbə]
organisieren to organize ['ɔːgənaɪz]
Ort place [pleɪs]
Osten east [iːst]
Ostern Easter ['iːstə]

D Dictionary

German – English

P

Paar pair [peə]
ein **paar** some [sʌm]; a few [ə 'fju:]
Päckchen packet ['pækɪt]
packen to pack [pæk]
Packung packet ['pækɪt]
Papa dad [dæd]
Papagei parrot ['pærət]
Papiere papers ['peɪpəz]
Papierförmchen paper case ['peɪpə ˌkeɪs]
Papierhut paper hat [ˌpeɪpə 'hæt]
parken to park [pɑ:k]
Parlament Parliament ['pɑ:ləmənt]
Partner/-in partner ['pɑ:tnə]
Party party ['pɑ:ti]
passieren to happen ['hæpn]
Person person ['pɜ:sn]
pfeifen whistling ['wɪslɪŋ]
Pferd horse [hɔ:s]
Pfund pound [paʊnd]
Picknick picnic ['pɪknɪk]
pink pink [pɪŋk]
Pirat/-in pirate ['paɪrət]
Pizza pizza ['pi:tsə]
Plan plan [plæn]
Planke plank [plæŋk]
Platz place [pleɪs]; room [ru:m]
plötzlich suddenly ['sʌdnli]
Plumpudding Christmas pudding [ˌkrɪsməs 'pʊdɪŋ]
Plural plural ['plʊərl]
Polizei police [pə'li:s]
Polizist policeman [pə'li:smən]
Pony pony ['pəʊni]
Popcorn popcorn ['pɒpkɔ:n]
Poster poster ['pəʊstə]
Postkarte postcard ['pəʊstkɑ:d]
Präposition preposition [ˌprepə'zɪʃn]
Präsens simple present [ˌsɪmpl 'preznt]
Präsentation presentation [ˌpreznˈteɪʃn]
präsentieren to present [prɪ'zent]
Preis price [praɪs]; prize [praɪz]
Premiere opening night ['əʊpnɪŋ ˌnaɪt]
Probe practice ['præktɪs]
probieren to try [traɪ]
Problem problem ['prɒbləm]
Programm programme ['prəʊgræm]
Projekt project ['prɒdʒekt]
Pronomen pronoun ['prəʊnaʊn]
Publikum audience ['ɔ:diəns]
Puffreis rice crispie [ˌraɪs 'krɪspi]
Pullover pullover ['pʊləʊvə]
putzen to clean [kli:n]

Q

Quiz quiz [kwɪz]

R

Rad wheel [wi:l]
Radiergummi rubber ['rʌbə]
Radio radio ['reɪdiəʊ]
Rap rap [ræp]
Rate mal! Guess what! [ges 'wɒt]
raten to guess [ges]
Ratespiel quiz [kwɪz]
Rätsel puzzle ['pʌzl]
Ratte rat [ræt]
Raum room [ru:m]
rechte/-r/-s right [raɪt]
rechts right [raɪt]; on the right [ɒn ðə 'raɪt]
reden to talk [tɔ:k]
Redewendung phrase [freɪz]
Refrain chorus ['kɔ:rəs]
Regel rule [ru:l]
regelmäßig regular ['regjələ]
regnen to rain [reɪn]
reich rich [rɪtʃ]
an der **Reihe** turn [tɜ:n]
Reihenfolge order ['ɔ:də]
reiten to ride [raɪd]
rennen to run [rʌn]
Rennen race [reɪs]
Rennbahn race ring ['reɪs ˌrɪŋ]
Rentier reindeer ['reɪndɪə]
Reporter/-in reporter [rɪ'pɔ:tə]
Rezept recipe ['resɪpi]
Rhombus diamond ['daɪəmənd]
Rice Krispie rice crispie [ˌraɪs 'krɪspi]
richtig true [tru:]; right [raɪt]; correct [kə'rekt]
Ring ring [rɪŋ]
Ritt ride [raɪd]
Rock skirt [skɜ:t]
Rolle part [pɑ:t]
Rollenspiel role play ['rəʊl pleɪ]
Rollschuh skate [skeɪt]
rosa pink [pɪŋk]
Rosine raisin ['reɪzn]
rot red [red]
rufen to shout [ʃaʊt]; to call [kɔ:l]
ruhig quiet ['kwaɪət]
rund um around [ə'raʊnd]
Russe/Russin Russian ['rʌʃn]
russisch, Russisch Russian ['rʌʃn]

S

Saal hall [hɔ:l]
Sache thing [θɪŋ]
Safari safari [sə'fɑ:ri]
Safarifahrt safari ride [sə'fɑ:ri ˌraɪd]
Saft juice [dʒu:s]
sagen to tell [tel]; to say [seɪ]
sah saw [sɔ:]
sah ... nicht didn't see ... ['dɪdənt ˌsi:]
sammeln to collect [kə'lekt]
Sammler/-in collector kə'lektə]
Samstag Saturday ['sætədeɪ]
Sandwich sandwich ['sænwɪdʒ]
Satz sentence ['sentəns]
sauber clean [kli:n]
sauber machen to clean [kli:n]
Schachtel box [bɒks]
Schaf sheep [ʃi:p]
Schatz dear [dɪə]; treasure ['treʒə]
schauen to look [lʊk]
Schauspiel drama ['drɑ:mə]
Schauspieler actor ['æktə]
Schauspielerin actress ['æktrəs]
Scheune barn [bɑ:n]
schicken to send [send]
Schiff ship [ʃɪp]
Schiffsjunge cabin boy ['kæbɪn ˌbɔɪ]
Schinken ham [hæm]
Schirmmütze cap [kæp]
schlafen to sleep [sli:p]
Schlafzimmer bedroom ['bedrʊm]
schlagen to chime [tʃaɪm]
Schlagzeug drum [drʌm]
schlecht bad [bæd]
schließen to close [kləʊz]
schließlich finally ['faɪnəli]
Schlüssel key [ki:]
schmelzen to melt [melt]
schmutzig dirty ['dɜ:ti]
schneiden to cut [kʌt]
schnell fast [fɑ:st]; quick [kwɪk]; quickly ['kwɪkli]
schneller faster ['fɑ:stə]
schnellste/-r/-s fastest ['fɑ:stɪst]
Schnurr! Purr! [pɜ:]
Schokocrossie chocolate crispie [ˌtʃɒklət 'krɪspi]
Schokolade chocolate ['tʃɒklət]
schon already [ɔ:l'redi]
schön nice [naɪs]; beautiful ['bju:tɪfʊl]
Schrank cupboard ['kʌbəd]
schrecklich awful ['ɔ:fl]
schreiben to write [raɪt]
Schreibtisch desk [desk]

Dictionary   D

German – English

schreien to shout [ʃaʊt]; to scream [skriːm]
Schuh shoe [ʃuː]
Schule school [skuːl]
Schüler/-in pupil [ˈpjuːpl]
Schulhof playground [ˈpleɪɡraʊnd]
Schulleiter/-in headteacher [ˌhedˈtiːtʃə]
Schulranzen school bag [ˈskuːl bæɡ]
Schultasche school bag [ˈskuːl bæɡ]
Schuppen shed [ʃed]
Schüssel bowl [bəʊl]
Schwanz tail [teɪl]
schwarz black [blæk]
Schweif tail [teɪl]
Schwein pig [pɪɡ]
schwer hard [hɑːd]
schwierig hard [hɑːd]
schwimmen to swim [swɪm]
schwimmen gehen to go swimming [ɡəʊ ˈswɪmɪŋ]
sechste/-r/-s sixth [sɪksθ]
seekrank seasick [ˈsiːsɪk]
segeln to sail [seɪl]
segelte sailed [seɪld]
sehen to see [siː]; to look [lʊk]
Sehenswürdigkeit sight [saɪt]
sehr very [ˈveri]; a lot [ə ˈlɒt]
Sei vorsichtig! Be careful! [ˌbiː ˈkeəfl]
seid are [ɑː]
Seide silk [sɪlk]
sein to be [biː]
sein/-e its [ɪts]; his [hɪz]
Seite page [peɪdʒ]
Sekunde second [ˈseknd]
selbst yourselves [jɔːˈselvz]
selbstverständlich of course [əv ˈkɔːs]
senden to send [send]
September September [sepˈtembə]
setzen to put [pʊt]
sich setzen to sit [sɪt]
sie she [ʃiː]; them [ðem]; her [hɜː]; you [juː]; they [ðeɪ]
siebte/-r/-s seventh [ˈsevnθ]
sind are [ɑː]
singen to sing [sɪŋ]
Situation situation [ˌsɪtjuˈeɪʃn]
sitzen to sit [sɪt]
Skateboard skateboard [ˈskeɪtbɔːd]
SMS text message [ˈtekst ˌmesɪdʒ]
Snack snack [snæk]
so so [səʊ]
sogar even [ˈiːvn]
Sohn son [sʌn]
Sommer summer [ˈsʌmə]
Sonnabend Saturday [ˈsætədeɪ]
Sonne sun [sʌn]

Sonnenbrille sunglasses pl. [ˈsʌnˌɡlɑːsɪz]
sonnig sunny [ˈsʌni]
Sonntag Sunday [ˈsʌndeɪ]
sortieren to sort [sɔːt]
Souvenirshop gift shop [ˈɡɪft ˌʃɒp]
sowohl ... als auch both ... and [bəʊθ]
Spaß fun [fʌn]
spät late [leɪt]
später later [ˈleɪtə]
Spaziergang walk [wɔːk]
Speisekarte menu [ˈmenjuː]
Spiel game [ɡeɪm]
spielen to act [ækt]; to play [pleɪ]
Spielkarte card [kɑːd]
Spielplatz playground [ˈpleɪɡraʊnd]
Spielzeug toy [tɔɪ]
Sport sport [spɔːt]
Sportfeld field [fiːld]
Sportfest sports day [ˈspɔːts deɪ]
Sporthalle sports hall [ˈspɔːts ˌhɔːl]
Sprache language [ˈlæŋɡwɪdʒ]
sprechen to talk [tɔːk]; to speak [spiːk]
Sprechgesang chant [tʃɑːnt]
springen to jump [dʒʌmp]
Stadt town [taʊn]
Stadtplan map [mæp]
Stall barn [bɑːn]
Stammbaum family tree [ˌfæməli ˈtriː]
Stand stall [stɔːl]
starren to stare [steə]
stehen to stand [stænd]
stehlen to steal [stiːl]
Stelle place [pleɪs]
stellen to put [pʊt]
Steuerrad wheel [wiːl]
Stil style [staɪl]
still quiet [ˈkwaɪət]
Stimme voice [vɔɪs]
stoßen to push [pʊʃ]
Straße street [striːt]
Streichelzoo pets corner [ˌpets ˈkɔːnə]
streichen to paint [peɪnt]
Streit fight [faɪt]
(sich) streiten to fight [faɪt]
Strumpf stocking [ˈstɒkɪŋ]
Stück piece [piːs]
Stuhl chair [tʃeə]
Stunde hour [aʊə]
suchen to look for [ˈlʊk fɔː]
Süden south [saʊθ]
super super [ˈsuːpə]
Supermarkt supermarket [ˈsuːpəˌmɑːkɪt]
süß sweet [swiːt]; cute [kjuːt]

Süßwarengeschäft (in einer Schule) tuck shop [ˈtʌkʃɒp]
Sweatshirt sweatshirt [ˈswetʃɜːt]
Szene scene [siːn]

T

Tabelle grid [ɡrɪd]
Tafel bar [bɑː]; board [bɔːd]
Tag day [deɪ]
Tagebuch diary [ˈdaɪəri]
Tante aunt [ɑːnt]
tanzen to dance [dɑːns]
Tasche bag [bæɡ]
Taschendieb/-in pickpocket [ˈpɪkˌpɒkɪt]
tätscheln to pat [pæt]
Taxi taxi [ˈtæksi]
Team team [tiːm]
Tee tea [tiː]
Teil part [pɑːt]; piece [piːs]
Telefon phone (= telephone) [fəʊn = ˈtelɪfəʊn]
Telefonnummer phone number [ˈfəʊn ˌnʌmbə]
teuer expensive [ɪkˈspensɪv]
Text text [tekst]
Theater theatre [ˈθɪətə]
Theaterklub Drama Club [ˈdrɑːmə ˌklʌb]
Theaterstück play [pleɪ]
Tier animal [ˈænɪml]
Tierfutter animal snacks [ˈænɪml ˌsnæks]
Tipp tip [tɪp]
Tisch table [ˈteɪbl]
Titel title [ˈtaɪtl]
Tochter daughter [ˈdɔːtə]
toll super [ˈsuːpə]; great [ɡreɪt]
Ton sound [saʊnd]
tot dead [ded]
töten to kill [kɪl]
Tourist/-in tourist [ˈtʊərɪst]
Touristik-Information tourist information centre [ˌtʊərɪst ɪnfəˈmeɪʃn sentə]
Tradition tradition [trəˈdɪʃn]
tragen to wear [weə]; to carry [ˈkæri]
Training practice [ˈpræktɪs]
Traktor tractor [ˈtræktə]
Traum dream [driːm]
treffen to see [siː]; to meet [miːt]
trinken to drink [drɪŋk]
Trommel drum [drʌm]
Truthahn turkey [ˈtɜːki]
tschüss goodbye [ɡʊdˈbaɪ]; Bye! [baɪ]
T-Shirt T-shirt [ˈtiːʃɜːt]

two hundred and thirteen   **213**

Dictionary

German – English

tun to make [meɪk]; to put [pʊt]; to do [duː]
Tunnel tunnel [ˈtʌnl]
Tür door [dɔː]
türkisch, Türkisch Turkish [ˈtɜːkɪʃ]
  Türkisch Turkish [ˈtɜːkɪʃ]
Turnschuh trainer [ˈtreɪnə]
Tüte bag [bæg]

U

üben to practise [ˈpræktɪs]
über above [əˈbʌv]; across [əˈkrɒs]; over [ˈəʊvə]
überall everywhere [ˈevriweə]
übernachten to stay [steɪ]
überqueren to cross [krɒs]
Überraschung surprise [səˈpraɪz]
Überschrift heading [ˈhedɪŋ]; title [ˈtaɪtl]
Übung practice [ˈpræktɪs]; exercise [ˈeksəsaɪz]
Uhr o'clock [əˈklɒk]
Uhr clock [klɒk]
Uhrzeit time [taɪm]
um at [æt; ət]
um … herum round … [raʊnd]; around … [əˈraʊnd]
sich umdrehen to turn [tɜːn]
umfallen to fall over [fɔːl ˈəʊvə]
Umzug procession [prəˈseʃn]
und and [ænd; ən]
unglücklich unhappy [ʌnˈhæpi]
unheimlich scary [ˈskeəri]
Uniform uniform [ˈjuːnɪfɔːm]
Unordnung mess [mes]
unregelmäßig irregular [ɪˈregjələ]
uns us [ʌs]
unser/-e our [aʊə]
unten (im Gebäude) downstairs [ˌdaʊnˈsteəz]
unter under [ˈʌndə]
Unterhaltung talk [tɔːk]
Unterrichtsstunde lesson [ˈlesn]
unterstrichen underlined [ˌʌndəˈlaɪnd]

V

Valentinstag Valentine's Day [ˈvæləntaɪnz ˌdeɪ]
Vater father [ˈfɑːðə]
Vati dad [dæd]
Veranstaltung event [ɪˈvent]
verärgert angry [ˈæŋgri]
Verb verb [vɜːb]

verbinden to connect [kəˈnekt]
Verein club [klʌb]
verfolgen to chase [tʃeɪs]
vergessen to forget [fəˈget]
vergleichen to compare [kəmˈpeə]
vergnügt jolly [ˈdʒɒli]
verheiratet married [ˈmærid]
sich verirren to get lost [ˌget ˈlɒst]
verkaufen to sell [sel]
Verkäufer/-in assistant [əˈsɪstnt]
Verkehrsmittel transport [ˈtrænspɔːt]
verlassen to leave [liːv]
sich verlaufen to get lost [ˌget ˈlɒst]
Verlaufsform der Gegenwart present progressive [ˌpreznt prəˈgresɪv]
verlor lost [lɒst]
Vermittlung communication [kəˌmjuːnɪˈkeɪʃn]
Verständigung communication [kəˌmjuːnɪˈkeɪʃn]
verstehen to understand [ˌʌndəˈstænd]
versuchen to try [traɪ]
Verwandte/-r kin [kɪn]; relative [ˈrelətɪv]
verwenden to use [juːz]
Verzeihung! Sorry! [ˈsɒri]
Video video [ˈvɪdiəʊ]
viel much [mʌtʃ]; lots (of) [lɒts]; a lot [ə ˈlɒt]
viel/-e a lot of [ə ˈlɒt əv]
viele many [ˈmeni]
Vielen Dank. Thank you very much. [ˈθæŋk ju ˌveri mʌtʃ]; thanks a lot [ˈθæŋks əˌlɒt]
vielleicht maybe [ˈmeɪbi]
Viertel quarter [ˈkwɔːtə]
vierte/-r/-s fourth [fɔːθ]
Vokabular vocabulary [vəˈkæbjəlri]
voll full [fʊl]
Volleyball volleyball [ˈvɒlibɔːl]
von of [ɒv]; from [frɒm]
vor before [bɪˈfɔː]
vor … … ago [əˈgəʊ]
vorbei over [ˈəʊvə]
vorbereiten to prepare [prɪˈpeə]
Vorhang curtain [ˈkɜːtn]
vorher before [bɪˈfɔː]
Vormittag morning [ˈmɔːnɪŋ]
vormittags am [ˌeɪˈem]
Vorsicht! Watch out! [ˌwɒtʃ ˈaʊt]

W

wahr true [truː]
Wand wall [wɔːl]
Wanderung walk [wɔːk]

wann when [wen]
war was [wɒz]
waren were [wɜː]
Warenhaus department store [dɪˈpɑːtmənt ˌstɔː]
warm warm [wɔːm]
warten to wait [weɪt]
warum why [waɪ]
was what [wɒt]
waschen to wash [wɒʃ]
Wasser water [ˈwɔːtə]
Wecker alarm clock [əˈlɑːm ˌklɒk]
Weg way [weɪ]
wegen about [əˈbaʊt]
weglaufen to run away [rʌn əˈweɪ]
wegrennen to run away [rʌn əˈweɪ]
Weihnachten Christmas [ˈkrɪsməs]
Weihnachtslieder singen carol-singing [ˈkærəl ˌsɪŋɪŋ]
Weihnachtsmann Santa Claus [ˌsæntəˈklɔːz]
1. Weihnachtstag Christmas Day [ˌkrɪsməs ˈdeɪ]
weil because [bɪˈkɒz]
weit far [fɑː]
weitere more [mɔː]
ein(e) weitere(-r/-s) another [əˈnʌðə]
weitermachen to go on [gəʊ ˈɒn]
Weitsprung long jump [ˈlɒŋ ˌdʒʌmp]
welche/-r/-s which [wɪtʃ]
Welt world [wɜːld]
wem who [huː]
wen who [huː]
wenden to turn [tɜːn]
wer who [huː]
  wer sonst who else [huː ˈels]
werden to become [bɪˈkʌm]
werfen to throw [θrəʊ]
Westen west [west]
Wetter weather [ˈweðə]
wie like [laɪk]; how [haʊ]
wieder again [əˈgen]
wiederholen to repeat [rɪˈpiːt]
Wiederholung revision [rɪˈvɪʒn]
Wiese field [ˈfiːld]
Willkommen … Welcome … [ˈwelkəm]
Wind wind [wɪnd]
windig windy [ˈwɪndi]
winken to wave [weɪv]
Winter winter [ˈwɪntə]
winzig tiny [ˈtaɪni]
wir we [wiː]
wirklich really [ˈrɪəli]
wissen to know [nəʊ]
Witz joke [dʒəʊk]

214 two hundred and fourteen

Dictionary

German – English

wo where [weə]
wohin where [weə]
Wohltätigkeitsverein charity ['tʃærɪti]
wohnen to live [lɪv]
Wohnung flat [flæt]
Wohnzimmer living room ['lɪvɪŋ rʊm]
wollen to want [wɒnt]
wollte wanted ['wɒntɪd]
Wort word [wɜːd]
Wörterbuch dictionary ['dɪkʃənri]
Wörternetz mind map ['maɪnd mæp]
Wortschatz vocabulary [və'kæbjəlri]
Wortschatztechniken vocabulary skills [və'kæbjəlri 'skɪlz]
wunderschön beautiful ['bjuːtɪfʊl]
wundervoll beautiful ['bjuːtɪfʊl]
wünschen to wish [wɪʃ]
wütend angry ['æŋgri]

Z

Zahl number ['nʌmbə]
zählen to count [kaʊnt]
Zartbitterschokolade plain chocolate [ˌpleɪn 'tʃɒklət]
zehnte/-r/-s tenth [tenθ]
zeichnen to draw [drɔː]
zeigen to show [ʃəʊ]; to point [pɔɪnt]
Zeit time [taɪm]
Zeitleiste time line ['taɪm laɪn]
Zeitung newspaper ['njuːsˌpeɪpə]
Zeitungsladen newsagent ['njuːzˌeɪdʒnt]
Zentrum centre ['sentə]
Zicklein kid [kɪd]
Ziege goat [gəʊt]
ziehen to pull [pʊl]
Zimmer room [ruːm]
zu to [tʊ]; too [tuː]

zu/nach … kommen to get to … ['get tʊ]
zu Ende gehen to end [end]
zu Fuß on foot [ˌɒn 'fʊt]
zu Hause home [həʊm]
zu spät late [leɪt]
Zucker sugar ['ʃʊgə]
zuerst first [fɜːst]
Zug train [treɪn]
Zuhause home [həʊm]
zuhören to listen ['lɪsn]
zumachen to close [kləʊz]
zuordnen to match [mætʃ]
zurück back [bæk]
zusammen together [tə'geðə]
zuschauen to watch [wɒtʃ]
zustimmen to agree [ə'griː]
zwanzigste/-r/-s twentieth ['twentiɪθ]
zweite/-r/-s second ['seknd]
zwinkern to wink [wɪŋk]
zwischen between [bɪ'twiːn]

two hundred and fifteen **215**

Numbers

Kardinalzahlen   Cardinal Numbers

1	**one** [wʌn]	eins		17	**seventeen** [ˌsevn'ti:n]	siebzehn
2	**two** [tu:]	zwei		18	**eighteen** [ˌeɪ'ti:n]	achtzehn
3	**three** [θri:]	drei		19	**nineteen** [ˌnaɪn'ti:n]	neunzehn
4	**four** [fɔ:]	vier		20	**twenty** ['twenti]	zwanzig
5	**five** [faɪv]	fünf		21	**twenty-one** [ˌtwenti'wʌn]	einundzwanzig
6	**six** [sɪks]	sechs		22	**twenty-two** [ˌtwenti'tu:]	zweiundzwanzig
7	**seven** ['sevn]	sieben		23	**twenty-three** [ˌtwenti'θri:]	dreiundzwanzig
8	**eight** [eɪt]	acht		…		…
9	**nine** [naɪn]	neun		30	**thirty** ['θɜ:ti]	dreißig
10	**ten** [ten]	zehn		40	**forty** ['fɔ:ti]	vierzig
11	**eleven** [ɪ'levn]	elf		50	**fifty** ['fɪfti]	fünfzig
12	**twelve** [twelv]	zwölf		60	**sixty** ['sɪksti]	sechzig
13	**thirteen** [θɜ:'ti:n]	dreizehn		70	**seventy** ['sevnti]	siebzig
14	**fourteen** [ˌfɔ:'ti:n]	vierzehn		80	**eighty** ['eɪti]	achtzig
15	**fifteen** [ˌfɪf'ti:n]	fünfzehn		90	**ninety** ['naɪnti]	neunzig
16	**sixteen** [ˌsɪks'ti:n]	sechzehn		100	**a / one hundred** ['hʌndrəd]	hundert

Ordinalzahlen   Ordinal Numbers

1st	**first** [fɜ:st]	erste (-r/-s)		15th	**fifteenth** [fɪf'ti:nθ]	fünfzehnte (-r/-s)
2nd	**second** ['seknd]	zweite (-r/-s)		16th	**sixteenth** [sɪks'ti:nθ]	sechzehnte (-r/-s)
3rd	**third** [θɜ:d]	dritte (-r/-s)		17th	**seventeenth** [sevn'ti:nθ]	siebzehnte (-r/-s)
4th	**fourth** [fɔ:θ]	vierte (-r/-s)		18th	**eighteenth** [eɪ'ti:nθ]	achtzehnte (-r/-s)
5th	**fifth** [fɪfθ]	fünfte (-r/-s)		19th	**nineteenth** [naɪn'ti:nθ]	neunzehnte (-r/-s)
6th	**sixth** [sɪksθ]	sechste (-r/-s)		20th	**twentieth** ['twentiɪθ]	zwanzigste (-r/-s)
7th	**seventh** ['sevnθ]	siebte (-r/-s)		21st	**twenty-first** [ˌtwenti'fɜ:st]	einundzwanzigste (-r/-s)
8th	**eighth** [eɪtθ]	achte (-r/-s)		22nd	**twenty-second** [ˌtwenti'seknd]	zweiundzwanzigste (-r/-s)
9th	**ninth** [naɪnθ]	neunte (-r/-s)		23rd	**twenty-third** [ˌtwenti'θɜ:d]	dreiundzwanzigste (-r/-s)
10th	**tenth** [tenθ]	zehnte (-r/-s)		24th	**twenty-fourth** [ˌtwenti'fɔ:θ]	vierundzwanzigste (-r/-s)
11th	**eleventh** [ɪ'levnθ]	elfte (-r/-s)		…		…
12th	**twelfth** [twelfθ]	zwölfte (-r/-s)		30th	**thirtieth** ['θɜ:tiəθ]	dreißigste (-r/-s)
13th	**thirteenth** [θɜ:'ti:nθ]	dreizehnte (-r/-s)		31st	**thirty-first** [ˌθɜ:ti'fɜ:st]	einunddreißigste (-r/-s)
14th	**fourteenth** [fɔ:'ti:nθ]	vierzehnte (-r/-s)		…		…

Mengen   Quantities

How much …?	Wie viel … ?	**a bag of** apples	eine Tüte Äpfel
How many …?	Wie viele … ?	**a bottle of** water	eine Flasche Wasser
a lot of money / books	viel Geld / viele Bücher	**a box of** eggs	eine Schachtel Eier
a packet of cheese	ein Päckchen Käse	**no** chocolate	keine Schokolade

In the classroom

Talking to your friends or teachers

Before the lesson
Good morning, Mr/Mrs/Miss … .	Guten Morgen, Herr/Frau … .
I'm sorry I'm late.	Tut mir Leid, dass ich mich verspätet habe.

Asking for help
Can you help me, please?	Kannst du / Können Sie mir bitte helfen?
How do you do this exercise?	Wie macht man diese Übung?
Is this right? I'm not sure.	Ist das richtig? Ich bin mir nicht sicher.
Sorry, I don't know. Ask … .	Tut mir Leid, das weiß ich nicht. Frag doch … !
Why don't you ask the teacher?	Frag doch den Lehrer / die Lehrerin!
Sorry. Can you say that again, please?	Wie bitte? Können Sie / kannst du das bitte wiederholen?
Can we open the window, please?	Können wir bitte das Fenster öffnen?
Can I go to the toilet please, Sir / Miss?	Herr … / Frau …, kann ich bitte zur Toilette gehen?
What's the homework?	Was haben wir als Hausaufgabe?

Asking for information
What's that in English/German?	Was heißt das auf Englisch/Deutsch?
What does that mean?	Was bedeutet das?
How do you spell …, please?	Wie schreibt man … , bitte?
What's the time, please?	Wie spät ist es, bitte?
Where's the … ? / Where are the … ?	Wo ist der/die/das … ? / Wo sind die … ?
What's today's date?	Welches Datum haben wir heute?

Working together
Can I borrow your book / …, please?	Kann ich mir bitte dein Buch / … ausleihen?
Thank you. / Thanks a lot.	Danke. / Vielen Dank!
You're welcome.	Bitte. / Bitte schön!
Now it's your turn.	Jetzt bist du an der Reihe.
Let's make / draw a … .	Lass(t) uns ein / eine / einen … machen / zeichnen.
Let's act the story / dialogue.	Lass(t) uns die Geschichte / den Dialog vorspielen.

Your teacher can say

Open your books at page … .	Öffnet eure Bücher auf Seite … .
Turn to page … .	Schlagt Seite … auf.
Do exercise … on page … for homework.	Als Hausaufgabe macht Übung … auf Seite … .
Where's your book, David?	David, wo ist dein Buch?
Sit down, please, and be quiet.	Setz dich bitte und sei ruhig. / Setzt euch bitte und seid ruhig.
Say that again, please.	Wiederhole es, bitte.
Try again!	Versuch es noch einmal!
That's really good!	Das ist sehr gut!
That's all for today. You can go.	Das wäre es für heute. Ihr dürft gehen.

Lösungen Check-out

Unit 1   Seite 25

1 A new school

Hello there,
Here **are** three pictures of my new friends and school in Greenwich. Picture number one **is** in the playground – it **is** big. I **am** with Lisa and Sam. They **are** nice. In picture number two we **are** in the cafeteria. The boy at the door **is** Terry. He **is** in Year 7, too. In picture three he and Lisa **are** in the classroom. Sam **is** not there. He **is** always late. My new school **is** OK but you **are** in Bristol an I **am** in Greenwich. That **is** not OK.
Love, Emma

2 Questions and answers

1. **Is** Thomas Tallis a big school?   – Yes, **it is.**
2. **Is** Mr Newman a teacher?   – No, **he isn't.**
3. Hi, Terry and Lisa! **Are** you from Greenwich?   – Yes, **we are.**
4. Oh, I'm sorry. **Am** I late?   – Yes, **you are.**
5. **Are** the girls in the classroom?   – No, **they aren't.**
6. **Is** your school bag new?   – No, **it isn't.**
7. **Is** Mrs Carter a teacher?   – Yes, **she is.**
8. Hello, Mrs Carter. **Are** we in the right classroom?   – No, **you aren't.**

3 What is different?

In A there is a football behind the door. – In B Tom is behind the door.
In A there is a pencil case on the table. – In B there are three pencils on the table.
In A there is a school bag on the chair. – In B there is a school bag under the chair.
In A there are two books in the cupboard. – In B there are four books in the cupboard.

4 Who, what or where?

1. **Who** is from Greenwich?
2. **Who** is Mr Newman?
3. **Who/What** is in the tree?
4. **Where** is Emma from?
5. **Who** is one?
6. **Where** is Greenwich?

Unit 2   Seite 39

1 Find the right words

Lisa: Let's look at **your** pictures from Bristol, Emma. Who's the girl here?
Emma: She's a friend from **my** old school. **Her** name is Fiona Green. The Greens have got a funny house. **Their** house has got a living room upstairs – and **its** walls are pink and yellow! And Fiona's dad is funny, too. He's always got funny pictures on **his** T-shirts!
Lisa: Ha, ha! Is that a dog with Fiona – or a mouse? We've got a dog, but **our** dog is big.
Emma: Yes, **your** dog is very big – but Fiona's dog is nice, too.

2 Six pictures

a)
2. That's Lisa's dog.
3. That's Tom's cupboard.
4. That's Sam's school bag.
5. That's Emma's CD.
6. That's Nasreen's T-shirt.

b)
2. Lisa has got a dog.
3. Tom has got a cupboard.
4. Sam has got a school bag.
5. Emma has got a CD.
6. Nasreen has got a T-shirt.

3 Funny questions

Example: Has my dad got drums in the car? – No, he hasn't.
1. Have my cousins got a shed in the playground? – No, they haven't.
2. Have we got a sofa in the bathroom? – No, we haven't.
3. Has my grandma got a computer in the garden? – No, she hasn't.
4. Has our school got a garden in the cafeteria? – No, it hasn't.
5. Have I got a cupboard in my school bag? – No, you haven't.
6. Has Barker got a window in his bed? – No, he hasn't.

Lösungen

Unit 3 Seite 53

1 What time is it?

b)
It's quarter past five./It's five fifteen.
It's eight fifty-seven./It's three minutes to nine.
It's nine forty-eight./It's two minutes to ten.
It's ten sixteen./It's sixteen minutes past ten.
It's three thirty-three.

It's seven o'clock.
It's two-oh-four./It's four minutes past two.
It's four ten./It's ten minutes past four.
It's half past one./It's one thirty.
It's quarter to one./It's twelve forty-five.

2 Tom's Sunday

On Sundays Tom gets up at **ten o'clock**. He makes breakfast at **half past ten**. Tom watches TV at **quarter past four**. He does his homework at **six o'clock**. Tom eats dinner at **half past seven**. He goes to bed at **quarter to nine**.

3 I never do!

1. We usually **meet** our friends in Greenwich on Saturdays.
2. He never **does** his homework at the weekend.
3. She often **watches** TV in the evenings.
4. I sometimes **call** my grandma on Sundays.
5. He usually **helps** his sister with her homework.

4 Put in this, that, these or those

1. **That** café over there is nice.
2. **These** crisps here are great.
3. Is **this** card here your card?
4. **Those** drums over there are Terry's.
5. **This** apple here is great!
6. **Those** boys over there are nice.
7. **That** teacher over there is nice.
8. **This** CD here is bad.

Unit 4 Seite 71

1 Find the pronouns

1. When does the bus leave? Emma rides the bus. Ask **her**.
2. Hey – We're lucky. My dad can take **us** on a tour of the sights!
3. The Cutty Sark is great. I like **it** because it's so beautiful.
4. I can find the tunnel. It's easy! Please give **me** the map.
5. OK, Terry. I can help **you** with your transport project today.
6. Mr Jackson knows the way. Ask **him**.
7. Lisa is always funny on the bus. I like **her**.
8. Mr Jackson drives the friends all round town. He takes **them** everywhere.

2 Questions

Do you go to the park on foot? – Yes, I do./No, I don't.
Do you go to town by underground? – Yes, I do./No, I don't.
Do you come to school by bike? – Yes, I do./No, I don't.
Do your friends go to the park by bike? – Yes, they do./No, they don't.
Do your friends go to town by train? – Yes, they do./No, they don't.
Do your friends come to school by bus? – Yes, they do./No, they don't.
Does your teacher come to school on foot? – Yes, he does./No, he doesn't.
Does your teacher come to school by train? – Yes, she does./No, she doesn't.

3 The friends and transport

Sam sometimes walks (to school).
He sometimes takes the train/goes by train.
He often takes the bus/goes by bus.

Terry sometimes rides his bike.
He never walks (to school).
He sometimes takes the train/goes by train.
He sometimes takes the bus/goes by bus.

Ben sometimes rides his bike.
He never walks (to school).
He often takes the train/goes by train.
He sometimes takes the bus/goes by bus.

Jade often rides her bike.
She often walks (to school).
She never takes the train/goes by train.
She never takes the bus/goes by bus.

Lisa often rides her bike.
She often walks (to school).
She sometimes takes the train/goes by train.
She never takes the bus/goes by bus.

Emma never rides her bike.
She often walks (to school).
She sometimes takes the train/goes by train.
She often takes the bus/goes by bus.

Nasreen never rides her bike.
She often walks (to school).
She often takes the train/goes by train.
She sometimes takes the bus/goes by bus.

two hundred and nineteen **219**

Lösungen

Unit 5 Seite 83

1 What are the customer's questions?

1. Customer: (Excuse me.) How much is the bag?
2. Customer: Where are the pencils, please?
3. Customer: (Excuse me.) What size is this T-shirt?
4. Customer: (Excuse me.) How much are the crisps?
5. Customer: (Excuse me.) Have you got magazines, too?

2 At school

1. A: Can I use your ruler, please? — B: Yes, I'm not using it right now.
2. A: Terry? He's in the school shop. — B: Again! What is he buying today?
3. A: Mrs Carter is late this morning. — B: No, she isn't. Look, she's coming now.
4. A: Aren't Lisa and Terry friends? — B: No. They aren't talking today.
5. A: This isn't the right exercise. — B: Oh no! Are we doing the wrong homework?
6. A: Do you want to play football? — B: No. I'm eating my sandwich.

3 What aren't they doing?

1. Barker isn't eating. He's sleeping.
2. Sam's grandma isn't drawing a picture. She's writing.
3. Emma and Lisa aren't playing computer games. They're dancing.

4 Put in the right words

Mrs Taylor: What do we need from the shops? How **much** flour have we still got?
Lisa: There is only **a little** flour here. And there isn't **much** sugar.
Mrs Taylor: And how **many** eggs have we got? I want to make a small cake so I only need **a few** eggs.
Lisa: We don't need eggs. But there's only **a little** cheese. It's not **much** for a big family!
Mrs Taylor: OK. I need flour, sugar and cheese. Oh, and **a few** bags of crisps, too. There aren't **many** in the cupboard.

Unit 6 Seite 97

1 Simple present or present progressive?

2. This Saturday they **are going** to the Cotswolds. 3. Sam's uncle usually **drives**, but today he **is reading** the map and Sam's aunt **is driving**. 4. Phil, Tracy and Susan always **sit** behind their parents. 5. Tracy usually **sleeps** and Phil often **plays** his computer games. What is Susan doing now? 6. She **is telling** jokes. 7. She always **tells** jokes.

2 Plurals: Regular and irregular

- child → children
- sandwich → sandwiches
- picture → pictures
- sheep → sheep
- goose → geese
- mouse → mice
- desk → desks
- cake → cakes
- island → islands
- pound → pounds
- pencil case → pencil cases
- shop → shops

3 Must and needn't

a)
2. Oh no! It's raining. I **must wear** my wellies.
3. Hurry! We **must be** at the bus stop at 2:00.
4. This room is really dirty. We **must clean** it!
5. Terry, you **must tell** jokes in the bus.
6. I **must send** a postcard to Grandma.
7. You **must listen** to your teacher in the lesson.

b)
2. Great! I **needn't wear** my uniform today.
3. Dad, you **needn't drive** us to school. We can walk.
4. Terry, you **needn't tell** your old jokes.
5. Lisa, you **needn't wait** for us. You can go to the shop without us.
6. You **needn't phone** your mum. She is not at home.

Unit 7 Seite 109

1 In the library

1. Terry is sitting **next to** Lisa in the library.
2. There are books **on** the table.
3. I cannot see Terry's and Lisa's bags. They must be **under** the table.
4. You can't have a library **without** books!
5. Mrs Carter is often **in** the library.
6. Terry has got a great book! There are a lot of interesting things **in** it.

220 two hundred and twenty

2 What does Terry say?

1. I like cats **but** I don't like dogs.
2. Next year I want to be in the play **and** I want to go to sports day.
3. At 3:30 I must play my drums **so** I can't go to the park.
4. This morning I want to go to Emma's shop **and** this afternoon I want to play computer games with Sam.
5. It's raining **so** I can't play basketball.
6. Today I must clean my room **but/ so** I needn't clean my shed.

3 Where and when?

1. I do my homework in the library after school.
2. I see my friends at the fair every year.
3. I have breakfast in the kitchen at seven o'clock.
4. I listen to music in the shed on Sunday mornings.
5. I have lunch in the cafeteria at twelve o'clock.
6. I eat dinner at home in the evening.
7. I sometimes watch TV in the living room after school.
8. I often meet my friends outside in the summer.

4 A Thomas Tallis quiz

1. The name of the school play is *Turn again, Whittington*.
2. You can buy or sell things at different stalls at the summer fair. You can play games and listen to music, too. You can eat cake, buy drinks or try on a T-shirt.
3. All the school year events are in the school planner.
4. The Lantern Procession is near the Thames.
5. Sports day is on the third Saturday in June.
6. Sam and Terry are a horse in the play.
7. You can play cricket on the big field at sports day.
8. The school year always starts in September.

Revision 1 Seite 54–55

1 The mouse house

Tom and **his** brother Tim have got a big bed in **their** room. **They** often play in the garden with **their** sister, Tess. **Their** mum is often in the kitchen, but Grandad Thomas is sometimes in the garden, too. **He** usually watches TV in the living room with Grandma Tilly. Grandma likes **her** family. **She** often says, "I've got all **our** pictures."
Tom says, "I like **my** picture!"
Tom's father's picture is good, too. **It** is on page 27 in this book. "Can **you** find **his** picture?" Tom asks.

2 Who has got it?

Emma: Nasreen, I **have got** my old CD with music but I **haven't got** my new CD. **Have** you **got** my new CD?
Nasreen: Oh, Emma, I **haven't got** your CD! Ask Mum. There are a lot of CDs in the kitchen. Maybe she **has got** your CD there.
Emma: Has Mum got it? No, she **has got** books and stories on CDs, but not music CDs.
Nasreen: Is it in the shop? Dad **has got** a lot of CDs there.
Emma: No, they're all computer CDs. He **hasn't got** music CDs in the shop. Mum and Dad **have got** all their music CDs in the living room, but they **haven't got** my CD there.
Nasreen: Well, then, it's in our room. Go and look again.
Emma: Oh, OK. (later) Hey, Nasreen, I **have got** my new CD! It's in my school bag.

3 Don't do it!

Don't put your magazines on my chair!
Don't put your shoes under my bed!
Don't put your dirty T-shirts in the wardrobe.
Don't make a mess in the room.

Don't forget your books.
Don't use my pens.
Don't take my new T-shirt!

4 What can they do?

1. Terry can play the drums in his shed.
2. Sam and Terry can play new computer games in Sam's room.
3. Terry can take Sam's old games to his shed.
4. Lisa can call Terry on her mobile from her room.
5. She can't play football in her room.
6. You can't watch TV in the garden.
7. Emma can't have her own room.
8. Lisa and Ben can take Barker to the park.
9. Jade can ride her bike in the park.
10. Emma can sing songs in her room.

5 Terry's friends

1. Terry often plays his drums.
2. Tiger usually sleeps on Terry's shed.
3. Mr Jackson never goes into Terry's shed.
4. Terry and Sam sometimes play computer games.
5. Barker always chases Tiger.

6 Tiger's day

Tiger **is** the Jacksons' cat. He **sleeps** on Terry's shed in their garden. Sometimes Tiger **goes** into the shed, but Terry **never likes** that. Tiger **sleeps** on the shed every morning. One Saturday morning at 11:30 Terry **opens** the door of the shed and **goes** out. He **goes** to the house. Tiger **gets up** and **looks** at the door. Terry and Mrs Jackson **are** in the house. Now Tiger **can go in**to the shed. He **looks** at Terry's drums. But drums **are** boring. You **can't (cannot) eat** them. What **is** that? There **is** a mouse behind the drums. Tiger **chases** the mouse, and it **runs away** into a corner but Tiger **sees** it. He **gets up** on a chair. He **washes** his face **and watches** the corner. Then Terry **comes** in! "Tiger!" he **shouts**. "No cats in my shed!"

Revision 2   Seite 84–85

1 At Sam's party

Sam: Where's Lisa, Emma? I can't see **her**.
Emma: She's in the kitchen. Look, your grandma's talking to **her**. They're next to the cake.
Sam: Oh, yes, I can see **them** now.
Emma: That cake is great! I really like **it**!
Sam: Thanks. Look, Lisa and Terry are coming.
Lisa: Hi, Sam, we're coming to talk to **you**.
Terry: Your grandma is giving **us** lots of cake. We can't eat **it** all!
Grandma: Hey, where's Terry? I've got cake for **him**!
Sam: Oh, Grandma!

2 Make a quiz

What does Lisa like? – She likes football.
Does Terry play computer games? – No, he doesn't. He plays the drums.
Does Emma play the guitar? – Yes, she does.
What does Sam play? – He plays computer games.
Does Barker like Tiger? – No, he doesn't. (He always chases Tiger).
What does Nasreen like? – She likes music CDs.
Does Tom like chocolate? – Yes, he does.
What does Sam's grandma like? – She likes apples.

3 Saturday

Mr Brook: What would you like to do, Farah?
Mrs Brook: I want to work in the flat. Then I want to go shopping at the supermarket. After that I would like to read a magazine.
Mr Brook: What would you like to do, Nasreen?
Nasreen: I want to work in the flat. Then I would like to watch TV. After that I want to go shopping in London.
Mr Brook: What would you like to do, Emma?
Emma: I want to go shopping at the supermarket. Then I would like to go to the park. After that I would like to listen to music.

4 Sam's party

1. Sam is **making** invitations on the computer. He is **inviting** all his friends to his birthday party.
2. Sam's dad is at the supermarket. He's **buying** eggs.
3. What's Sam **doing** now? – He's **making** a cake.
4. They're all at the party. They're **eating** the cake.
5. Now it's seven o'clock and they're **going** to the school disco.
6. It's great. They're all **dancing**.
7. The music stops. What's **happening**?
8. All the people at the disco are **singing** "Happy Birthday" to Sam!

5 Terry's Saturday

It's 9:30.   Is Terry playing the drums? – No, he isn't, he's having breakfast.
It's 9:40.   What is Terry doing? – He is helping his dad in the garden.
It's 10:30. Is Terry helping his mum? – No, he isn't, he's going to the park.
It's 10:40. What is Terry doing? – He's talking to Emma and Sam in the park.
It's 11:30. Is Terry playing football? – No, he isn't, he's playing his drums in the shed.
It's 12:30. What is Terry doing? – He's having lunch.
It's 1:00.   What is Terry doing now? – He's cleaning the kitchen with his mum.
It's 1:30.   Is Terry reading a book? – No, he isn't, he's playing a computer game.
It's 2:15.   What is Terry doing? He's going to the park again.
It's 2:30.   Is Terry going home? – No, he isn't, he's playing football with Lisa.
It's 4:20.   What is Terry doing? – He's going home for tea.
It's 5:30.   What is Terry doing now? – He's watching TV.
It's 6:00.   Is Terry making a cake? – No, he isn't, he's doing his homework.
It's 7:00.   What is Terry doing? – He's watching a video.

Bild-/Textquellen

Bildquellen:

Umschlag: Ernst Klett Verlag (Hacker), Stuttgart; VVS: 1-4 Ernst Klett Verlag (Fletcher), Stuttgart; S.12: Ernst Klett Verlag (Hacker), Stuttgart; S.13: 1-2 Ernst Klett Verlag (Fletcher), Stuttgart; 3 Ernst Klett Verlag (Hacker), Stuttgart; 4-6 Ernst Klett Verlag, Stuttgart; S.15: 1 Ernst Klett Verlag (Fletcher), Stuttgart; 2-4 Bananastock (RF), Watlington; 5 Corbis, Düsseldorf; 6 Bananastock (RF), Watlington; 7 Ernst Klett Verlag (Hacker), Stuttgart; S.17: 1 Ernst Klett Verlag (Fletcher), Stuttgart; 2 Corbis, Düsseldorf; S.21: Ernst Klett Verlag (Fletcher), Stuttgart; S.28: 1-2 Ernst Klett Verlag (Fletcher), Stuttgart; S.29: 1 Alamy Images (Arcaid/Churchill), Oxfordshire; 2 Alamy Images (Elizabeth Whiting Associates), Oxfordshire; 3 Alamy Images (Harding), Oxfordshire; 4-5 Ernst Klett Verlag (Fletcher), Stuttgart; S.30: 1, 9 Corbis (RF), Düsseldorf; 2, 4, 7 Ernst Klett Verlag (Fletcher), Stuttgart; 3, 5-6, 8, 10 Bananastock (RF), Watlington; S.31: Ernst Klett Verlag (Hacker), Stuttgart; S.42: 1-4, 6-7 Ernst Klett Verlag (Fletcher), Stuttgart; 5 Fotosearch (BRAND X PICTURES RF), Waukesha; S.43: 1 Fotosearch (BRAND X PICTURES RF), Waukesha; 2 Mauritius (Gilsdorf); 3 Avenue Images GmbH (Image 100 RF), Hamburg; 4 Picture-Alliance (dpa/Wolfgang Weihs), Frankfurt; S.44: Ernst Klett Verlag (Hacker), Stuttgart; S.46: Avenue Images GmbH (Image 100 RF), Hamburg; S.49: Ernst Klett Verlag (Fletcher), Stuttgart; S.58: 1 Ernst Klett Verlag (Hacker), Stuttgart; 2 Picture-Alliance (Picture Press/Frank), Frankfurt; 3 Corbis (Colin Garratt/Milep), Düsseldorf; S.59: 1 Getty Images (PhotoDisc); 2 Bananastock (RF), Watlington; 3 Getty Images (PhotoDisc); 4 Alamy Images (FCL Photogr. RF), Oxfordshire; 5 National Maritime Museum, London; 6 Topham Picturepoint (UPPA Ltd), Edenbridge Kent; S.60: 1-2 Ernst Klett Verlag (Fletcher), Stuttgart; S.61: 1 Corbis, Düsseldorf; 2 Mauritius (Vidler), Mittenwald; 3 Mauritius (age Fotostock), Mittenwald; 4 Alamy Images (SHOUT), Oxfordshire; 5 Jupiterimages/photos.com RF; 6 Corbis (Colin Garratt/Milep), Düsseldorf; 7 Getty Images (PhotoDisc); S.64: Ernst Klett Verlag (Hacker), Stuttgart; S.65: 1 Picture-Alliance (Picture Press/Frank), Frankfurt; 2 Topham Picturepoint (UPPA Ltd), Edenbridge Kent; 3 National Maritime Museum, London; 4 Ernst Klett Verlag (Hacker), Stuttgart; 5 Corbis (Colin Garratt/Milep), Düsseldorf; 6 Stefanie Schmidt, Weingarten; 7 Jupiterimages/photos.com RF; S.67: Ernst Klett Verlag (Fletcher), Stuttgart; S.71: Ernst Klett Verlag (Fletcher), Stuttgart; S.72: 1 Alamy Images (Gianni Muratore), Oxfordshire; 2 Image Source (RF), Köln; 3 Alamy Images (Don Jon Red), Oxfordshire; 4 Alamy Images (Creatas RF), Oxfordshire; 5 Alamy Images (Paula Solloway/Photofusion), Oxfordshire; S.73: 1 Fotosearch (BRAND X PICTURES RF), Waukesha; 2 Image Source (RF), Köln; 3 Avenue Images GmbH (Stockbyte RF), Hamburg; 4 Ernst Klett Verlag, Stuttgart; S.76: 1-3 Ernst Klett Verlag (Hacker), Stuttgart; S.77: Ernst Klett Verlag (Hacker), Stuttgart; S.86: 1, 4 Ernst Klett Verlag (McGeoch), Stuttgart; 2 Creativ Collection Verlag GmbH; 3 istockphoto/RF/Ramos; S.87: 1 Avenue Images GmbH (IndexStock), Hamburg; 2 Corbis (Tom Stewart), Düsseldorf; 3 ZEFA (Kormann), Düsseldorf; S.93: 1-2 Ernst Klett Verlag (McGeoch); 3-4 Corel-Corporation, Unterschleissheim; S.98: 1 Ernst Klett Verlag (Hacker), Stuttgart; 2 Fotosearch (BRAND X PICTURES RF), Waukesha; 3 Das Fotoarchiv (Markus Dlouhy), Essen; 4 Ernst Klett Verlag (McGeoch), Stuttgart; 5 Mauritius (Pöhlmann), Mittenwald; 6 Topham Picturepoint, Edenbridge Kent; 7 Education Photos (John Walmsley), Albury Heath Guildford Surrey; S.99: 1 Education Photos; 2 Alamy Images (Philip Wolmuth), Oxfordshire; 3 Corbis (Richard Olivier), Düsseldorf; S.101: 1 Avenue Images GmbH, Hamburg; 2 Ernst Klett Verlag (Fletcher), Stuttgart; S.105: Ernst Klett Verlag (Fletcher), Stuttgart; S.109: Ernst Klett Verlag (Fletcher), Stuttgart; S.110: Bananastock (RF), Watlington; S.113: Picture-Alliance, Frankfurt; S.114: Ernst Klett Verlag, Stuttgart S.128: 1 NewsCast; 2 Picture-Alliance, Frankfurt; 3 Corbis, Düsseldorf; S.129: 1 Avenue Images GmbH, Hamburg; 2-3 Corel-Corporation; S.161: Ernst Klett Verlag (Fletcher), Stuttgart; S.162: Getty Images (DigitalVision), München; S.163: 1 Ernst Klett Verlag (Fletcher), Stuttgart; 2 Ernst Klett Verlag (Mel Smith), Stuttgart; S.165: Ernst Klett Verlag (Fletcher), Stuttgart; S.166: Ernst Klett Verlag (Fletcher), Stuttgart; S.169: 1-4 Ernst Klett Verlag (Fletcher), Stuttgart; S.170: 1 Ernst Klett Verlag (Fletcher), Stuttgart; 2 MEV, Augsburg; S.172: Ernst Klett Verlag (Fletcher), Stuttgart; S.177: Ernst Klett Verlag (Fletcher), Stuttgart

Textquellen:

S.3: Hi, hi, hi, hello!, K.-H. Böttcher S.11: Let's get started, Sheila McBride; S.35: We're a funny family, Ernst Klett Verlag; S.41: Seven days in a week, K.-H. Böttcher, Sheila McBride; S.67: A jolly fine pirate, Sheila McBride; S.81: It's your day, Sheila McBride

Every effort has been made to trace owners of copyright material. However, in a few cases this has not proved possible and repeated enquiries have remained unanswered. The publishers would be glad to hear from the owners of any such material reproduced in this book.